MW01485116

"Hibbs has given us an excellent book to present in accessible form the biblical basis for the centrality of language in God's communion with us, in God's creation and providence, and in human living. The book combines biblical exposition, practical examples, and clear, winsome writing. There is nothing like it on the subject of language!"

—VERN S. POYTHRESS
Author, *In the Beginning Was the Word: Language—A God-Centered Approach*

"The last century has witnessed a major preoccupation with language among philosophers. Theologians, too, have tried often to understand the language of God—his word… Hibbs stresses the centrality of language to reality and to human life, and he persuasively expounds his view that language is *communion behavior*. This thesis has huge importance, and therefore I hope that the book finds many readers."

—JOHN M. FRAME
Author, *Systematic Theology: An Introduction to Christian Belief*

"What a bracing theology Pierce Taylor Hibbs has given those of us who have been called to preach the word! Those who read and meditate on *The Speaking Trinity and His Worded World* will find their knowledge of God and his word expanded and elevated. Preachers will find their hearts on fire to preach God's holy word."

—R. KENT HUGHES
Author, *Disciplines of a Godly Man*

"This extraordinary book brings together themes from linguistics, biblical theology, and apologetics, arguing that human language derives from the communion behavior of the divine Trinity… No one is more qualified to accomplish this task than Pierce Hibbs. His years of experience both as a theologian and a language instructor bear fruit in this profoundly edifying study. Accessible to the specialist and the non-specialist alike, the book bristles with insights. It has the makings of a classic."

—WILLIAM EDGAR
Author, *Created and Creating*

"In a post-post-modern age that despairs of language, meaning, and truth, Pierce Hibbs's reminder that language—communicative and expressive behavior—is ultimately rooted in the triune God comes as a welcome Christian relief. Of particular importance is the claim that language is always personal and covenantal, oriented to communion, and that God is a speaking, communicative being. Anyone interested in God and language will profit from this book."

—KEVIN J. VANHOOZER
Author, *Is There a Meaning in This Text?*

"Building on the work of Van Til, Frame, and Poythress, Hibbs has written a fascinating account of the Trinity as communicative, with language integral to creation and the nature of humanity in communion with God. Superbly written, his highly accessible discussion should do much to stimulate thought about God as Trinity… he mounts a credible case that the Trinity is discernible all around us."

—ROBERT LETHAM
Author, *The Holy Trinity*

"God created the world by speaking and his own Son is identified as the eternal Word. God's works of creation, providence, redemption, and consummation are all attributed to his powerful speech. So biblical faith is bound up with words—with language—in a unique way. That's why this is such an important book. Regardless of whether one agrees with all of the arguments, I expect it to strike up a fresh and crucial conversation about God and language."

—MICHAEL HORTON
Author, *The Christian Faith*

"This is a well-written book with a provocative thesis. Whether one ultimately agrees with all of Hibbs' contentions, his is a voice worth taking seriously."

—JONATHAN MASTER
Editor, *Place for Truth*

The Speaking Trinity
& His Worded World

TYPING ERRORS - P. 5
↳ OWEN LACKS IN BIBLIOGRAPHY

The Speaking Trinity
& His Worded World

Why Language Is at the Center of Everything

PIERCE TAYLOR HIBBS

WIPF & STOCK · Eugene, Oregon

THE SPEAKING TRINITY AND HIS WORDED WORLD
Why Language Is at the Center of Everything

Copyright © 2018 Pierce Taylor Hibbs. All rights reserved. Except for brief quotations in critical publications or reviews, no part of this book may be reproduced in any manner without prior written permission from the publisher. Write: Permissions, Wipf and Stock Publishers, 199 W. 8th Ave., Suite 3, Eugene, OR 97401.

Wipf & Stock
An Imprint of Wipf and Stock Publishers
199 W. 8th Ave., Suite 3
Eugene, OR 97401

www.wipfandstock.com

PAPERBACK ISBN: 978-1-5326-5647-7
HARDCOVER ISBN: 978-1-5326-5648-4
EBOOK ISBN: 978-1-5326-5649-1

Manufactured in the U.S.A.   APRIL 4, 2019

Scripture quotations are from the ESV® Bible (The Holy Bible, English Standard Version®), copyright © 2001 by Crossway, a publishing ministry of Good News Publishers. Used by permission. All rights reserved.

For Jesus

*　*　*

And for Kenneth Pike and Vern Poythress,
men of God and lovers of language

Our Father—to whom
All speech is one
And tongues of man
But image thin of Thine—
Help me now.

—Kenneth L. Pike

Contents

Figures for The Speaking Trinity

OTHER BOOKS BY THE AUTHOR

The Trinity, Language, and Human Behavior: A Reformed Exposition of the Language Theory of Kenneth L. Pike

In Divine Company: Growing Closer to the God Who Speaks

Theological English: An Advanced ESL Text for Students of Theology

Finding God in the Ordinary

Visit piercetaylorhibbs.com to read more from this author and to receive updates about new publications.

- ALL OF REALITY IS TRISTRUCTURAL & EXPRESSIVE
- STABILITY, VARIATION, RELATIONSHIPS ARE IN DECISION, WHICH IN TURN ARE ROOTED IN CHARACTER.

Introduction

I HAVE NEVER CONSIDERED myself to be cavalier. I am a simple Christian who looks to the inerrant and infallible words of Scripture for guidance and formation—spiritual and intellectual. I have studied under men who love God and keep his word with vigilance, drawing their theology not from existential experience or from philosophical speculation but from God's revelation, as that revelation has been understood in the Reformed tradition. In the broader theological world, some would no doubt consider me a rather boring theologian. I do not make it a point to seek out novelty.

Nevertheless, what you find in this book may appear to be novel. It may *appear* that way, but I can assure you that it is not. It is merely an extension and application of the clear teaching of Scripture, which I feel continues to go unnoticed, or at least is seldom given its full weight in the broader fields of linguistics, philosophy, theology, and, most importantly, everyday Christian life.

I have always appreciated when authors are up front with me, so let me get right to it. This book has a single purpose: to argue that *language is central to reality because the Trinity is linguistic (communicative) and has formed, shaped, and continues to direct everything through his speech*. All of reality reflects the word of its maker, and because its maker is triune and communicative, all of reality is what we might call *tristructual* and expressive.[1] That is, it can be understood as in some sense reflecting the Trinity and communicating a message that goes back to the character of its creator.

If you understand all of that, then I suppose you do not need to read this book. But seeing as how the men from whom I have learned this (Cornelius Van Til, Kenneth Pike, Vern Poythress, and John Frame) consistently foregrounded the depth of mystery and complexity in God and in language itself, I will assume that you do not. I mean no insult by this. In fact, no one

1. I am borrowing the term "tri-structural" from Kenneth Pike's language theory.

understands it fully—nor could they, since it is a divine truth. But what I do understand I want to share for the sake of Christ and his church.

BASIC ASSUMPTIONS

Before we get into the content of the book, I believe it is important for me to be candid about my basic assumptions. This is necessary, in my view, since all discussions begin not with ideas but with *persons*, and if you do not know anything about the person whom you are reading, you will likely misinterpret what he or she says. So, what follows are my basic theological assumptions. You may disagree with them if you like, but you will not properly understand what I am about to say if you are unaware of them.

1. I believe that Scripture is the inerrant, infallible word of God. I realize that this position sounds stale in a pluralistic age, but it is part and parcel of the Reformed faith, and my reasons for holding it can be laid out briefly, since here is not the place to develop them.[2]

Every person must have some basis for knowing anything (i.e., every person functions with at least an implied epistemology). That basis must be able to account for the stability, variation, and relationships we find in ourselves and in the world around us. Many people today are either practical empiricists or analytical rationalists, though they certainly would not label themselves that way. The former group says that nothing can be accounted for except by the senses. Testing and verification are prerequisites for claims that one knows anything. In other words, for something to be known it must be experienced. The latter group is similar, but proponents of this group believe that what can be known must be grasped with the hands of reason. They might say that for something to be known it must be rationally perceivable. We cannot know what we do not understand, can we?

Of course, all of us fall into these two tendencies (and others) from time to time. But these two epistemologies—one empirical and the other rational—cannot ultimately account for the stability, variation, and relationships in the world around us. Empiricists claim stability can be found in experience, and there is some truth to that. We almost always act based on our previous experience, based on what we can test and measure. But what happens when there is something that we claim to know which cannot be measured or tested? I do not think anyone would contest that humans have

---

2. For those looking for a fuller defense of the inerrancy and infallibility of the Bible, I recommend Warfield, *Inspiration and Authority of the Bible*; Conn, *Inerrancy and Hermeneutic*; Lillback and Gaffin, *Thy Word Is Still Truth*; and, for a more accessible discussion, DeYoung, *Taking God at His Word*.

an imagination, but if you cut open a brain, you will not find daydreams and devious thoughts. You will find blood and brain tissue. Not all of what we know can be measured, weighed, and counted.[3] Our stability of knowledge must have a deeper foundation. It must go beyond us.

The same goes for variations in our experience. Empirically, we can track variation and learn about patterns and deviations in the natural world and in human lives. But what is to say that this deviation is not just a sign that reality is chaotic? And if it is a sign of chaos, can we ever talk about stability of knowledge to begin with? How can we be sure that we know anything if all we know are unstable patterns and their deviations? This was the problem that David Hume introduced, and it was not solved by Immanuel Kant, despite his valiant efforts.

Empiricists also encounter difficulty when they try to account for relationships in reality. Interconnectivity—the relationships between countless people, places, and things—is notoriously complex, and this complexity can, for some people, make it almost impossible to say that they truly know anything. Their difficulty is not baseless. In fact, when we think about it, in order to truly understand relationships between one thing and another—between me and my wife, for example—one would ultimately have to know about the relationship of every fact to every other fact in reality.[4] In order to really know the relationship between me and my wife, you would have to know everything about me and everything about her. But because our thoughts and actions are not contained to us (they affect many other people and things), you would have to also know about everything that we have affected in our lives, and how all of those effected elements of reality relate to one another.[5] It is endless. No one can empirically account for all of the relationships in reality, and so, for empiricists, nothing can ever truly be known in full.

In the end, empiricists find themselves in a quandary when it comes to stability, variation, and relationships.

The same can be said for rationalists. At first glance, it may seem that rationalists can account for stability, since the principles of reason and logic appear to be steadfast and immoveable. But a closer look reveals problems. Take stability, for example. Certainly, there seem to be many logical laws (or natural laws) at work in the world. These laws appear to account for the stability we find around us and within our own thought patterns. "There is ice

3. For an atheist's perspective on this, see Nagel, *Mind & Cosmos*.

4. Cornelius Van Til emphasized this point consistently throughout his writings.

5. You would also have to account for the thoughts and actions that my wife and I have committed across time, and since thoughts cannot be traced this closely, it makes the task once again insurmountable.

on the road, so I cannot drive safely to work." There is a simple cause and effect relationship in a sentence like this. The ice on the road is the cause of my
not being able to drive safely, the effect. Logic might appear to account for
this stable relationship between cause and effect, but it cannot account for
the personal variations that are woven into real life situations. For instance,
there are many personal factors that must be taken into consideration in the
context of that sentence. (1) How do I tend to drive? Do I obey the speed
limits? Do I roll through stop signs? Do I forget to signal my turns? If the
latter is the case, then it may not matter whether there is ice on the road or
not. Either way, I may not get to work safely. Or, even if I follow the law to
the letter, I cannot control the decisions and driving habits of my neighbor
who lives down the street. So, there enters another question: (2) How do my
neighbors tend to drive? And of course, I cannot account for this with any
precision. Even if I could, there is nothing to say that one of my neighbors
might violate the norms of his or her behavior and drive more recklessly
one morning. Reason cannot account for or control the choices of others.
Reason and logic capture generalities that have been formed on the basis of
countless particulars. But if we think that logic or reason is some neutral
entity or power at work in the world, we will be sorely disappointed. Logic
and reason begin with concrete *persons*, not with abstract *principles*. We can
use logic and reason in many ways, but logic and reason themselves do not
account for the stability we find in the world. They simply give us tools to
measure what is, in the end, beyond them.

Variation, as well, is difficult for rationalists to explain. Certainly, any
reasonable person could predict that there are variations for any given event,
utterance, or entity. The Red Maple tree outside of my window looks slightly
different today than it did yesterday. It has fewer leaves and perhaps its roots
have grown a bit during the night. The tree, in other words, varies from day
to day. Reason, in following common stages of plant development (recorded
by the empiricist), could certainly *predict* that, but it could not ultimately
explain it (i.e., account for it by uncovering its ultimate purpose). In the
end, a rationalist would say that such development happens simply because
this is the way the world works. That is not an explanation.[6] Rationalists can

---

6. Now, I know that many atheists would say that "God" is not an explanation either.
We seem to be at an impasse here. But this should be resolved based on which position
makes the most sense of how reality functions. Atheists might claim that there is no
ultimate reason why the world has stable laws of logic, or variation, or relationships.
Thus, atheistic rationalists are ultimately *irrational*. Christians, on the other hand, claim
that a tri-personal God is responsible for the way the world functions—in its stability,
variation, and relationality. It seems to me that Christians are more consistently rational
than rationalists. See Frame, *The Doctrine of the Knowledge of God*, 361–63.

notice variation and even predict it, but that is not the same as *accounting for it*—giving an ultimate reason for why this is the way the world works.

Relationships, too, pose problems for rationalists, sometimes because of the sheer mass of relationships that encompass us. There are relationships between persons, between places, between moments, between elements, between cells, between molecules, and so on. It is not possible to notice all of these relationships, let alone rationally explain their existence. But if we cannot rationally explain all relationships, then can we truly say with confidence that we can know any of them exhaustively?

As you might predict, I believe that only God and his spoken word can account for the stability, variation, and relationships around us. One of the primary reasons for this is that there must be a personal explanation for stability, variation, and relationality. Without a personal explanation, we are left only with patterns and observations that might be subject to change. That was the bomb that Hume exploded on the playground of philosophy. This personal explanation, however, is actually *tri-personal*. As I will show in the pages ahead (echoing the teaching of Scripture and the thoughts of Kenneth Pike and Vern Poythress), stability, variation, and relationships are rooted in the self-communicating Trinity.

Stability, in the end, is not the result of natural laws or principles of logic. As we said, the latter are simply tools for measuring what lies beyond them. *Stability is rooted in decision, which in turn is rooted in character.* This seems clear for two reasons. First, for stability to be what it is—reliable, immovable, trustworthy, predictable—it must be set in motion and controlled by something or someone that transcends reality. It must be decided by a personal (choosing) being. Otherwise, stability is a groundless principle; it is only an abstract label for patterns. Second, lest stability be founded on the capricious whim of some divine being, stability must be simultaneously rooted in the character of this personal, divine being. In short, stability must be both decided by and derived from the character of the one who set it in motion.

The same can be said for variation and relationships. *Stability, variation, and relationships are rooted in decision, which in turn are rooted in character.* In what follows, we will see the Father as the source of stability, the Son as the source of variation, and the Spirit as the source of relationality. Yet these three persons are one God, and so stability, variation, and relationships are coinherent, i.e., bound up with one another. What's more, only this tri-personal God accounts for the two things noted in the previous paragraph. The triune God is a God who chooses—a God who has a will and who exercises it (cf. Ps 51:18; Matt 7:21; 12:50; 18:14; Luke 12:32; John 6:40; 7:17; Rom 1:10; 15:32; Phil 2:13; 1 Pet 3:17; 4:19). The triune God is likewise the only one whose character reflects the decisions he has made. This leads to my next assumption.

2. I believe in the Trinity. This is a more nuanced way of saying, "I believe in God," which is behind my first assumption. However, I prefer the latter wording. The Trinity *is* God. There is no such thing as a generic or basic deity to which we can attach descriptors and characteristics. We would not say, in other words, that God exists and that he happens to be triune. Rather, we would simply say, "The Trinity exists." There is nothing deeper than that. I state this at the outset because I see everything in existence as reflective of the Trinity, to varying degrees.[7]

3. I believe that language is a properly divine behavior. I have written elsewhere what I mean by "language" when it comes to the Trinity. I will summarize that by saying that each of the persons in the Godhead expresses himself to the other persons exhaustively and is thus known exhaustively by them. Cornelius Van Til writes that the divine persons are "exhaustively representational" of one another.[8] What he meant is that whenever we look at one person of the Trinity, the other two persons are exhaustively and felicitously represented as well. You never have one without the other two. You cannot tear one person of the Trinity away from the others, for God is essentially one. Moreover, each person eternally lifts up the others with accolades of love and glory. That mutual expression of love and glory is what I have in mind when I think of language as a properly divine behavior. I use "behavior" because I believe that language, on the divine and crea-turely level, includes more than words, phrases, and sentences. Language is part of a spectrum of personal action that is structurally integrated with everything else that personal beings do. Because of this, everything can be looked at through the lens of language and can be understood as expressive or communicative. This does not discount the truth that language is always embedded in a web of many other distinguishable behaviors. I simply want to acknowledge that language is not structurally separate from all that per-sonal beings do. This is the case for God; it is also the case for us, which leads to the next assumption.

4. I believe that language is an imaging behavior.[9] Though some might view it as an exaggeration, I believe that language is the heart of the *imago Dei*, the image of God in us. By that, I mean that our ability to communicate

---

7. Of course, we cannot perceive this until our minds are illumined by special reve-lation. Special revelation is the lens through which we properly view general revelation.

8. Van Til, *A Survey of Christian Epistemology*, 78.

9. I will define language as *communion behavior*. This definition fits well with Geer-hardus Vos's understanding of the *image Dei*. For Vos, the essence of our image is our disposition for *communion* with God. See Vos, *Anthropology*, 13.

personally and powerfully—expressing meaning, exercising control, and evoking our presence—is what marks us quintessentially as image-bearers.[10] When we use language for God's glory, we are a breath-taking light to the world; when we use it for self-serving purposes, we descend into the darkness of depravity. When we use language for God's glory, we illuminate his image in us; when we use language for merely human ends, we darken that image. In both scenarios, however, it is language that lies at the heart of who we are as God's creatures.

5. *I believe that language is covenantal.* Actually, I believe that all of reality is covenantal, but because I believe that all of reality is linguistic (spoken into being and sustained by the Trinity), it is more fitting in this book to say the former. Here is what I mean: All of our sundry uses of language—in every moment of every day—occur in the context of a covenant between God and man. This is a covenant that God has graciously and in his good will condescended to implement (WCF 7.1), suffered to uphold, and labored to fulfill with his own blood. By implication, because we are all either covenant keepers or covenant breakers, we are accountable for every linguistic action we take. In this sense, all of our communication happens in consonance with or in violation of our covenantal obligations.

6. *I believe that language is representational.* I do not mean by this that language is a system for representing thoughts (though there is obviously truth to this). Instead, I mean that *we* are represented in our language. For this reason, Jesus could say, "on the day of judgment people will give account for every careless word they speak, for by your words you will be justified, and by your words you will be condemned" (Matt 12:36–37). We are fooling ourselves if we assume that language is merely the trappings of thought, that what really counts are our ideas or motives. Ideas and motives are certainly important, but they are formed and expressed by language, and that expression is vital to our spiritual health, even to our eternal destiny. There is a very real sense in which what we say reflects how we think (epistemology) and who we are (metaphysics). Our communicative acts represent us faithfully to other people and to God, who searches the heart (1 Sam 16:7; Jer 17:10), but also hears every whisper that echoes in its chambers.

Those are my assumptions. You can disagree with them, analyze them, critique them however you like. The only thing you cannot do is claim to have understood what I say in the following pages if you are unaware of them.

---

10. I am here drawing on Vern Poythress's work where he describes man as imaging the meaning, control, and presence of God's words analogically (on a creaturely level). Poythress, *In the Beginning Was the Word*, 24–31.

ORGANIZATION

The discussion in this book is organized as follows, in two main sections.

I. Why Language is at the center of everything

   a. Defining language

   b. The communicative Trinity

   c. Creation through speech and reality as linguistic

   d. Image-bearing creatures, image bearing speakers

II. What that means for you and me

   a. Relying on the Trinity for our understanding of language

   b. Creation and the purpose of language

   c. The fall in language: sin as linguistic

   d. The redemption of language: the eternal Word entering the temporal world

   e. The consummation of language

   f. Principles for living in a worded world

In the first section, I define language in general, both for God and for us. Then, I focus more narrowly on how the Trinity is communicative. From there I move on to consider creation as a product of God's words, exploring how all of reality is thus linguistic and marked structurally by trinitarian speech. I end the first section by applying what we have learned about the trinitarian Creator to his image-bearing creatures.

In the second section, I move on to consider what all of this means for us. Picking up where the first section ends, I explore how and why image bearers must rely on the Trinity for our understanding of language. Then I survey the fall of language, considering what we learn about sin by viewing it as linguistic in nature. This will naturally lead to a discussion of the redemption of language, specifically considering how the eternal Word entered and began redeeming the temporal world. Next, I present what the ultimate goal of language is, the consummation of language. I end with a chapter more pragmatically focused on the implications all of this has for our use of language, outlining principles for living in a "worded world." I explain what I mean by that expression in the chapters ahead.

A WORD ABOUT THE STYLE AND CONTENT

I wish to make it abundantly clear that my purpose is to put my thoughts into accessible prose. My thinking is heavily influenced by the four men I mentioned earlier: Cornelius Van Til, Kenneth Pike, Vern Poythress, and John Frame.[11] So, nearly all of what I say can be traced back to their work in one way or another. However, in my effort to present this to a less specialized readership, I have refrained from filling up pages with footnotes. Where I feel that background information might be necessary, or when I quote or paraphrase an author explicitly, you will see a footnote. But my goal in this book is not to present a piece of work for academia; it is to offer the truth of Scripture to the church as a whole—to the layman, pastor, theologian, *and* academic. Those who wish to explore some of the ideas in this book in more detail may consult the Recommended Reading List at the end of the book, or reference some of my own scholarly articles.[12] To use a phrase from Thomas and Turner, I want my message in this book to be "clear and simple as the truth."[13] To that end, I have done my best to keep the pages clear of clutter. But behind every one of them is the thought and theology of the men under whom I have studied—whether on paper or in person.

One technical point about pronoun use: I sometimes use "I" to express my thoughts, conclusions, or intentions; other times I use "we." This use of "we" is meant to be inclusive of you, the reader, since I consider reading an interpersonal activity. So, when I use "we," I am not implying that there are additional authors for this book.

Lastly, if you find anything in the following pages that inspires you or draws you to marvel at the truth of Scripture, that is the result of the Spirit's work in continuing to sanctify my own mind. If you find anything pompous, shallow, egotistical, short-sided, unbiblical, inaccurate, ambiguous, or poorly worded, I take full responsibility for these things.

---

11. I am also indebted to K. Scott Oliphint for his work on covenantal apologetics and Christian epistemology.

12. Hibbs, "Imaging Communion"; "Where Person Meets Word Part 1"; "Where Person Meets Word Part 2"; "Closing the Gaps: Perichoresis and the Nature of Language"; "Words for Communion."

13. Thomas and Turner, *Clear and Simple as the Truth.*

Why Language Is at the Center of Everything

1

Defining Language

LET ME BEGIN BY defining language.

Language is difficult to define because our entire lives are immersed in it. We have to use language to define language, which is a strange thing when you think about it. We do not use paint to define paint or gravel to define a road—we use language to define these things. But when we are dealing with language itself, we are dealing with something so basic to our existence that it must be used *as* it is being understood. When we begin discussing language, we are already caught up in its current. In later chapters, I will suggest why this is the case theologically.

Language is also inherently difficult to define because of the array of purposes it serves. At a local business, language might be commonly perceived as a means of information transfer. In an undergraduate course on Romantic literature, language might be praised as a poetic medium. For parents trying to shepherd a toddler through a season of temper tantrums, language often serves an instructional purpose, expressing boundaries for acceptable behavior and solutions for frustration or emotional overload. Considering its sundry purposes, when we define language, we run the risk of either being too narrow or too broad. On the one side, too narrow a definition would not account for the range of purposes that language serves, and it might also segregate language from other parts of life in an unnatural way. For instance, the greeting "hello" is virtually unintelligible if we do not account for the contextually appropriate actions and environments in which it is embedded. "Hello" could be a casual greeting, if two strangers are passing on a street. Or it could signal the beginning of a conversation if the two persons are friends. It would not, however, be spoken by a man to his family as he was getting into a taxi and leaving them behind. In this last example, "goodbye" (or some similar expression) would suite that social and physical environment. Thus, we cannot ignore other parts of life—even physical environments—when we define language. A narrow definition would run the risk of just that. On the other side, too broad a definition would end up being useless, since language would then not be distinguishable from everything else that we do. If we define language as "an action performed by humans and directed towards other humans," then language would be no different from throwing a football. How do we settle this? How do we define language neither too narrowly nor too broadly?

We should stop here before going any further, since we are getting ahead of ourselves in trying to address such questions before opening the good book. What does Scripture reveal about how we might define language? The very word of God should be our starting place for every definition. Of course, Scripture is not a dictionary, but it does have much to say about human communication—in fact, an overwhelming amount! Let us start with just one passage.

One passage that has been historically referenced by theologians as having unique significance for our understanding of language is John's Prologue, especially John 1:1–3 and 1:14.

> In the beginning was the Word, and the Word was with God, and the Word was God. 2 He was in the beginning with God. 3 All things were made through him, and without him was not any thing made that was made.

> And the Word became flesh and dwelt among us, and we have seen his glory, glory as of the only Son from the Father, full of grace and truth.

As I will explain more fully in the following chapter, in calling the second person of the Trinity "the Word," John is showing us that language has divine origins. In the beginning was not just "God" but *the Word*, and this Word was "toward God" or "facing God." The Word—both as a divine person and as some high form of divine interpersonal discourse—was in the beginning. As one theologian remarked, we might translate John's verses more poetically: "In the beginning was Discourse, and Discourse was with God, and Discourse was divine." The Word as eternal Son and as divine discourse, eternally communicated by the Father in the hearing and power of the Spirit, indicates that language is not a human invention; it is a divine disposition, a disposition to express, in the highest sense, mutual love and glory among the persons of the Godhead.

However, what is less attended to in this passage is how John 1:14 intersects with John 1:1–3, and what this suggests about the nature of human language. The Word, the eternal foundation for interpersonal discourse, became a fully human *person*. There are many implications of this that are worth drawing out here, some of which lead to a weighty conclusion about human language.

First, we must remember the connection between the eternal Son of the Father and humans as created sons and daughters. The Gospel of Luke refers to Adam, the first human, as the "son of God" (Luke 3:38), and Israel is referred to corporately as God's son (e.g., Hos 11:1–2). As Scripture unfolds, we find that people who profess faith in Jesus Christ are named "sons and daughters of God" (2 Cor 6:18), a title they can only acquire *in Christ*, the eternal Son (Gal 4:5–7) through whom they have been adopted. In light of the connection between the eternal Son and God's created sons and daughters, what is said of the eternal Son might be analogically applicable to creaturely sons and daughters. So, we must pay close attention to this eternal Word, the Son, taking on a human nature.

Second, Paul tells us in his letter to the Romans that we are "predestined to be conformed to the image of [God's] Son" (Rom 8:29). This truth builds upon earlier biblical revelation, namely Genesis 1:27, where we are told that humans are made in the image and likeness of God. God's Son, however, is the ultimate "image of the invisible God" (Col 1:15) and "the exact imprint of his nature" (Heb 1:3). As far as is possible for creatures, we are to conform to him—his disposition, his speech, his social behavior.

Third, in the context of John's Prologue it is important to keep in mind the allusion to Genesis 1, which tells us that we are products of God's speech in a manner analogous to the way in which the eternal Son is the Word, or speech, of God the Father, spoken in the power and hearing of the Spirit. We are not divine, as the eternal Word is divine. Rather, we are *the products* of God's speech. This reinforces the distinction between God as Creator and humanity as his creatures. Yet, at the same time it also shows us that there is a connection between the Son as the Word of the Father and creatures as products of the Father's Word.

Let us bring these three implications together to recognize something truly magnificent about human language. We are sons and daughters of God, called to conform to God's Son, who is the divine Word that took on flesh. As the divine Word in the flesh, Jesus Christ has divine language embedded in his very personhood. Put differently, as the Word incarnate, Jesus has language—interpersonal discourse—as the beating heart of his identity. He does not just use language in his earthly ministry; he *is* language: divine discourse from the Father, uttered in the power of the Holy Ghost. Because

Christ never ceases to be the divine Word of the Father, language is at the foundation of *everything* that he does on earth.

This truth is worth re-expressing, for I have not seen it emphasized in much of the Reformed theology I have read. Recall the orthodox teaching that Christ has two natures (one divine and one human) that are both fully present in his person. That means the divine Word of the Father is simultaneously present with the fully human person born of the virgin Mary by the power of the Spirit (Matt 1:18; Luke 1:35). Divine discourse (the eternal Word) tabernacled among us in human flesh! Thus, all that Christ thought, said, and did was undergirded and directed by his divine identity as the Word. Let me say it again: Christ did not just *use* language; he *is* language, the root of all interpersonal communication—divine and human. And so language is bound up with everything in his life.

Now, because we are creatures made in the image of the Son and are products of God's Word, language is, in a derivative way, embedded in our personhood, too. All that Christ thought, said, and did was undergirded and directed by his divine identity as the Word. All that we think, say, and do is undergirded and directed by our identity as products of that Word. Language is not just something we use; it is an essential part of who we *are* as creatures crafted by the speech of the tri-personal God.

Because of this, language is intertwined with all of the other behaviors we carry out as creatures. This is my weighty conclusion about human language—one that is often rejected or forgotten in contemporary discussions. *We cannot segregate language from other human behaviors because it is the base of those behaviors and the base of our identity.* This truth is divinely established in Scripture and rooted in God himself. We cannot sunder what God has joined together. So, if we try to separate language from other human behaviors, we will either be frustrated or we will simply misinterpret and misuse it. We can distinguish elements of language, such as verbal discourse in speech or writing, from other human behaviors, but we cannot structurally separate them. Thus, these two small sections of John's Prologue reveal why language as a behavior is related to everything else that we do. The Word incarnate is holistically engaged with every facet of life. All of what Christ thought, said, and did was colored by his divinely linguistic identity—as the communicated and communicating Word of the Father. By implication, because we are the products of God's speech, which specifies our identify, human language is likewise engaged with every facet of life. Language is a window on all that we do.

Now, it may seem that we have complicated things by arriving at this conclusion. We were trying to find a definition for language that was neither too broad nor too narrow, but now we also must factor into the equation the centrality of language to all that we do! While it might seem that we have made things more difficult for ourselves, this was a necessary step in moving toward our definition, for we must begin with Scripture. Given what we have seen in John's Prologue, we can at least say that, because language is at the heart of our identity as products of God's speech, language must be considered in conjunction with everything that we do. If we are going to define language, we must think about where language fits in relation to the rest of life. Only then will we arrive at a definition that is faithful to the biblical witness and to our divinely governed identity.

Still, to situate language in relation to the rest of our behavior we must begin with a bare definition—for practical reasons. Let us for the moment say that language is "communicative behavior." We can take this bare definition and relate it to many other common human actions before further refining it. Only if it is seen in relation to such actions can language simultaneously be distinguished from and integrated with all of life. Going about it this way, and checking ourselves against the teaching of Scripture, will provide us with a definition that is sufficiently broad and yet still nuanced enough to be helpful.

Let us start by asking ourselves a simple question: What do we do *besides* use language? Figure 1 suggests some of the many sorts of human action that are distinguishable from language as communicative behavior and yet, in one way or another, related to it.

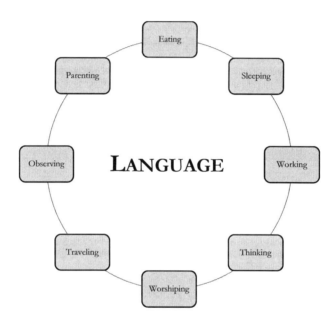

Figure 1: Language in Relation to Other Human Behaviors

Language, as "communicative behavior," is not *equal to* any one of the actions in figure 1. When we see someone driving a car (traveling), we do not say, "He's using language." The same goes for our observations of a person eating or sleeping or watching a basketball game. Yet, language can be clearly related to all of these behaviors. Scripture itself attests to this.

Take parenting, for example. In Ephesians, Paul exhorts his readers to follow an ancient command from Deuteronomy: "Honor your father and your mother." In addressing fathers more specifically, he says "do not provoke your children to anger, but bring them up in the discipline and instruction of the Lord" (Eph 6:4). Provoking, discipline, and instruction all presuppose the use of language. We often use words to provoke another person; discipline and instruction require verbal commands and exhortations; they require communicative behavior on the part of parents. Thus, the action of parenting is both distinct from and yet intimately related to language.

Or consider sleeping. Dreaming is a common part of sleeping, and throughout Scripture God uses dreams to communicate with his people (Gen 20:3; 28:10; 31:11, 24; 37:5; Num 12:6; 1 Kgs 3:5; Matt 1:20; 2:12, 13, 19, 22; 27:19). In several cases, he speaks to people in their dreams, relaying messages or warnings. In the New Testament, Joseph was told in a dream to take Mary as his wife (Matt 1:20). The wise men who traveled from distant lands were warned in a dream not to report to Herod, but to return to their land by another route (Matt 2:12). Even outside the bounds of Scripture, in our own lives we have all had numerous dreams that communicate something to us—fears, desires, lusts, and so on. Dreams are communicative, and so sleep is bound up with language. Even if we do not dream in our sleep, we are resting from a day full of communicative interactions, processing what we have heard and said. Dreamless sleep is still surrounded on all sides by language.

A less obvious example might be observing or thinking. How are these behaviors related to language? Thought, of course, lies beneath all communicative behavior. We cannot express anything before first thinking of what words we want to say or write, even when we are not conscious of the thought processes that are occurring in our minds. Not only this, but language actually structures our thought: it gives us a framework for thinking. We think in words, phrases, sentences, paragraphs, and so forth. When we reason, we logically arrange propositions or hypotheticals that are channeled through language. So, language and thought have a deep and reciprocal relationship. Scripture also testifies to this in statements such as Ps 139:4, "Even before a word is on my tongue, behold, O Lord, you know it altogether." Thoughts flow into words, and God sees and knows every thought we have even before it finds its way into phonemes and rolls off of our tongue. We can just as well say that God knows how every word we speak and hear affects the thoughts we have. So, thinking and language are bound up with one another.

Observation is similar to thought. When we observe the world around us, we process it mentally; we *interpret* it. We do not, strictly speaking, give the world new meaning in our interpretation. Rather, as Cornelius Van Til taught, we *re-interpret* the world that God has already interpreted for us in Scripture. In other words, we are called to recognize the meaning that God has already instilled in every fiber of reality, as much as we are able to as finite creatures. When we observe the world, then, we are interpreting it, which is patently linguistic. To interpret is to derive meaning, and meaning is always understood and expressible to some degree in communicative behavior, in language. In everyday life, consider how many times you hear the question, "What does that mean?" The person asking this question is always hoping that the other person will formulate in words the significance of an utterance, action, or event. Meaning is bound up with language, and so interpretation is bound up with language. Because interpretation is a core part of observation, we can say that language and observation are bound up together.

Scripture, once again, confirms this. The author of Proverbs expresses a deep desire for his son to look, interpret, and receive his teaching. "My son, give me your heart, and let your eyes observe my ways" (Prov 23:26). The son is called to observe the patterned behavior of his father (his "ways") and to interpret this as instruction. This instruction presupposes language—the communicative behavior of one person passing on a moral lesson to another. Moreover, this phenomenon—observing, interpreting, learning—would be an expression of total commitment on the part of the son, who in this process is giving his "heart" to his father. Note here that receiving instruction through the communicative behavior of the father (i.e., through language) is *all-encompassing* for the son; it involves the giving of his *heart*. This parallels on a creaturely level the all-encompassing submission of Christ to the plan of his heavenly Father. The whole person of Christ—his "heart"—was offered up to his Father as he carried out his will, even to death on a cross at the hands of crooked men. Throughout his entire life, Jesus is the perfect model of observing, interpreting, and acting as he witnesses the work of his Father (his Father's "ways"), both in his own interpretation of Scripture and in the engagements he has with those around him. He tells his disciples, "My Father is working until now, and I am working" (John 5:17). The implication is that Christ, as the perfect Son, is observing what his Father has done and is doing. He is then receiving divine instruction as he carries out his Father's will in his earthly ministry. Language for the Son of God incarnate is thus inextricably intertwined with interpretation and observation. The same is the case for us as creatures. When we observe, we interpret, and are thus receiving communication that is controlled by God, who is present everywhere and is the Lord of all meaning.

We could go on. Eating, working, worshiping, traveling, and parenting all have clear ties to language, some of which have been implied already. Eating, all throughout Scripture and into the present day, is the occasion for conversation between friends and family members. Meal times were and continue to be an opportunity to commune with loved ones, and language as communicative behavior plays a central role in this. We all use language in one way or another in our work—that's true for the businessman and school teacher as much as it is for the stay-at-home parent. And what is worship without words? The songs we sing—the psalms and hymns that the church has sung for centuries—are filled with language that communicates our gratitude for and worship of the Trinity: for the Father's mercy and grace in sending his Son and Holy Spirit for the sake of sinners. Traveling, too, is bound up with language, since we almost always travel in order to commune with others via language. Or, even if we travel without plans to see anyone, we rely on language in our thinking (as already mentioned) and will find it hard to avoid personal contact with others—whatever our destination might be.

It is clear from these examples that language is tied in some way to every other human behavior. Yet, Scripture also treats language as a behavior that is distinct. There are many verses and passages in Scripture dealing with our words (what we might call *verbal behavior*), with the use of the tongue, particularly in Psalms and Proverbs (Ps 19:14; 34:13; 36:3; 64:3; 119:103; Prov 10:19; 12:6, 25; 15:1, 23, 26; 16:24; 17:27; 18:4; 21:28; 25:11). Our words can be both brilliantly redemptive, if we use them to build one another up in grace (Eph 4:29), and dishearteningly destructive (James 3:5–6), if we use them to burn bridges and break apart what love has joined together. In both cases, our communicative behavior is distinct from various other human activities.

So, as Scripture itself confirms, language is related to all other human behaviors and is still distinguishable from them. The follow-up question is this: "Is there something about language—some purpose for it or effect of it—that helps us to see how it is related to and distinguished from all other human behaviors?" By this question, I hope to help us see the core of language: its primary and eternal purpose, both for God himself and for us as his image-bearing creatures.

Here is my answer to that question: *Language, as communicative behavior, always represents or fosters interpersonal connections.* Language is, at base, always personal. This is the case for all the examples we have just considered. Recall the initial examples of how language might be perceived in business, in a course on Romantic literature, and in parenting. In business settings, there is no such thing as purely propositional (informational) language. Language can never be reduced purely to information transfer, because information transfer ultimately transpires between persons, and those persons will, as a result of the information being conveyed, be either cognitively or spiritually closer to or further from one another. Language always goes back to interpersonal connections.

What about the course on Romantic literature? Despite the prevalent assumption that reading is an individual activity, every time we read something we are engaging with the words of another person. Written words are not dead; they are alive and well, offering us the presence of the person who wrote them. When we read, we are actually growing closer to the author, coming to a deeper understanding of his or her meaning, values, and desires. Reading is a communal activity, even when we find ourselves sitting alone in a sofa chair with a good book. There is interpersonal engagement between author and reader, though this is not as fluid and full as that which occurs in verbal conversation.

Parenting, too, relies on the interpersonal connections that language fosters. Shepherding children through a spell of temper tantrums (as my wife and I have experienced) requires strong interpersonal connections, both between parents and children and between siblings. I must use language to connect with my son, Isaac, and show him that I have his spiritual and social growth at heart when I reprimand him. When I tell him that he cannot hit his sister with a plastic hammer, I am not just trying to prevent her from being harmed. I am trying to show him the interpersonal connection he has with her, and with me. As her older brother, he has the privilege of guarding and protecting his younger sister, just as I have the privilege of guarding and protecting my children. Both of these interpersonal connections are established by our heavenly Father, who through Christ and the Holy Spirit guards and protects us from evil. What's more, God often does this by calling us to follow his word, Scripture. So, provided that our words align with the truth of Scripture, we can rightly guard and protect others with the words we speak.

Psalm 91 is a beautiful picture of this. Here we read words that have power to engulf our souls with heaven-sent confidence. This is a psalm about God's unparalleled protection of the one who trusts in him. In verse 14, we read, "Because he holds fast to me in love, I will deliver him; I will protect him, because he knows my name." Knowing God's name is the result of reading God's word. As we read and meditate on God's word, our *yes!* knowledge of him (of his name) grows deeper and more secure. Thus, God reveals himself so that we might know him by name and trust in his protection and deliverance. He uses language to shepherd and protect us as his sons and daughters, fostering interpersonal connections between himself and his creatures. Parents stand upon this foundation of God's personal communication when they use language to foster interpersonal connections with their children. Our parenting, in other words, is a finite image of God's parenting of his children—and both levels of parenting are mediated through language.

So, in all of these situations language represents or fosters interpersonal connections. But we can go further.

The phrase "interpersonal connections" can sound a bit stiff to some people. I have written elsewhere that language as communicative behavior not only fosters *connections;* it fosters *communion.* We might think of interpersonal connections as strands of rope that bind us to one another. God's revealing his name to us, for instance, is an example of an interpersonal connection: a bridge between persons. But these connections are meant to draw us into closer fellowship with God and with one another. The connections point toward communion. This is illustrated in figure 2.

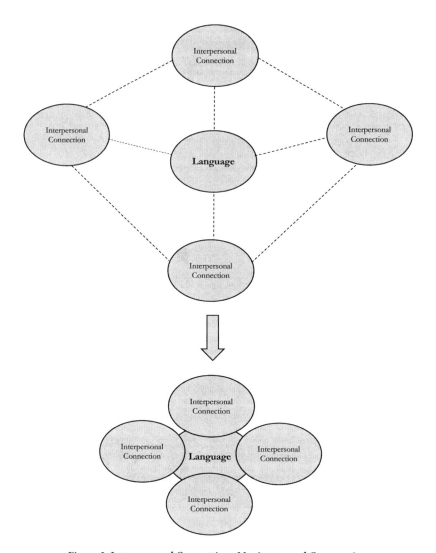

Figure 2: Interpersonal Connections Moving toward Communion

This communion is something that has its roots in the Trinity, which we will explore in the next chapter. In light of this, let us revise our earlier definition of language so that we can account for its ultimate purpose: *Language is communion behavior*. If this definition does not seem to distinguish language adequately from other human behaviors (recall our earlier discussion), we can go on to say that this communion behavior is either *verbal* or *nonverbal*. I have tried to explain what I mean with this distinction below, noting the different senses in which I understand communion behavior (divine and human). We will explore these concepts in more detail as the chapters unfold.

COMMUNION BEHAVIOR DEFINED

Communion behavior: (1) an interpersonal, trinitarian divine behavior amongst the Father, Son, and Holy Spirit, whereby they express mutual and intimate love and glory to one another; (2) an image-bearing human behavior that has the goal of (a) drawing persons into fellowship with God and (b) drawing persons into fellowship with each other

Verbal: The use of written or spoken language to foster communion or fellowship between God and humanity or between human persons

Nonverbal: Any other communicative behaviors (aside from written and spoken language) that are substitutable for verbal behavior and serve the purpose of drawing people into more intimate fellowship with God or with each other.

In this book, I will use the terms *language, communion behavior*, and *speech* sometimes interchangeably.

We set out in this chapter to define language, and now we have a working definition: Language, i.e., verbal and nonverbal communion behavior, is a phase of human behavior that fosters connections between persons who are ultimately meant to grow closer to one another and to the God who communes with himself.[1] This leads us to the next chapter.

---

1. I am taking the phrase, "a phase of human behavior" from Pike.

2

The Communicative Trinity

DEFINING LANGUAGE AS COMMUNION behavior naturally calls us back to the hearth of communion itself: the eternal Trinity.

This chapter is focused on a universal question: Who is God? There is nothing more basic than the answer to this question, though others certainly vie for our attention. I once had a youth pastor who said that there are three fundamental questions all people have: (1) Who am I? (2) What am I doing here? (3) Where am I going? It seems to me that these questions presuppose an answer to the initial question of who God is. We cannot define ourselves in isolation from our maker (question 1); nor can our ultimate purpose be meaningful if it is self-directed (question 2); nor can we have a sense of our ultimate purpose (question 3) unless we know who God is.

We can only answer this universal question, however, based on what God himself has told us. On a creaturely level, we cannot know much at all about another person unless he discloses his identity. I will not know what my wife's favorite flower is unless she *tells* me. On the divine level, we cannot know the character or nature of God unless he reveals himself to us. Thus, we begin answering our question with Scripture.

GENESIS: THE BEGINNING OF OUR KNOWLEDGE OF GOD

The very first page of Scripture reveals perhaps one of the most central identifying markers of God.

In the beginning, God created the heavens and the earth. 2 The earth was without form and void, and darkness was over the face of the deep. And the Spirit of God was hovering over the face of the waters. 3 And God said, "Let there be light," and there was light. 4 And God saw that the light was good. And God separated the light from the darkness. 5 God called the light Day, and the darkness he called Night. And there was evening and there was morning, the first day. (Gen 1:1–5)

How easy it is to gloss over these words as a mere opening to a narrative! But think of this: what is the first of God's actions recorded in Scripture? Creation, yes, but creation *through speech*. God speaks!

It is worth taking a few moments to consider the implications of this. We often marvel at the *power* of God's words in creation. His words manifest reality. All things have their being, their existence, because he spoke them. Surely, we will never plumb the depths of this truth.

But what about speech itself—the fact that *this* is how God chose to create all things? In our own experience, we know that an artist's medium plays a defining role in who he or she is as an artist. Someone who works with clay or stone or metal or wood is a sculptor. Someone who works with paint is a painter. The medium in which the artist works is definitive of the artist as such. This is true on a divine level with God himself. The medium of creation—divine speech—reveals something definitive about him; it reveals that God is a speaking, communicative being.

This is the very first thing we learn about who God is. He is one who speaks. We might be tempted to move on and make other observations, but consider this in light of the first chapter. We defined language as *communion behavior*. Provided that our definition of language is true and biblical, the natural question here would be, with whom is God communing when he speaks at the dawn of creation? Or, perhaps more strikingly, with whom *has God been communing*? Nothing in the Genesis account suggests that this is the first time God spoke. In fact, given the quick-handed way in which the author refers to God's action, it is more likely that this is something *expected* of God.

The short answer is that God is communing (and has been communing) with himself. To our ears, that may sound strange or even egotistical. What kind of a being communes with himself? But, difficult as it may be, we must strive to respect that God is *qualitatively* different from us. Scripture tells us that God's ways are "higher" than our ways, and his thoughts are "higher" than our thoughts (Isa 55:9). This statement would be true even if we lived in a sinless world. It was true for Adam and Eve before they fell into sin.[1] God is God; he is divine, all-knowing, all-powerful, ever-present. We are not. We are, in the language of Genesis 1:27, made in his *image* and *likeness*. In other words, we are derivative creatures that reflect God's glory. All that we think, say, and do is thought, said, and done as image-bearers.[2] If this was true in a sinless world, how much more so in a world riddled with sin and corruption?! We fall woefully short of being able to understand just how high and lofty God is. Instead of thinking of and worshiping him as the one whose ways and thoughts are higher than ours, we tend to take our own experiences and map them onto God. For us, anyone who "communes with himself"—that is, meditates on, talks to himself—is either egotistical or ludicrous. But God has eternally existed before and beyond our sinful earthly experience, so we cannot take our own sin-ridden understandings and actions and pin them onto God. God is God, and we are not. God is *qualitatively* different from us. It is not as if God is simply a greater kind of human—a human without limitations. That would make God *quantitatively* different. Rather, God is of a different *quality* than we are. He is the eternal and unchangeable Creator. We are finite creatures.

Now, there are two reasons why we must be careful in understanding just how God communes with himself. The first one is what we have just mentioned: God is a qualitatively different being as compared to finite, limited creatures. The second reason is related to the first. Though I hesitate to use this language because it sounds abstract, humans are *unipersonal* while God is *tripersonal*. All I mean by this is that each of us is one person. That much is obvious. The mind-boggling part is what makes God a qualitatively different being: He is one God in *three* persons. We would not recognize this truth in the first few verses of Genesis (hence the following section). It took the church several hundred years before it truly understood what Scripture was saying about who God is and then translated that into the language we have today (*being* and *persons*).

This second reason should shift our perception of what we mean by saying that God communes with himself. There are three *persons* in God: the Father, the Son, and the Holy Spirit. These persons have eternally spoken, or communed, with each other. Later in this chapter we will explore what that communion looks like. For now, it is important to note that these persons are certainly not to be understood in the same sense that we understand human persons.[3] Remember, God is a qualitatively different being;

---

1. As we will explore in a later chapter, their sin can be understood as a "linguistic sin." They exchanged the true language of the triune God for the false language of the serpent.

2. Oliphint, *Reasons for Faith*, 179.

3. Theological discussions about the definition of "person" abound throughout

what is "person" to us is not the same as what is "person" to him, but there is some correspondence—otherwise, it would be meaningless to call the Father, Son, and Spirit "persons."

What we can say about these divine persons based on Scripture is that they are distinct, self-conscious agents. If they were not distinct, there would not really be authentic communion amongst them. The same would be true if they were not self-aware. The very concept of communion assumes distinct, self-conscious agents drawn together in intimate fellowship. So, when we understand that God is tripersonal, it makes a bit more sense to see how or why he would commune with himself. Yet, the distinct persons of the Godhead nevertheless constitute *one* God, not three Gods. Each of the persons is fully God and shares in the single divine essence. Given this unity and trinity, there is certainly mystery in our understanding of who God is, but this mystery is biblically mandated for creatures, not something to be overcome or rationalized.

SEEING THE ONE AND THE THREE IN SCRIPTURE

There is more to say about this, but given that we began this chapter with Scripture, it makes sense to continue on that path.[4] However, before we note several passages in the Old and New Testaments, I should say that our discussion will be brief—not because it is unimportant; in fact, it is the most important. But many other theologians have done a fine job in presenting biblical support for the Trinity in the Old and New Testaments.[5] It is not necessary to attempt to reproduce what has been done so well by others.

First, let us summarize the foundational truth that has come to light in Genesis 1:1–5. From the very beginning, Scripture sets before us a God who speaks, a God who is in part defined and identified for us by the fact that he practices what we called communion behavior. God, we said, communes

church history. Now is not the place to get into those. But it is worth noting that much of the debate rides on whether a person is defined primarily as a rational being or a relational being. In other words, is a 'person' properly understood as a rational individual or as a being in relation to others? There is truth to both positions, but I believe that the second position is more emphasized in Scripture. Genesis 2:18 is evidence of this on the human level. The creation of Adam as "good" was not complete until Eve was made as "a helper fit for him." Intrinsic personhood, it seems, requires personal *relationships* to like-minded beings. And because God makes us in his image, it is safe to assume that divine persons are also to be understood relationally.

4. In what follows, I rely on the biblical discussion by Robert Letham and the passages he provides in *The Holy Trinity*, 17–85.

5. Warfield, "The Biblical Doctrine of the Trinity"; Frame, *Systematic Theology*, 421–73; Bray, *God Has Spoken*.

with himself. Yet, because he is qualitatively different from his creatures, the Father, Son, and Spirit do not have interpersonal connections that move towards communion, as is the case with us. For God, his communication simply *is* communion. In other words, God was, is, and always will be the perfect and eternally sustained embodiment of communion, which sets him apart from us. We might say that the Trinity is the hearth of communion, the wellspring that feeds our longing for communion in a broken and fragmented world.

However, that God is a being who communes with himself in three persons is made clear only through the *progressive* unfolding of Scripture. He revealed what he wanted to reveal about himself, when and where he wanted to reveal it. In Scripture, there is an organic revelation of who God is—his unity is foregrounded in the Old Testament, while his plurality is backgrounded. B. B. Warfield famously referred to the Old Testament as a chamber richly furnished but dimly lit. The light grows brighter in the New Testament, allowing us to see what was already there, though perhaps shrouded in shadow. In the New Testament, the three persons are brought more into the foreground. God's chamber of self-revelation is then more fully lit, but God was God all along. He was always Father, Son, and Holy Spirit.

Let us start by looking at a few Old Testament passages that foreground God's unity and yet suggest something of God's plurality or threeness.

Several passages in Genesis are good examples. Perhaps the most famous starting point for trinitarian discussions in the Old Testament is Genesis 1:26, when God uses the first person plural form: "Then God said, 'Let us make man in our image, after our likeness.'" Let *us*? Who is "us"? There has only been one speaker at this point in the narrative. The author repeats, "and God said" several times (Gen 1:3, 6, 9, 11, 14, 20, 24), using a singular verb. Why would God himself say, "Let *us*"? Many explanations have been offered throughout history, but none of them, in my opinion, fits as naturally in the biblical context as the one suggesting that this is an indication of some sort of plurality in God. This interpretation would also make the most sense with regard to later biblical revelation, and it coheres with our biblical understanding of language and of God as one who speaks. As mentioned earlier, communion behavior requires distinct, self-conscious agents. It is my view that the Father is here communing with the Son and Holy Spirit. This fits seamlessly into the larger context of Scripture, where the Son or Word is referenced as the medium through whom creation comes (e.g., Ps 33:6; John 1:1–3; Col 1:16), and the Spirit is referenced as God's life-giving power (Gen 2:7; Job 33:4; John 6:33; 2 Cor 3:6). So, with the words "let us" the Father is encouraging the Son and Spirit to join him in doing what they already want to do (for the will of God is one): create man as an image bearer. In a later chapter, we will explore one of the primary marks of humanity as God's image, the very subject of this book: language.

Later in Genesis, we encounter passages that, once more, foreground God's unity but hint at or even portray plurality. In Genesis 16:7–13, we meet the "angel of the Lord," who seems at first to be a divine messenger, but this angel promises to do what only God has earlier promised to Abraham (Gen 12), that is, to multiply his offspring (Gen 16:10). A similar event occurs with "the angel of God" in Genesis 21:17–18, where again the angel promises to do what God has already promised in Genesis 12. Then as the narrative of God's people continues, we read about Jacob's great wrestling match with a mysterious figure. In refusing to let go of this figure until he is blessed, Jacob receives a new name, Israel, and is marked as one who has striven with *God* (Gen 32:28), indicating the divine nature of his wrestling partner. A few verses later, Jacob names the location of his supernatural wrestling match and claims to have seen "God face to face" (32:30). What's more, this figure *renames* Jacob, and in the immediate context changing a person's name is a right given only to God (Gen 17:5, 15). Plurality in God is thus hinted at and even portrayed within a context that assumes God's unity as the only true God.

The angel of the Lord also appears in Judges 2:1–5, again taking ownership for actions that were already explicitly ascribed to God: "Now the angel of the LORD went up from Gilgal to Bochim. And he said, 'I brought you up from Egypt and brought you into the land that I swore to give to your fathers. I said, "I will never break my covenant with you"'" (Judg 2:1). It was the Lord himself who had brought the people of Israel from the land of Egypt (Exod 3:17; 7:4; 12:51). It was also the Lord who promised never to break his covenant (Gen 9:12, 15; Gen 17:7, 19). This latter point is evidence against the position that the angel of the Lord is simply a messenger doing God's bidding. The Lord himself always stands behind his covenant promises as the sole and responsible actor; he does not send his messengers to make covenants in his stead (Exod 6:4; 34:10, 27; Lev 26:9; Deut 5:2, 3; 2 Kgs 17:38; 1 Chr 16:16; Ps 89:34; Isa 42:6; 55:3; 61:8; Jer 34:13; Ezek 16:8, 62). God may send his messengers (Moses and the prophets) to announce what he is doing, but he remains the primary actor in his covenant with his people.

A figure similar to the angel of the Lord appears in Josh 5:13–15. It is important to note in this passage how this figure does *not* reject the worship that Joshua offers him, as angels do elsewhere in Scripture (Rev 19:10; cf. Heb 1:14), indicating that this figure is identified with God himself.

Of course, in Deut 6:4 we find perhaps the boldest declaration of God's unity: "The LORD our God, the LORD is one." There has been much debate over what exactly is meant by the Hebrew word often translated as "one" here. Some translate it as "alone," meaning that only God is God. That interpretation certainly has biblical support. Perhaps what is more significant than the precise meaning of this word, given our current discussion, is the name of God in this passage, YHWH. This name is not to be understood as excluding all plurality. One scholar writes that the relation between YHWH and the figure with whom Jacob wrestled (Gen 32), along with the Old Testament descriptions of God's Spirit and his Word or Wisdom, "indicates an overlap of identities and a simultaneous distinction between persons" (Gen 41:38; Exod 31:3; 1 Sam 11:6; 16:15; Job 33:4; Ps 143:10; Isa 48:16; Ezek 8:3; 11:24; Ps 56:4, where the word receives praise; Prov 1:20; 3:19, where wisdom is linked to the divine Word by whom creation was brought into being).[6] YHWH is not thus an exclusive reference to unity. Based on later biblical revelation, the name YHWH also allows for distinctions or plurality within God.

Other passages later in the Old Testament, such as Ps 110:1, Isa 63:8–14, and Hos 11:1 clearly suggest a plurality of persons in God: God is one, but God is not what we might call a "monistic" unity. Throughout the Old Testament, God is consistently referenced as one, and yet this oneness whispers of plurality, of the eternal presence of essentially united, self-aware agents who receive the praise and honor worthy of God alone.

One passage in the Old Testament that whispers of God's plurality with striking clarity does so in the context of language, which, of course, is of special interest to us. In Ps 33:6, the psalmist writes, "By the word of the LORD the heavens were made, and by the breath of his mouth all their host." This verse calls us back to Genesis 1 and suggests how the Trinity is foreshadowed in the Old Testament via the concept of language. The Father utters his Word in the power of the Spirit, and creation bursts into being. Later in the Bible, we learn that this word and breath are references to *persons*: the Son and the Spirit, respectively. In fact, all of the references to God speaking in the Old Testament imply the presence of the Son and the Spirit as the Word and Breath of the Father. We can go even further: all of the references to God speaking imply the presence of distinct (but not separate or independent), self-conscious agents within the Godhead, for language is communion behavior, and this behavior is not possible with a monistic God (a God who has no plurality or diversity within himself).

---

6. Gignilliat, "The Trinity and the Old Testament," 185.

As many theologians have noted, while the oneness of God is fore-grounded in the Old Testament and plurality is backgrounded, the three-ness of God is foregrounded in the New Testament and given equal weight with God's unity. Following Warfield's illustration, we might say that the New Testament turns up the wick in God's oil lamp of revelation, brighten-ing the room in which the Father, Son, and Holy Spirit have always dwelt.

The best place to start is with the relationship often referenced between Jesus and his Father. Throughout his life, Jesus constantly speaks about and references his Father, and the Father consistently speaks to and about Jesus as his beloved Son (Luke 2:49; Matt 3:17; John 2:16; 6:27; 5:30; 17; Matt 26:39ff; Luke 23:34; John 20:28). There is no longer in the New Testament any ambiguity as to God's plurality. God is the Father, and also the Son, and also the Spirit (Matt 1:20; Luke 3:16; 4:1; John 14–16). This revelation is complemented by continual references to the linguistic, communicative nature of God, which seems most pronounced in John's Gospel (John 1:1–14; 8:28; 12:49; 14:10; 16:13), but is clear also in Heb 1:1–3, among other passages.

The texts which bring into view all three persons of the Godhead si-multaneously are especially instructive. In chapter 14 of John's Gospel, Jesus consoles his anxious disciples. While he is leaving to return to the Father, he will not abandon them; he will send them another: "the Helper, the Holy Spirit, whom the Father will send in my name, he will teach you all things and bring to your remembrance all that I have said to you." Here we have distinctly personal actions attributed to the Father, Son, and Holy Spirit. Je-sus, as the Son incarnate, *has spoken* to the disciples throughout his ministry ("all that I have said to you") and is now going to the Father (14:28), leaving peace with his disciples. The Father is *sending* the Spirit in Christ's name, and the Spirit will *teach* the disciples about all that Christ has said to them. Speaking, sending, and teaching are distinctly attributed to the Father, Son, and Holy Spirit. Yet, these are not three Gods, for God is one (John 17:11, 21, 22). God is the speaker, sender, and teacher. These actions are attributed to three essentially united divine persons.

Paul, as well, often brought the three persons of the Godhead to light in his epistles, for example, in 1 Corinthians, Romans, and Galatians.[7] In 1 Corinthians 12:4–6, he tells his audience, "Now there are varieties of gifts, but the same Spirit; and there are varieties of service, but the same Lord; and there are varieties of activities, but it is the same God who empowers them all in everyone." Many times, Paul's references to "God" in general are meant to be taken as references to the Father. In this case, we have references to the

---

7. A recent helpful study of this has been provided by Hill, *Paul and the Trinity*.

Spirit as divine gift-giver, the Son as the Lord of all creaturely service, and the Father as the one who empowers all creaturely activity. Paul ends his letter to the Romans with a plea for prayer that similarly draws our attention to three distinct persons: "I appeal to you, brothers, by our Lord Jesus Christ and by the love of the Spirit, to strive together with me in your prayers to God on my behalf." He asks the recipients of his letter to offer prayers to the Father by appealing to Jesus Christ and the love of the Holy Spirit. Lastly, in his epistle to the Galatians, he draws our attention to adoption by referencing the work of these three persons: "But when the fullness of time had come, God sent forth his Son, born of woman, born under the law, to redeem those who were under the law, so that we might receive adoption as sons. And because you are sons, God has sent the Spirit of his Son into our hearts, crying, 'Abba! Father!'" (Gal 4:4–6). God sent his Son so that, in him, we might be adopted into God's family. To confirm the adoption, the Father sends the Spirit of his Son into our hearts so that we break out in glorious recognition of our newfound, eternal family.

Much more can be said about the New Testament's teaching on the three persons and the unity of the Godhead, but this very brief discussion simply confirms that Scripture speaks of God as both one and three.[8] In other words, Scripture reveals God as the Trinity. For this reason, throughout church history, "the Trinity has been understood to be a robustly *biblical* doctrine."[9]

THE COMMUNION BEHAVIOR OF THE ETERNAL TRINITY: MUTUAL GLORY AND LOVE

Now that we know a bit more about the biblical roots of God being both one and three, we are in a better position to answer the question posed at the beginning of this chapter: Who is God? At the least, we can use the historic language of the church to say that God is one in *essence* and three in

8. I think it is helpful to remember John Frame's comment on this: "[Scripture] distinguishes among Father, Son, and Holy Spirit; yet very often it speaks of God as a person without mentioning those distinctions. It is true, as the traditional formulae suggest, that God is one in one respect, three in another respect. Such language is necessary to guard against the possibility of a 'real contradiction,' a chaos, in the Godhead. Yet Scripture does not clearly specify the 'respect' in which God is three as over against the 'respect' in which God is one. In other words, Scripture leaves us with an 'apparent contradiction' here. God is one, and God is three. And Van Til's view [that God is in a sense both one person and three persons] gives us an important warning not to go beyond Scripture in this matter." Frame, "The Problem of Theological Paradox," 307.

9. Crowe and Trueman, "Introduction," in *The Essential Trinity*, 19; emphasis added.

persons. Again, much has been written on the precise meaning of "essence" and "person." But it is sufficient here to say that God's essence is his divinity and its associated characteristics (his spiritual nature, along with his being all-powerful, all-knowing, and ever-present). When we say "persons" we mean distinct and yet interdependent self-conscious agents who are defined in relationship to each other. The Father is who he is as the Father of the Son in the love and power of the Spirit. The Son is who he is as the Son of the Father in the love and power of the Spirit. The Spirit is who he is as the Spirit of the Father and the Son.

Still, for many people today, defining or identifying God as one essence in three persons seems abstract and impersonal. That does not mean that we should abandon this language, for it is based on the teaching of Scripture and has served the church well for a few thousand years. Yet, there are ways in which we can draw out of this language something more relatable for everyday people, those who are not pastors or theologians. As I have argued from the beginning, we might do this by identifying God through his communion behavior, through language. Who is God? God is the one who speaks and dwells in eternal self-communion. Out of that self-communion, he speaks to us, revealing that he is a *communicative being*—and, more importantly, that he wants to communicate with his creatures.

The remainder of this chapter will be devoted to spelling out what it means more precisely for God, as the Trinity, to speak to himself, that is, to exercise communion behavior of the highest order.

One question that I have often been asked by people who are fascinated by the idea that God speaks to himself is this: *how* does God speak to himself? What does this look like? Can we really say that language is a necessary part of God's identity, that language is rooted in the Trinity? I began pondering these things myself after reading a passage from my friend and teacher, Vern Poythress:

> The New Testament indicates that the persons of the Trinity speak to one another. This speaking on the part of God is significant for our thinking about language. Not only is God a member of a language community that includes human beings, but the persons of the Trinity function as members of a language community among themselves. Language does not have as its sole purpose human-human communication, or even divine-human communication, but also divine-divine communication.[10]

If the persons of the Godhead are part of their own divine language community, what do they discuss with one another? This is not just an

10. Poythress, *In the Beginning Was the Word*, 18.

exercise in theological speculation; it gets at the heart of who God is *in himself*, so it deserves a thoughtful, biblical response. I have found such a response in the work of John Frame. Because his thought on this has had such a profound influence on my own thinking, it is worth reproducing here.

> There is no conflict in the Trinity. The three persons are perfectly agreed on what they should do and how their plan should be executed. They support one another, assist one another, promote one another's purposes. This intra-trinitarian "deference," this "disposability" of each to the others, may be called *mutual glorification.*
>
> In the gospel of John, the Father glorifies the Son (John 8:50, 54; 12:23; 17:1) and the Son the Father (7:18; 17:4). The Spirit glorifies the Son (16:14), who in turn glorifies the Father.
>
> To my knowledge, no text says precisely that the Father or Son glorifies the Spirit, but Father and Son do honor the Spirit in his particular work. In John 16:7, Jesus tells the disciples:
>
>> It is to your advantage that I go away, for if I do not go away, the Helper will not come to you. But if I go, I will send him to you.
>
> The Spirit, the Helper, has his special work, which is different from that of the Son. The Spirit can do that work only after the Son has ascended to the Father. So the Son defers to the Spirit. He "goes away," so that the Spirit may come. Jesus testifies, indeed, that after he is gone and the Spirit is come, the disciples will do "greater works" than the works Jesus performed on earth (John 14:12). So Jesus pays honor to the Spirit: he rejoices that in one sense the Spirit's ministry will be greater than his own. So the Father and Son glorify the Spirit by giving him a distinctive and great role in the work of redemption.[11]

I would argue that this glorification and deference within the Trinity also extends to the expression of love. The Father's self-proclaimed love for the Son (Matt 3:17; Luke 3:22; John 5:20) is not something we can restrict to creation and redemption. Surely, it reflects how the Father always views the Son. And we find many passages about the Son's love for the Father (John 3:35; 5:20; 15:9). We can also infer with certainty that the Spirit loves the Father and the Son, for the fruit of the Spirit is love (Gal 5:22). That which comes about because of the Spirit's work must be inherent in the Spirit himself, and if the Spirit inherently *loves*, there must be eternal objects for that

---

11. Frame, *Systematic Theology*, 480–81.

love: the Father and the Son. So, there is also such a thing as *mutual love* within the Trinity. Thus, we can say there is mutual love and glorification within the Godhead. It is this phenomenon that I would deem the communion behavior of God. Each of the divine persons eternally expresses love and glory towards the others.

Now, it is important to make some clarifications here. Frame is discussing what theologians refer to as the *economic* Trinity, the Trinity in its work of creation and redemption. But God chose at some point to create. He was not forced to do so. Before creation, there was God—just God. To refer to God in this sense, we use the terms *immanent* or *ontological* Trinity. The question is, do Frame's statements apply to only the economic Trinity? Can we say that God, apart from creation, mutually loves and glorifies himself?

I believe we can. In John 17:5, Jesus says, "And now, Father, glorify me in your own presence with the glory that I had with you before the world existed." The Son asks the Father to glorify him with the glory that he had been given *before* the world existed. Even before the Father uttered creation into being through his Word and in the power of his Spirit, he glorified the Son. The Father also loved the Son before creation. When Jesus says, "The Father loves the Son and has given all things into his hand" (John 3:35), he does not mean that the Father began loving the Son once creation started. The simple present tense "loves" conveys an eternal truth, not a temporal event. Even more compelling is the wonderful statement from 1 John 4:8, "God is love." Love is not something that God takes on or practices in relation to his creation. Love is something God *is essentially*. In addition, we should note that many theologians have affirmed the biblical teaching that "what God does in time reflects who and what he is in eternity."[12] In terms of God's communication, Kevin Vanhoozer writes, "it is on the basis of God's communicative presence and activity in history that we come to understand divine communicative perfection in eternity."[13] All this is to say that God expresses love and glory within himself even *apart from* creation and redemption. Self-love and self-glory constitute the *essential* nature of the tripersonal God.

Each of the persons in the Godhead, then, glorifies and loves the others without end. These expressions of love and glory represent what we have called communion behavior. As stated earlier, God's communion behavior does not serve to bring the Father, Son, and Holy Spirit into deeper

12. Bray, *God Is Love*, 29.

13. Vanhoozer, *Remythologizing Theology*, 245. Note, however, that Bray and Vanhoozer are not suggesting that *everything* God does in history reflects who he is *essentially*. In the person of Christ, God suffered in history, but this does not mean that God is essentially a suffering God.

communion, since God is already perfect. He already dwells in unparalleled intimacy with himself.

Though we can never quite understand this as creatures, there are spiritual benefits to imagining from our limited human perspective what this could look like. The "trialogue" below is not meant to replicate the expressions of love and glory in the Godhead or to represent the divine persons as human persons. God, as we said, is qualitatively different. But the imagined discourse that follows may help us better understand and marvel at the communion of the Trinity in eternity, leading us to a more concrete appreciation of who God is.[14]

> **The Father**: Son, I love you to the depths of myself. What a perfect image you are of me! You sound so beautiful as I speak you in the hearing of our beloved Spirit! You are all I wish to say.
>
> **The Son**: My Father, you know my love for you runs deeper than the oceans we will hew out of stone for the sons of men. You speak me fluently, in the pure power of our Holy Ghost. Is not the Spirit so wondrous in his energy, as he resonates my sound back to you without residue?! We are one with him, and he with us.
>
> **The Father**: Yes! Spirit, you are simply . . . glorious. As you proceed from me, I rest in your harmony with my Son, and his harmony with me—our harmony with one another.
>
> **The Spirit**: Father, how sweet your Word is as you utter him in the echoes of our essence! I chase around the syllables of your Son in his glory, and *we* revel in *you*! You are our glory! We rest forever in the greatness of your love.

Again, I want to be very careful here. It is not as if God is simply like three human persons who sit in a circle for eternity exchanging compliments. While God is a community unto himself, we must be careful not to import our human understanding of "community" into the Godhead.

14. I am by no means a "social trinitarian." Social trinitarians understand the persons of the Godhead to be relatively independent persons who have unity mainly in their harmonious interaction with each other. This, I believe, goes too far in rationalizing the being of God. The persons of the Godhead are distinct, self-aware agents, but they are also one *in essence*, as the church has always affirmed. Because of this, we will never be able to comprehend God as creatures. Nevertheless, assigning speaking and hearing roles to each of the divine persons is something that occurs in Scripture. The Father speaks (Matt 3:17; 17:5; Mark 1:11); the Son obviously speaks throughout the gospels in the person of Christ; and the Spirit speaks through believers (Matt 10:20). The Son also hears (John 12:49–50), as does the Spirit (John 16:13). We have a duty to reflect this truth in our theology.

God's ways are *higher* than our ways. Nor, by supplying the discourse above, am I implying that we can know precisely what words or expressions God exchanges within himself. We cannot fathom the depths of divine interpersonal communication. Yet, the witness of Scripture confirms that a trialogue of love and glory is at the heart of who God is. This is communion behavior of the highest order. It is personal in the purest sense of the word, going beyond what we can understand or even imagine. The discourse I have written above is only a creaturely attempt to give shape to a biblical truth that we will never—not even in eternity—grasp completely.

Now, it is critical to remember God's communion behavior (language) in the context of creation. *This* medium is what God uses to create all things. God *speaks* creation, and speaking is an essential attribute of God.[15] This has magnificent implications for the nature of reality as we know it.

We began this chapter with a foundational question: Who is God? God is the self-communing Trinity, one being in three persons, each of whom eternally glorifies and loves the others so deeply that our earthly reflections of glory and love pale in comparison. In himself, God is an others-focused, praise-giving, love-extending being. He is one who has eternally and will forevermore *speak*, exercising communion behavior so pure and powerful that it illuminates our world and calls us to know him, seek him, and pour ourselves out in love for him and for others.

This leads us to a discussion of God's communion behavior in relation to us, his creatures. In the next chapter, we explore how language is central to creation.

15. On speech as an essential attribute, see Frame, *Systematic Theology*, 522–23.

3

Creation through Speech and Reality as Linguistic

On the very first page of Scripture, we learn that God created all things through his speech. He spoke the world into being, as we saw in Gen 1:1–5. But we cannot stop there. What does it mean for creation to come through God's communion behavior? This chapter is meant to provide two answers to that question: (1) all of creation is marked by God's communion behavior and thus expresses something about the personal, self-communicating God; and (2) because creation has been brought about through God's communion behavior, and because God is triune, we can perceive a trinitarian structure to reality.

THE TRINITY AND CREATION

Let us first consider how creation relates to the Trinity more broadly. Several theologians have pointed out that creation would not have been possible for what we earlier called a "monistic" deity, a god in whom there is no plurality or diversity. Herman Bavinck, the Dutch Reformed theologian, wrote about this extensively. For him, "the self-communication that takes place within the divine being is archetypal for God's work in creation."[1] What does he mean by this? God's internal communication in eternity is the model (archetype) for his external communication in creation (ectype).[2] If God were

---

1. Bavinck, *God and Creation*, 333.

2. Theologians have used the language of "archetype" and "ectype" to distinguish

not triune, if he were incapable of internal communication as one being in three persons, then he would be incapable of external communication, which includes both creation and redemption. In addressing the essentiality of speech within God, of the eternal Word uttered in the power of the Spirit, Bavinck writes, "By the word God creates, preserves, and governs all things, and by the word he also renews and re-creates the world. . . . John calls Christ the Logos because it is he in whom and by whom God reveals himself both in the work of creation and that of re-creation (John 1:3, 14)."[3] Thus, the Word (John 1:1), which draws our attention to God's self-communication, is central to creation and redemption.

But for now let us focus more narrowly on creation (leaving redemption for a later chapter). Bavinck writes elsewhere about what theologians call "the eternal generation of the Son." The Father eternally generates, or, we might say, *speaks* the Son in the presence and power of the Spirit. Bavinck refers to this as God's "fecundity" (the quality and power to produce something), which we can interpret simply as the Father's ability to eternally speak the Son (John 1:1).

> God's fecundity is a beautiful theme, one that frequently recurs in the church fathers. God is no abstract, fixed, monadic, solitary substance, but a plentitude of life. It is his nature (*ousia*) to be generative (*gennaetikae*) and fruitful (*karpogonos*). It is capable of expansion, unfolding, and communication. Those who deny this fecund productivity fail to take seriously the fact that God is an infinite fullness of blessed life. All such people have left is an abstract deistic concept of God, or to compensate for this sterility, in pantheistic fashion they include the life of the world in the divine being. Apart from the Trinity even the act of creation becomes inconceivable. For if God cannot communicate himself, he is a darkened light, a dry spring, unable to exert himself outward to communicate himself to creatures.[4]

For Bavinck, if God were not trinitarian, if he did not eternally generate or speak the Son in the presence of the Spirit, he could not create. His act of creation derives from his being self-generative. Understand, however, that this does *not* mean that God could simply multiply himself indefinitely. There is and could only ever be three persons in the Godhead, as one

what is proper to God from what can be said about his creatures, since God's creation reflects him on a finite level.

3. Bavinck, *God and Creation*, 273.

4. Bavinck, *God and Creation*, 308–09.

theologian has argued recently.[5] Rather, we only mean that God the Father eternally generates the person of the Son, and this eternal generation is what allows for God's temporal "generation," or creation.

Other theologians confirm Bavinck's biblical sentiment. In a different sense, Ralph Smith has written about God's creation and subsequent revelation through speech. Creation is itself revelation from God. The psalmist writes, "The heavens declare the glory of God, and the sky above proclaims his handiwork" (Ps 19:1). But then God follows his creation with verbal revelation (verbal communion behavior) to Adam and Eve. This act of revelation is integrally related to God's creation (and later redemption) through the Word, in the life-giving power of the Holy Ghost. In light of all this, Smith poses the question,

> Why should God reveal himself? Because He is a triune God for whom the eternal fellowship and mutual communication of Father, Son, and Spirit is essential. It is not possible to imagine the Christian God not communicating because communication is an aspect of His covenantal life as God. Why would God reveal Himself in words? Because there is something about human language this is so perfectly analogous to the communication of the Persons of the Trinity that the Second Person may be called the Word of God. Human language is an analogue of one of the modes, perhaps the most important, of divine communication. For God to have given us verbal revelation, then, is what we would have expected.[6]

Note how Smith points out what we noticed in our earlier discussion of Genesis 1:1–5: It is *expected* that God would create through speech, through communion behavior, because God is a communicating being who eternally communes with himself in three persons. The Father has always spoken the Son in the power of the Spirit, so we would expect God to create the world and reveal himself by communicating through the self-same Word and Breath who are essential to him.

Now, let us move further with this truth. If God has created all things through his divine Word and in the life-giving power of the Holy Spirit, then that means that some mark of God's eternal self-communication—his communion behavior—is reflected in creation. We cannot divorce the medium of God's creation from the message that it communicates (God's glory and divine nature; Rom 1).[7] The medium through which creation comes is

---

5. Bosserman, *The Trinity and the Vindication of Christian Paradox*, 176–82.

6. Smith, *Trinity and Reality*, 72.

7. In the secular world, Marshall McLuhan drew special attention to this in his

part of the message of God, part of his communication. So, this is far from a theological abstraction. In fact, it opens up the first answer offered to the question we asked at the outset of the chapter: What does it mean for creation to come through the medium of divine speech? Is this relevant to our knowledge of God and the world he has made? Indeed, it is. The first answer I wish to develop is that *all of creation is marked by God's communion behavior and thus expresses something about the personal, self-communicating God.*

This will require some unpacking, especially since it sounds abstract. How is all of creation, all of reality, communicative?

REALITY AS COMMUNICATIVE

When I say that all of reality is marked by God's communion behavior and thus expresses something about him, all I am really saying is that every fiber of God's Word-created world reflects his communicative nature in one way or another. The medium (communion behavior) is bound up with the message (the glory of God that creation reveals). And consider this: everything was not only made by God's verbal communion behavior but is continuously sustained by it. In the first chapter of Colossians, Paul goes off on a wondrous tangent glorifying the preeminence of Christ. In 1:16–17, he tells us something that can and should be read in light of John 1:1. He says that *everything holds together in him*, that is, in *the Word* (John 1:1). Reality is not only created by the Word; it is sustained and held together by him. In the same vein, the writer of the book of Hebrews tells us that the Son of God, the Word of the Father, "is the radiance of the glory of God and the exact imprint of his nature, and *he upholds the universe by the word of his power*" (Heb 1:3). Because of this, every part of reality expresses something about its self-expressive maker and sustainer. Put differently, everything in reality is revelational of the God who spoke it—not just people, who are God's image bearers, but animals, plants, the sky, and so on.[8]

Perhaps the clearest biblical support for this comes from Ps 19:1–4.

> 1 The heavens declare the glory of God,
> and the sky above proclaims his handiwork.
> 2 Day to day pours out speech,
> and night to night reveals knowledge.
> 3 There is no speech, nor are there words,
> whose voice is not heard.

---

media theory. What he noted and applied in media studies is a derivative of the truth we are considering here.

8. Van Til, *Introduction to Systematic Theology*, 266.

4 Their voice goes out through all the earth,
and their words to the end of the world.

The heavens "declare"; the sky "proclaims"; time itself and everything that occurs within it ("day to day") "pours out speech." And here is the best part: we hear all of it, for the voice of this speech, its message, cannot escape the ears of image-bearing creatures!

Just think of the concrete implications of this truth: *everything in reality is expressing something about God's glory and his handiwork.* In other words, everything that the trinitarian God has made expresses the glory of the one who communes with himself. Every pebble, every strand of hair, every skin cell *speaks*. It speaks about its triune, self-communicating Lord.

Some examples should draw us into wonder at the wealth of revelation we have been given all around us, and how this revelation points to the communicative nature of God himself. Consider any object you like: a blade of grass, rolling hills, a house—all of them have no choice but to speak of the triune God.

A blade of grass seems like an insignificant thread of vegetation, but remember that it is pouring forth speech, speech about God. So, here is the natural question: what is it saying? Much more than we might think! First, consider the process of photosynthesis that takes place within that blade of grass. If you can remember your early science education, photosynthesis is "the process used by plants, algae and certain bacteria to harness energy from sunlight into chemical energy."[9] A single blade of grass soaks up sunlight and converts it into the energy it needs to thrive. Place this process in its context of divine speech: God spoke the sun and the oxygen surrounding the grass into being, and he sustains the sun, atmosphere, and blade of grass by the word of his power (Heb 1:3). By drawing on the light of the sun and converting it into life-sustaining energy, the blade of grass proclaims God's glory and handiwork. It *speaks* about God, telling us of his grace in choosing to create all things; it tells us of his generosity in providing what the blade of grass needs to survive and grow. It tells us of his steadfastness in setting the laws of nature in place so that the process of photosynthesis is possible.[10] It tells us that God governs all growth—physical growth, of course, but by implication spiritual growth as well. It tells us that God has created life to be embodied; in this case, the embodiment of life takes the form of a single blade of grass. All of this is what the blade of grass is saying about God.

9. Aparna Vidyasagar, "What Is Photosynthesis?" LiveScience, accessed January 18, 2017, http://www.livescience.com/51720-photosynthesis.html.

10. Note that the laws of nature are themselves words of God. See Poythress, *Redeeming Science*, 15.

We can go still further. The blade of grass also contributes to the world around it, since "it takes in the carbon dioxide produced by all breathing organisms and reintroduces oxygen into the atmosphere."[11] So, the blade of grass also suggests that God has embedded life in creation to be relational and integrated. The blade of grass does not exist and dwell by itself; it contributes to the atmosphere around it, and so it is intrinsically relatable to that atmosphere, to its environment. The blade of grass thus tells us that life is relational—all things are integrated. This is a finite reflection of the relational nature of God in three persons. The Father, Son, and Spirit are gloriously and integrally related—in a way we cannot even fathom as creatures. This glorious, integral relation of God manifests itself in the world he has made because he created it through speech, through his communion behavior. It has no choice but to tell of him. A single blade of grass, as it turns out, has much to say about the trinitarian God.

Try the same thing with rolling hills—not rolling hills in general, but a particular series of them in your part of the world. I live in a suburban area of Pennsylvania, so I see a lot of rolling hills. One stretch of them that has impressed itself on me is between Quakertown, where I live, and Doylestown, which is to our southwest. A little road, Route 313, runs through the countryside like a rope laid down in the grass. As I leave Quakertown, I look out into the distance and see a series of waves in the land, a rising and falling topography. The winding road makes the world seem smaller for a moment, since I can see various places connected to a single line of pavement: the intersection at Paletown Road, the edge of Nockamixon State Park, a hint of Dublin in the distance—these and a thousand other things linked to this one road running up and down the land.

I ask the same question of these rolling hills as I ask of the single blade of grass. What are they saying? Again, much more than we might think. The earth that forms the topography has been spoken into being. In fact, mankind was created from the very earth, having life breathed into him by the triune God (Gen 2:7). The land is not just sediment and soil; it is a substance precious to God, something he made and saw fit to use in creating his image bearers. So, the earth beneath my car tells of God's goodness (Gen 1:9–10) and his creativity. The wave-like topography, the peaks and valleys in the land stretching out before me, tells of God's power in making and moving mountains (Judg 5:5; Job 9:5; 14:18; Ps 18:7; 46:3; 65:6; 90:2; 95:4; 97:5; 104:8; Prov 8:25; Isa 40:4, 12; 49:11; Amos 4:13; Micah 1:4; Matt 17:20; 21:21; Mark 11:23; Luke 3:5; Rev 6:14). The hills also tell me of God's diversity in *not* making the world an utterly flat place. And at the same

11. Vidyasagar, "What Is Photosynthesis?"

time, the winding road shows me unity in the land—the interconnectivity of many places. This reminds me of the unity and diversity in the Trinity; God is one being in three persons. The earth that he has formed is comprised of topography that simultaneously express unity and diversity. Once again, because the Father, Son, and Holy Spirit worked via communion behavior to utter the world into being, that world reflects him. It *speaks* about him. Its mountains (and rolling hills) even "sing" about God (Isa 44:23; 49:13). They sing of the glorious redemption he has provided for his people. In the waving topography between Quakertown and Doylestown, the hills tell me that God is good and that he follows his people into valleys and over peaks to redeem them, to reconcile them to himself and draw them into communion.

Or consider your own house. The natural world (grass, rolling hills) speaks of God, but what about parts of reality that have been synthesized or constructed by mankind? Floor boards, two-by-fours, drywall, electrical wires, plumbing pipes—these are all constructed elements that comprise a house. Do they speak of God? Because these elements are drawn from the raw materials that God has spoken into being, and because they have been further crafted by humans (God's language-using image bearers), yes, they too *speak* of God's glory and handiwork. Once again, we can ask, what is my house saying about God?

I currently live in an old home, built in 1902. Like any house, it has many parts, and each part has something to say about God. Perhaps my favorite part of the house is its wood floors. They were laid out in an intricate design with three different kinds of wood: maple, ash, and walnut. What is more impressive than the variation in the wood is the fact that all of the boards were cut to size and installed before the use of electric power tools. Someone did all of this work by hand. Running close to each cutline was not a blade but a person's fingers. Because of this, there are some hairline differences in length for some of the boards, and the spacing between them varies ever so slightly. The personal craftsmanship of the floors tells me of God's overwhelmingly gracious and intricate work of personal spiritual formation. God is both transcendent and immanent, above the world and yet intimately involved with it. He loves person-specific details—features that make each of us unique. Some of the floor boards in my house seem a tad short, but they are sturdy and still fit into a beautiful pattern of woodwork. Analogously, in some of my interactions with my children, I am a tad impatient. Yet, God does not therefore rip me out of my family structure and replace me because I am imperfect. He knows that I am "sturdy" and can hold the weight of my family—not because of any strength on my part but because I am *in* his Son. In fact, I am indwelt by the entire Trinity, by the Father, Son, and Holy Spirit (John 14:23; 15:4–7; 1 Cor 3:16). The Father

sees his Son when he looks at me and finds the Holy Spirit lifting up my con-
science and enlivening my repentance, helping me to be more patient. We
are all short boards in one way or another, but God keeps us in the houses
he has built (Heb 3:4). God is personally gracious in intricate ways for each
of us. That, among many other things, is what my floorboards say of God.

My house also has plaster walls—which, quite frankly, I frequently
complain about. Plaster is brittle; it chips and cracks and shatters at a hammer stroke. It is no friend of nails and does not take kindly to screws either.
Whenever my wife and I want to hang something on the wall, we have to
predrill holes and use what they call "molly bolts" to avoid cracking the
plaster. What do these plaster walls say of God? Many things, but I am most
aware of their message about God's glorious sensitivity. Plaster, you see, is
frustrating to me because it responds more broadly to pressure at a particular point. A hammer stroke at the bottom of the wall can easily lead to a
crack that runs several feet. I respond to this by claiming that plaster is too
fragile, but the problem is actually in my own hands. *I* am the one who is
hitting the wall and causing the fractures. *I* am the one who is not patient
enough to get out my drill and use more caution. *I* am the one causing the
damage, but I blame the plaster. I balk about its composition and nature.

In all of this, the plaster has something to say of God. First, by con-
cealing the inner wall, with all of its electrical cords and rusty, nail-ridden
two-by-fours, the plaster protects me and my family from danger. It makes
us almost wholly ignorant of the electrical threat that lies in the wires behind the wall. In a similar way, God protects us from dangers of which
we are almost wholly ignorant. The greatest threats to us, after all, are not
physical. As terrible as they are, it is not cancer or crones or heart attacks
that pose the greatest threat to us. It is something we cannot see. In fact, it
is a *war* in which we are engaged, whether we realize it or not. There is a
war going on right now for our soul. Our adversaries in this spiritual war
pose the greatest threat to us. Paul writes in his letter to the Ephesians, "We
do not wrestle against flesh and blood, but against the rulers, against the
authorities, against the cosmic powers over this present darkness, against
the spiritual forces of evil in the heavenly places" (Eph 6:12). For many of
us, we go about the day as if we were free from war (which, by the way, the
devil is quite happy about). We are unaware of the evil that lies in wait for
us because God, in his grace, only gives us what we can bear (1 Cor 10:13).
The hideous nature of spiritual evil massed against us is concealed by a wall
of God's mercy and grace. He helps us, day by day, to combat the evil that
emerges. So, he is *sensitive* to our limitations.

Second, though God is certainly not brittle like a plaster wall, he is
also *sensitive* to our daily behaviors and responds to us in a way that does

not compromise his immutability.[12] He is not obligated to respond, and his responses do not compromise his nature as the eternal, unchanging God.[13] God is *both* infinite and personal, as only he can be.[14] Thus, throughout the Old Testament, various emotions are attributed to God: grief, wrath, pity, love.[15] The same is the case throughout the New Testament. When Scripture attributes emotions to God, it does not compromise his eternal unchangeability because "although God's eternal decree does not change, it ordains change. It ordains a series of events, each of which receives God's evaluation."[16] In this sense, God has ordained to be sensitive to the way in which his creatures respond to him.[17] While emotion in God must be understood differently from emotion in human beings, God is not a passionless stone. When we rebel against him and his kingdom of light by acting in darkness—speaking corruptly, fueling bitterness or wrath, slandering others—it *grieves* the Holy Spirit (Eph 5:29–31).[18]

In condescending to create and subsequently reconcile all things to himself, God is not a titanium wall, repelling the marks that creatures might make on him; he is, in a sense, like a plaster wall: He responds with sensitivity to our decisions. In fact, his sensitive response to our decisions is forever marked in the very hands of Christ, God's only Son. The holes in his hands are unmistakable evidence of God's loving, unforced, freely willed response to his sinful creatures. In all that we think, say, and do, God is *sensitive* and responds in the gracious and loving offer of Christ through the Holy Spirit. And perhaps if we meditated more on God's sensitivity, we would be less inclined to swing a hammer at him when we feel frustrated or impatient. Of course, the analogy here breaks down rather quickly. We pose no threat to the Lord of all creation. Though in some senses the plaster wall reminds me of God's sensitivity as he absorbs the marks I make on him in the nail holes of his incarnate Son's hands, the weakness of the plaster also (thankfully) reminds me that God's strength is unparalleled. He is never *essentially*

12. See Vos, *Theology Proper*, 177–78. God takes on a "new relation" when he creates, but this new relation does not necessitate any essential change in God.

13. Frame, *Systematic Theology*, 412–19.

14. Grudem, *Systematic Theology*, 167.

15. Grudem, 166.

16. Frame, *Systematic Theology*, 413.

17. In Vos's language, this means that the "relation" God has to creation changes, but not God himself.

18. We must constantly balance two truths with regards to anthropomorphic language: God is both immutable and yet this emotive language that seems to indicate change is somehow "real." This parallels the mystery of the incarnation, where Christ is *both* the eternal Son *and* truly human.

changed. That is why we can rely on him so heavily. In the end, the plaster walls of my home tell of the paradox of God's sensitivity and unfathomable strength and constancy.

We could go on, but I believe the point is clear. You can look at everything in reality and ask, "What is this saying of God?" You can do this because all things have been spoken into being by the self-communicating Trinity, are sustained by his eternal Word (John 1:1; Col 1:17), and therefore speak *of* him (Ps 19:1–4). What's more, though we can ask this question about every object every day for the rest of our lives, we still will not exhaustively know all that reality is saying about God. Because every speck of reality is marked by God's communion behavior, and God himself is incomprehensible, there is untold mystery in the world. In a lecture delivered several decades ago, Cornelius Van Til said something quite provocative: "We certainly cannot penetrate intellectually the mystery of the Trinity, but neither can we penetrate anything else intellectually because all other things depend on the mystery of the Trinity, and therefore all other things have exactly as much mystery in them as does the Trinity."[19] Because everything around us, including ourselves, has been created through trinitarian communion behavior, everything speaks of God but is also irrevocably marked with mystery.

Now, in drawing this part of the discussion to a close, let me make something very clear. I am *not* trying to advocate for some form of pantheism (thinking of reality as divine), or panentheism (arguing that reality is part of God's being), or animism (attributing self-conscious life to every part of material reality). Reality is not divine, and only some of God's creatures are what we would call "animate." There is and always will be an immoveable distinction between the Creator and his creation, and animate creatures are set apart from inanimate parts of creation.[20] But the fact that God spoke creation into being has an effect on that creation: it keeps testifying *to* him because it was made and is continually sustained *by* his Word (Col 1:16–17), by his speech, by his communion behavior. Reality, as created by God, is expressive of him because it is the product of his communion behavior. The expressive quality of the medium has been imbibed by creation itself. That is what I want to accent here. Because of this, we must constantly remind ourselves that we live in a *worded world* (part of the title of this book), a world that speaks of God's glory. As John Calvin wrote hundreds of years ago,

> Whichever way we turn our eyes, there is no part of the world, however small, in which at least some spark of God's glory does

19. Van Til, "Christ and Human Thought: Modern Theology, Part 1."
20. Poythress, *Philosophy, Science, and the Sovereignty of God*, 21–24.

not shine. In particular, we cannot gaze upon this beautiful masterpiece of the world, in all its length and breadth, without being
completely dazzled, as it were, by an endless flood of light. Ac-
cordingly, in Hebrews, the apostle aptly calls the world the mirror of things invisible, because the structure of the world serves
as a mirror in which we behold God, who otherwise cannot be
seen (Heb 11:3).[21]

For Calvin, all of reality—its length and breadth—is communicative
in the sense that it speaks of God's glory; it shines for him. However, reality
is not only communicative of God's glory and handiwork. It also reflects
the Trinity more specifically in what we might call its *structure*. Because it
was brought into being by God's communion behavior, and God is triune,
the structure of reality (both the world itself and our perception of it) is
trinitarian.

PERCEIVING THE TRINITARIAN STRUCTURE OF REALITY

At this point, I would like to introduce the work of Kenneth L. Pike, whose
thought I have presupposed in the previous pages. For me, Kenneth Pike is
almost unparalleled in his perception of the trinitarian structure of reality,
especially when we consider language as a lens for all of life. Pike studied
many languages for most of his career. His theory of language eventually
solidified into a window through which we can view the world. Let me try
to explain some of Pike's thought and how it reveals the trinitarian structure
of reality.[22]

Let me start by acknowledging that the phrase "trinitarian structure
of reality" sounds quite abstract. I do not want it to be received this way, so
I will try to specify what I mean by it. We have already discussed the most
foundational question, "Who is God?" The answer that we uncovered in the
previous pages is that God is the three-in-one, self-communicating Trinity.
We do not know who God truly is unless we know him as one God in three

---

21. Calvin, *Institutes of the Christian Religion*, 10.

22. In the following pages, I will be drawing on Pike, "Language and Life 4: Tristructural Units of Human Behavior," 36–43; *Language in Relation to a Unified Theory of the
Structure of Human Behavior*; *Linguistic Concepts*; and *Talk, Thought, and Thing*. I will
also be relying on the theological development of Pike's work found in Poythress's text,
In the Beginning Was the Word. I am indebted to Poythress for many conversations on
this topic and his development of the idea that all of reality (metaphysics) is specified by
God's speech. Poythress, *Redeeming Philosophy*, chaps. 5 and 12–14.

persons (Father, Son, and Spirit) who eternally loves and glorifies himself. This God is the hearth of interpersonal communion.[23]

Based on our understanding of who God is, we can ask ourselves what difference this makes in how we see the world. All of reality has been spoken into being by *this* God. As we have stated throughout the book, God has used an intimately personal medium—communion behavior—to create and uphold all things. And because all things reflect God's glory, that is, because all of creation pours forth speech about this God (Ps 19:1–4), would we not expect reality to reflect God's tripersonal nature in some sense?[24] That is what I am getting at with the language "trinitarian structure of reality." Reality has been structured or put together in such a way that, upon the redemption of our minds and spiritual rebirth (Eph 4:23; John 3), we can see the Trinity imprinted on everything—even on our own minds and behaviors.

This last point is an important one. We can only perceive the trinitarian structure of reality when our minds have been renewed by the power of the Holy Spirit, who unites us to Christ, reconciling us with God the Father and drawing us into deeper, personal fellowship with him. Those who reject the saving revelation of God in Scripture are blind to truths that God has instilled in the world around us (Rom 1:21, 28).

Now, the first step to perceiving the trinitarian structure of reality is to begin with *persons as observers.* The title of this section is "Perceiving the trinitarian Structure of Reality." *People* are the ones who *perceive*, so we begin with them. It goes without saying that every person has a perception, a view of reality.[25] That view of reality is created and sustained by the triune God and thus reflects him. At the same time, this reflection is limited. God perceives everything in every way. All of time and space is ever present

---

23. Compare John Calvin's words here: "[God] so proclaims himself the sole God as to offer himself to be contemplated clearly in three persons. Unless we grasp these, only the bare and empty name of God flits about in our brains, to the exclusion of the true God" (Calvin, *Instit.* 1.13.2).

24. There is a tradition in the church of people recognizing what they call *vestigia trinitatis*, "vestiges of the Trinity" in creation. Augustine is perhaps the most famous advocate of this in the Western tradition, drawing out connections between faculties of the human mind and persons of the Godhead. The Eastern tradition tended to focus more on interpersonal analogies. I have set out my own example for vestiges of the Trinity in the article, "Do You See How I See? The trinitarian Roots of Human Perception," 59–76. It is important to note that no vestige of the Trinity is free from error, since we cannot encompass the Creator with examples from creation. For a short explanation of this, see "A Note on trinitarian Analogies," Place for Truth, January 4, 2015, accessed January 19, 2017, http://www.placefortruth.org/content/note-trinitarian-analogies-1.

25. For background on this, see Frame, *Theology in Three Dimensions* and Poythress, *Knowing and the Trinity.*

to him from every perspective imaginable. As John Frame put it, God is *omniperspectival.*[26] Just as God is all-knowing (omniscient), all-powerful (omnipotent), and ever-present (omnipresent), so he is conscious of all perspectives on every part of reality simultaneously. In contrast, as creatures we usually operate based on a single perspective, though we can change our perspective or add to it or refine it when we read the Bible and see the world through God's word. When we sympathize with others through conversing with them or through reading great works of literature, we can develop a range of perspectives on a given issue, or at least become aware that there *is* a range of perspectives available to us. However, this is but a shadow of the omniperspectival God. God sees all in every way. We are scarcely aware of what goes on around us in a ten-foot radius!

As finite creatures of God, we must *focus.* This focus is not negative, for we are made to function as a unified body of believers in Christ (Rom 12:5; 1 Cor 12:27), and our unity and diversity is reflective of the unity and diversity in God.[27] In fact, our capacity to focus is evidence of our finitude and dependence on the God who sees all (Gen 16:13).

Beyond this, we might ask *how* we focus and what this reveals about the triune God. Kenneth Pike used a triad of terms to express how people often focus on pieces of reality: *particle, wave,* and *field.* He called these *observer perspectives.*

We use the particle perspective when we view some part of the world or our daily activity as a discrete particle, with relatively neat borders that separate it from other parts of life. For example, I have some precious time with my family after we eat dinner each night—call it, "post-dinner family time." I can view this time as a unit or particle, preceded and followed by other units of action. Our post-dinner family time seems to have a somewhat discrete beginning and end and is clearly separate from other events of the day (figure 3).[28]

---

26. John M. Frame, "A Primer on Perspectivalism (Revised 2008)," Frame-Poythress.org, accessed January 19, 2017, http://frame-poythress.org/a-primer-on-perspectivalism-revised-2008/.

27. Van Til, *The Defense of the Faith*, 45–53.

28. I use dotted lines in figure 3 because these units are not, in fact, separated with exact precision, as the wave perspective makes clear.

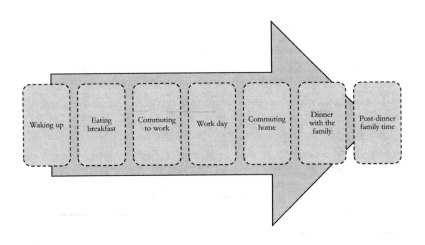

Figure 3: Particle Perspective of the Post-Dinner Family Hour

Viewing family time with the particle perspective helps me to cherish the time I have with my wife and kids because I know it is only a very small part of the day. So, the particle perspective—in helping me view this time as a recurring, but small unit of each weekday—deepens the love I have for and joy I find in my family. By looking at post-dinner family time in *relative* independence from everything else (hence the dotted lines in figure 3), I notice more easily how precious it is. The post-dinner family hour quickly transitions to bedtime routines and late night work projects, once the kids are asleep. I have a treasury of memories from these post-dinner family hours—some make my heart swell with gratitude; others are painful reminders that I am spiritually broken and self-centered. Both sorts of memories, however, are used by the indwelling Holy Spirit to call me to the good works that God has ordained for me to walk in (Eph 2:10). I can compare and contrast my memories to remind myself of what sort of behavior in that hour would be the greatest blessing to my wife and children. By helping me to focus on memories from this relatively discrete time period each day, the Spirit works to sanctify my behavior and align it with that of Christ. In this sense, God uses the particle perspective (which he has created and sustains by his word) to conform me to the image of his Son (Rom 8:29), helping me to emerge wiser and more reflective of him in each post-dinner family hour as his Spirit works in me to manifest the mind of Christ (1 Cor 2:16). Certainly, the progress I make is not continuous. There are setbacks and stumbles, but those become part of God's plan to redeem me. This is one of the many spiritual benefits of the particle perspective.[29]

However, I can also view the post-dinner family hour from the *wave* perspective. Perhaps our family time is spent by running circles around the middle wall of the house: through the living room, around the kitchen, down the hallway, and back into the living room (a common activity for a toddler and a two-year-old). For my wife and I, this time is often the highpoint of the day, like the crest of a wave. Our running around the house is preceded and followed by other actions and conversations: waking up, eating breakfast, driving to work, driving home, greeting my wife, eating dinner, and going to bed. I can perceive waking up as the beginning of the wave, and all of the other events as part of the initial margin of the wave that is leading up to post-dinner family time, which is the highpoint or crest of the wave (Pike used the term "nucleus"). What follows the highpoint would be the other side of the wave, which eventually becomes the margin of another wave with its own nucleus (figure 4). We can perceive our time each day as

29. Kenneth Pike thought that the particle perspective is the most commonly used perspective, since we seek to manage and understand the world around us by breaking it up into separable bits.

a series of such waves—some waves incorporating nearly the whole day (as this example suggests) and others focusing more narrowly on a smaller time frame.

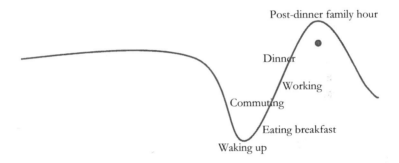

Figure 4: Wave Perspective of the Post-Dinner Family Hour

The wave perspective allows me to focus on the fluid nature of reality: the movement from one action or event to another. With this view, the relatively fixed borders of units in the particle perspective drift into the background. My focus shifts from the static to the dynamic, from stillness to movement, from the world as a series of particles to the world as a series of waves with more fluid borders. God has used this perspective in my own life to teach me in several ways. The wave perspective allows me to see that not everything in a day deserves the same amount of attention. It is more important, for example, that I focus on playing with my children and speaking with my wife than it is for me to focus on what I might eat for breakfast. The former actions are others-focused and part of my calling and passion as a father and husband (Eph 5:25; 6:4). The latter is self-focused and, while good and enjoyable in itself, also has the potential to distract me from what is really important. Remember when Jesus's disciples asked him to focus on eating?

> 31 Meanwhile the disciples were urging him, saying, "Rabbi, eat." 32 But he said to them, "I have food to eat that you do not know about." 33 So the disciples said to one another, "Has anyone brought him something to eat?" 34 Jesus said to them, "My food is to do the will of him who sent me and to accomplish his work. (John 4:31–34)

Jesus did not condemn eating; he knew that food is necessary for survival and that it is often the context for communion with others. But he did put it in a different place on his priority list as compared to his disciples (and to most of us today). In a similar way, God can help us to use the wave perspective to prioritize certain events and actions. Because God has taught me to sometimes view the world through the wave perspective, I can be a better steward of my family by pouring more time and attention into the highpoints. That does not mean I ignore other parts of the day (the margins of this wave) or give less of myself to others during those times. My goal is to be fully present wherever I am and to bring Christ's love and passion to bear on the work I do and the conversations I have. But, for each of us as persons, life is not a flat line; every day has peaks and valleys, and God uses these patterns to teach us when and how we can be good stewards of the time he has given us.

Lastly, I can view post-dinner family time from the *field* perspective, seeing it in relation to other parts of reality: other people, places, and events that have occurred in the past or are occurring simultaneously or will occur in the future. As I am running around the house with my kids, my brother in Montana is likely engaging with his children in a similar way, or speaking to his wife. My other two brothers may be taking photographs or painting or playing music. All of these events might be occurring at the same time, and all of them are in some way related to each other in the complex web of God's plan and providence.

Other outings or family visitations we did on the weekend are in the background of our post-dinner family hour. Our shared experiences as a family inform (explicitly or implicitly) this particular time, as do our individual experiences and conversations from that day. Post-dinner family time is thus placed in a complex web of relations with other events and actions occurring simultaneously, in addition to past and future actions that, in God's providence, are or will be related to that hour. The field perspective draws our attention to the relationships and connections we find all around us (figure 5). Only God has exhaustive knowledge of these relationships, for he is in control of all things and knows precisely how every detail of history, every moment of our lives, is meaningful in relation to his plan to redeem his people and renew all things (Rev 21:5). Amen.

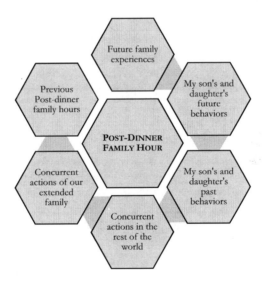

Figure 5: Field Perspective of the Post-Dinner Family Hour

Now, we began discussing these perspectives because we wanted to show how our understanding of who God is might be reflected in the structure of reality. Well, these perspectives are actually rooted in the persons of the Trinity. The particle perspective reflects the Father, the wave the Son, and the field the Spirit.

> The particle perspective is closely related to stability, which is established by the unchanging stability of the plan of the Father. The wave perspective is closely related to the controlling work of the Son, who brings about action in history: "he upholds the universe by the word of his power" (Heb 1:3). The field perspective is closely related to the Spirit's presence. . . . The Spirit, as present to us, and indwelling us who are believers in Christ (Rom 8:9–11), expresses God's relation to us.[30]

We can say a bit more about the relationship between these perspectives and the persons of the Trinity. In relation to the particle perspective, the Father is described throughout Scripture as changeless and immovable, which corresponds to the stability and fixity we see in the particles we perceive all around us. James describes the Father as the one "with whom there is no variation or shadow due to change" (1:17). Nothing in creation can perfectly mirror this quality of the Father, but creation can certainly reflect it on the creaturely level. In fact, as we have said all along, the communion behavior by which God created and specified the nature of all things means precisely this.

In relation to the wave perspective, we have already noted how the Son is the *Speech* or *Word* of God. As Bavinck wrote, "both in creation and re-creation God reveals himself by the word. By the word God creates, preserves, and governs all things, and by the word he also renews and recreates the world."[31] The Word, as Son, is the dynamism of God—both in eternity and in the incarnation. The incarnate Son is the "servant sent to effect the work of the Father, obedient even unto death and one day delivering up his kingdom to the Father."[32] All of what Christ did, however, was also done in union with the Spirit of God, who bore him and was always upon him (Matt 1:18; Luke 1:35; 4:18; cf. Isa 61:1). Because the Son carries out the work of his Father in the power of the Spirit, it is possible to view the salvific work of Christ as a wave: his life and teaching the *initial margin*, his crucifixion and resurrection the *crest*, and his following ascension the *final margin*. And even within that initial margin, we see the human nature of Christ in

---

30. Poythress, *In the Beginning Was the Word*, 56–57.
31. Bavinck, *God and Creation*, 273.
32. Bavinck, 276.

dynamic development within a field of relationships, as he "increased in wisdom and in stature and in favor with God and man" (Luke 2:52).

In relation to the field perspective, the Spirit proceeds from the Father and the Son and "stands in the closest possible relation to both of the other persons."[33] As such, the Spirit associates the Father and the Son in eternal fellowship. The deep association between the Father and the Son, a "mutual fellowship and indwelling," is what "reflects the character of God the Holy Spirit, who indwells us."[34] As the Spirit brings out the communion of the Father and the Son, so he also brings out the communion between members of the body of Christ. In Christ, we are all "being built together into a dwelling place for God by the Spirit" (Eph 2:22). Because of the person and work of the Spirit, all of reality coheres and is interrelated in a way that reflects the glorious relations and coinherence of the Father and Son.

Now, just as the Father, Son, and Holy Spirit are intimately related to one another in communion, the perspectives with which we view the world (particle, wave, and field) are intimately related.[35] Theologians use the term *perichoresis* or *coinherence* to refer to the intimate union of the divine persons. St. Augustine described the biblical teaching of perichoresis as the notion that, with regards to the Father, Son, and Holy Spirit, "each is in each, and all are in each, and all are one."[36] We can say the same, analogously, about the particle, wave, and field perspectives.

The particle perspective is clearly distinct, but even in our example, we can see that the other perspectives are in the background. As we noted, our post-dinner family hour is preceded and followed by other events, each of which is part of a wave-like structure. In fact, we need these other events to provide some sort of border for the post-dinner family time. In other words, for particles to exist, there must be waves in which we can identify them—waves comprised of other particles that are separable from the one on which we are focusing. Similarly, the field perspective is in the background because there is no such thing as a "decontextualized unit." *Every unit of behavior has a context.* That context enables us to identify both the unit and the wave-like structures in which we might view it. So, we can

---

33. Berkhof, *Systematic Theology*, 97.

34. Poythress, "Reforming Ontology and Logic in the Light of the Trinity," 192. "No communion with God is possible except by the Spirit. . . . By the Spirit we have communion—direct and immediate communion—with no one less than the Son and the Father themselves." Bavinck, *God and Creation*, 278.

35. Poythress, *In the Beginning Was the Word*, 56–59.

36. Augustine, *The Trinity*, 6.10. For the biblical grounds of this teaching and a survey of its history, see Hibbs, "Closing the Gaps: Perichoresis and the Nature of Language."

focus on the particle perspective, but not at the expense of the wave and field perspectives. Analogously, we can focus on the Father and give him the worship that he deserves, but not to the exclusion of the Son, whom he has given for our redemption, and the Spirit, who indwells us because of what the Son has done.

In sum, the trinitarian structure of reality is reflected in how we, as God's image bearers, perceive the world around us in particles, waves, and fields. Yet, there is more in the world that reflects God's triune nature. We can move from our general perspectives on the world to more specific features of the various elements within that world.

Kenneth Pike used the terms *contrast, variation,* and *distribution* to describe these features.[37] Everything that we can perceive around us contrasts with something else, has various manifestations (variants), and is distributed in a broader context.

Let us choose another example to consider: my favorite writing instrument. I like using mechanical pencils, and my current favorite is a Pentel Twist-Erase GT, with 0.5mm lead. (I know: I am a huge nerd.) This pencil contrasts with other pencils of a different color, brand, lead thickness, and so on. Even if I had a second one of these pencils of the same color, there would be minor variations between them. One might have the grip slightly frayed at the bottom, or the pocket clip might be a little bowed out from the barrel of the pencil. No two things are *exactly* alike. There is contrast, and this contrast establishes *identity* in both negative and positive ways. There are certain features of my blue pencil that are *not* present in other pencils (negative); and there are certain features that I notice more positively as belonging to this particular pencil (e.g., some of the hairline scratches on the plastic barrel). In other words, we identify parts of the world around us both by what they are and what they are not. "My blue pencil is not a mountain." That statement does not really help someone understand what my pencil is used for or looks like. To fill in the missing pieces of the definition, I must add positive specifics. "My blue pencil is a six-inch, well-worn writing instrument that I use to mark up the books that I read." Now you have a better sense of what my blue pencil is; in other words, you can identify it by distinguishing it from what it is not and also by attributing positive features and purposes to it. That is all part of the concept of identity.

At the same time, my blue pencil has what Pike called *variation.* My pencil is not the same today as it was several months ago. In fact, each day it is a little bit different. Each day, it is a unique *manifestation* of the same pencil. When I pick up my pencil on Friday, it is the same pencil I was using

37. Pike, *Linguistic Concepts,* 42–65.

on Monday (identity), but it is slightly different. There may be new scratches on the shaft or the pocket clip. The rubber grip is worn a bit more, as is the eraser. Each day, my pencil is a unique manifestation of the same object.

Lastly, my blue pencil has a *distribution*. That term sounds abstract, but the idea it represents is quite simple. In plain terms, we might just say that my blue pencil has a *place* or *context*. It has a physical place that varies from day to day, based on whether I take it with me to work or leave it on my desk, or on top of my night stand. It has a place or context with regards to its purpose. It is part of a network of instruments I use for particular ends. I pick up a fork to eat food, a mug to drink coffee, and a pencil to take notes. Each instrument has its purpose, and each purpose fits into a network of functions and greater purposes that God is governing.

As with the particle, wave, and field perspectives, the elements of contrast, variation, and distribution reflect the persons of the Trinity.

The element of contrast reflects the Father, whom *no one* knows exhaustively but the Son. Recall Matthew 11:25–27.

> At that time Jesus declared, "I thank you, Father, Lord of heaven and earth, that you have hidden these things from the wise and understanding and revealed them to little children; 26 yes, Father, for such was your gracious will. 27 All things have been handed over to me by my Father, and no one knows the Son except the Father, and no one knows the Father except the Son and anyone to whom the Son chooses to reveal him.

Remember that contrast and identity involve both positive and negative descriptions. Negatively, the Father is he whom only the Son knows exhaustively; thus, the Father is *not* known exhaustively by his creatures, though he is certainly known truly according to their limited capacity as image bearers. As we said earlier, God's thoughts are higher than our thoughts and his ways higher than our ways (Isa 55:9). There is a clear contrast, but because God has made us in his image, the contrast does not exclude overlap. We do have true knowledge of God (Rom 1), but we will never know the Father as the Son knows the Father in the intimacy of the Holy Spirit. Positively, the Father is described by Jesus as "Lord of heaven and earth," which labels the Father not in terms of what we do *not* know but in terms of what we *do* know. The Father is sovereign over the celestial and earthly realms. This is part of the *identity* of the Father that we recognize even when we are not specifically considering him in his relationship to the Son.

In linking the Father with the element of contrast, however, we must be careful not to suggest that the contrastive and identifying features of the Father segregate him from the other divine persons; rather, they actually allow for unity, since "unity" is an empty term apart from the context of diversity. We see this unity brought to our attention when some of the actions that are prominent in the personhood of the Father do not exclude the Son. For instance, in Matthew 11:25–27, "a comparable revealing function is attributed to both the Father and the Son." And because Matthew clearly expresses that "Jesus' position is squarely on the Creator side of the Creator-creature divide," we know that the Son shares in the Lordship of the Father (as passages such as 1 Cor 15:28 make plain).[38] Thus, while we can link the Father with the element of contrast, his contrastive and identifying features serve the gloriously deep harmony of the Godhead.[39]

The element of variation reflects the Son, since he is a "variant" or "manifestation" of the divine essence, eternally begotten (or spoken) by the Father. We hinted at this when we referenced Herman Bavinck's statements about the fecundity of God. We might phrase Bavinck's point here with the language of Pike's theory. God's ability to manifest himself and produce the eternal "variant" of the Son is part of what makes God trinitarian and what allows for creation.

Lastly, the element of distribution reflects the Spirit. The Spirit is the *context* for the relation between the Father and the Son. The Father and the Son are in harmony *through the Spirit*, who proceeds from them both. Without the Spirit, whom theologians have called "the bond of love" between the Father and the Son, God would be incomplete.[40] The Spirit is thus the *context* for the Father-Son relationship, since the Father-Son relationship flourishes in an eternal bond of Spirit-wrought love. As written by the Greek Orthodox theologian Dumitru Stăniloae, "The Father and the Son unite as Father and Son even more through the Spirit. They are three Persons, but the third does not stand to the side of the other two; He unites Them. He is in each, uniting Them and reinforcing Them in Their distinct qualities even when they speak with us."[41] Especially noteworthy for our purposes is the fact that Stăniloae reaffirms that the Spirit is united to the Father and the Son *through divine language* (communion behavior).

38. Crowe, "Trinity and the Gospel of Matthew," 30.

39. There is also a sense in which all of the contrastive-identificational features that we might have of the Father are in some sense related to the Son and the Spirit, since the very word "Father" presupposes sonship. This has been evident at least since the time of Augustine. He addresses this issue in the first few books of *De Trinitate*.

40. Levering, "The Holy Spirit in the trinitarian Communion," 129–30.

41. Stăniloae, *The Holy Trinity: In the Beginning There Was Love*, 65. Given Stăniloae's theological tradition, Reformed readers must guard against the subordinationism that still lies in eastern theology, since most eastern theologians have never accepted the *filioque* clause of the Nicene Creed. Nevertheless, Stăniloae's work is helpful in showing the bond of love that unites the Father, Son, and Spirit.

Both the Son and the Spirit speak with the other—and the Father—in Themselves. This is why we say that the Spirit is not a "He" about whom the Father and Son speak, but each speaks of the other two inseparably. Neither the Father nor the Son speaks about the Spirit as about a third who is apart from Them, but the Father has the Spirit within Himself when he speaks with the Son, and the Son has the Spirit within Himself when He speaks with the Father, just as when He speaks with us.[42]

The Spirit is thus the divine person fostering and partaking in communion behavior among the persons of the Godhead.

As with the particle, wave, and field perspectives, the elements of contrast, variation, and distribution interpenetrate one another in a way that mirrors the interpenetration of the Father, Son, and Holy Spirit (perichoresis). This is summarized in figure 6.

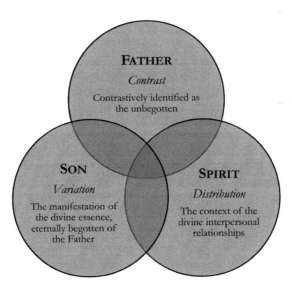

Figure 6: Father, Son, and Spirit as Contrast, Variation, and Distribution

42. Stăniloae, 65

Now, though I have used the terminology above—particle, wave, and field perspectives; contrast, variation, and distribution—more generally, it is important to note that Kenneth Pike first used them in his study of language. It was language, for Pike, that brought out the particle, wave, and field observer perspectives. It was linguistic units that showed elements of contrast, variation, and distribution. This should be easy for us to accept, given what we have seen about the linguistic or communicative nature of created reality. If all of reality is linguistic or communicative because God has brought it about by his communion behavior, then the study of language would be the natural avenue to perceive the trinitarian nature of God in the world around us.

Let me end this chapter by restating why we have examined all of this. The terminology can seem unnecessary and intimidating, so I want to make it clear that this has practical implications for every believer.

We noted earlier in the chapter that, for theologians such as John Calvin, all of reality is communicative in the sense that it speaks of God's glory. Psalm 19:1–4 confirmed this for us. However, we wanted to see if all that God has made might communicate something about who he is as triune. Reality, I noted, has a "trinitarian structure." This applies both to how we perceive that reality (particle, wave, and field perspectives) and to the nature of reality itself, everything having elements of contrast, variation, and distribution. So, both for us as image bearing creatures and for reality itself, the communion behavior of the Trinity has a profound impact. All of reality is indelibly marked by the Trinity. Christians who have been born of the Spirit and are walking in newness of life have the Spirit-wrought ability to see the Trinity everywhere.

But we ourselves, as communicative creatures, image the Trinity in far deeper ways than the rest of creation. Only humans are made in the image and likeness of God, and language is the greatest testament to our being made in that image. This leads us to the final chapter of this section.

4

Image-Bearing Creatures,
Image-Bearing Speakers

PEOPLE COMPRISE A UNIQUE part of God's creation precisely because we are made in his image and likeness. But it can be difficult to understand precisely what this means. Theologians throughout the history of the church have often defined the image of God (*imago Dei*) more broadly as consisting in *knowledge, righteousness,* and *holiness.* The Westminster Confession of Faith says that God "created man, male and female, with reasonable and immortal souls, endued with knowledge, righteousness, and true holiness, after his own image" (WCF 4.2). This is certainly true and plain from certain passages of Scripture, such as Colossians 3:10 and Ephesians 4:24. Our ability to know anything on a creaturely level, to live a righteous life by the Spirit of God, and to set ourselves apart from the sinful world mark us as image bearers. Another part of our image is our dominion over creation (Gen 1:26). God rules over all things, but he has given ruling privileges to his creatures that reflect his own dominion.

However, there is an element of God's image in man that presents itself in the immediate context of the creation account (Gen 1–2), and this element follows from all that we have witnessed so far: we image God in our ability to use language, that is, in our exercise of communion behavior.[1] In fact, I would argue that this is the burning core of God's image in us and the

---

1. Recall Vos's words: "That man bears God's image means much more than that he is spirit and possesses understanding, will, etc. It means above all that he is disposed for communion with God, that all the capacities of his soul can act in a way that corresponds to their destiny only if they rest in God." Vos, *Anthropology*, 13.

basis for all of our other imaging attributes (i.e., knowledge, righteousness, holiness). Language is thus a very special reflection of God in us. It is the prism through which divine light refracts and illuminates the world around us. Richard Gaffin seems to bring this out when he writes,

> As our being itself is derived from God (we exist because he exists), and as our knowledge is an analogue of his knowledge (we know because he knows), so, too, our capacity for language and other forms of communication is derivative of his. We speak because God speaks, because he is a speaking God; that is his nature and so, derivatively, it is ours. In other words, man in his linguistic functions, as in all he is and does, is to be understood as the creature who is the image and likeness of God (Gen 1:26). In fact, should we not say that especially in his language man reflects the divine image he is?[2]

Yes, "*especially* in his language." We can better understand this once we have a sense of who we were created to be. We have answered the question, "Who is God?" But now it is time to address the follow-up question: "Who are we?" The church's teaching on the image of God is meant, in part, to answer this question with Scriptural fidelity. So, let us follow in that path and first try to understand who we are by looking at the creation of Adam and Eve as persons. This will help us better appreciate how language is central to our being made in God's image.

A GENESIS DEFINITION OF 'PERSONS'

Much has been written about the meaning of the word 'person' over the centuries. This was a particularly important word for the church, since 'person' (with its variations in Latin and Greek) has long been used as a reference for humans and yet, since the formation of the Nicene Creed in the fourth century, it has also been used in a distinct sense to refer to the Father, Son, or Holy Spirit. So, we must be careful in how we define human persons in distinction from divine persons. Remember that there is a *qualitative* distinction between God and his creatures, but amidst that distinction there is also continuity and analogy. Thus, when we say that the Father, Son, and Holy Spirit are divine *persons*, we are simultaneously separating them from humans and yet relating them to humanity in some way. This is required by the biblical teaching of God's image in us.

---

2. Gaffin Jr., "Speech and the Image of God," 182–83.

So, what does Genesis have to say about who we are as human persons, as image-bearing creatures of the tripersonal God? As we have already noted, Genesis 1:26 tells us that we were made in God's image and after his likeness, and that we were given dominion over all else that God had spoken into being. It also tells us that we were created "male and female" (1:27). Then, after offering abundant, sustaining resources to his image bearers (1:29–30), God makes his pronouncement: all that he had made was "very good."

We might ask, in what sense were persons created as "very good"? There are many senses that we could explore, but let us focus on the sense that involves communion behavior: persons *as male and female* constitute the image of God as "very good." As Bavinck writes, "It is not man alone, or woman exclusively, but both of them, and those two in interdependence, who are the bearers of the image of God."[3] He goes on to say that Adam's nature "inclines to the social—he wants company. He must be able to express himself, reveal himself, and give himself. He must be able to pour out his heart, to give form to his feelings. He must share his awareness with a being who can understand him and can feel and live along with him."[4]

You might notice the parallels here that are drawn between God as the self-communicating Trinity and man as his communicating image bearer. Even before the creation of Eve, Adam had interpersonal communication with God. In that sense, part of his personhood—in fact, the foundation of his personhood—was communion behavior with his maker. God's creation of Eve complements rather than establishes the centrality of communion behavior to Adam's identity. As persons, we long to *express, reveal,* and *give* ourselves to God and to others. And in that expressing, revealing, and giving we long to grow closer to the God who made us in his image and to our fellow human beings who are also in relationship with God. In other words, people long to practice communion behavior in a way that parallels God on the creaturely level. God is three divine persons in one essence who eternally commune with each other in love and glory; his finite image bearers are endowed with a capacity and longing for communion with him and with other finite persons. To put it briefly, God is supernaturally relational in himself; we are derivatively relational with him and with one another.

Colin Gunton, among other recent theologians, has reinforced this notion that personhood is intrinsically relational. Following the thought of the Scottish philosopher John Macmurray, Gunton writes, "As persons we

3. Bavinck, *Our Reasonable Faith*, 184–85.

4. Bavinck, 188.

are only what we are in relation to other persons."[5] Gunton finds this truth professed most emphatically in the Eastern church (which, admittedly, has its own theological problems to wrestle with).[6] For him, "The logically irreducible concept of the person as one whose uniqueness and particularity derive from relations to others was developed by the Eastern Fathers in the heat of their concern for the loyalty of the Christian church to the biblical understanding of God."[7]

Now, this may sound novel to some readers. In the history of western orthodox Christianity, this understanding of personhood has not been emphasized. Much of the time, the *rational* nature of humans has been the focal point in defining persons as individuals.[8] But what I hope our brief discussion of Genesis 1–2 has pointed out thus far is that understanding persons as intrinsically relational is patently biblical. Adam and Eve *together* constitute the image of God. They are pronounced "very good" as relational creatures.

Genesis 1–2 reveals that we are communing creatures—spoken into being so that we might speak back to God and to other persons made in his image.

CONSCIOUS AND INTERPERSONAL SPEAKERS

The previous discussion helps pave the way for a deeper understanding of the image of God in us as it relates to language (communion behavior).

There are two senses in which we image God in our use of language. The first sense is what I will call the *consciousness analogy*. That phrase, again, sounds abstract, but here is what it means. In Genesis and all throughout Scripture, we see that God the Father speaks the Word in the power of the Spirit. Recall our reference to Psalm 33:6 earlier, "By the word of the LORD the heavens were made, and by the breath of his mouth all their host." At creation, the Father spoke his Word in the power of the Spirit and uttered reality into existence. This was a reflection, we noted, of the eternal

---

5. Gunton, *The Promise of Trinitarian Theology*, 88.

6. Eastern theologians still trend toward the ancient teaching known as subordinationism. In short, subordinationism suggests that the Son and Spirit are *subordinate* (and many consider this to connote inferiority) to the Father. They derive their essence or being from him. The Western church has, I believe on solid biblical grounds, always rejected this position. The Father, Son, and Spirit relate to one another in an ordered equality, not in a hierarchy of being.

7. Gunton, *The Promise of Trinitarian Theology*, 96.

8. See Kelly, *The God Who Is: The Holy Trinity*, 493–518; and Gunton, *The Promise of Trinitarian Theology*, 84–87.

communion behavior of God in himself. In eternity, God forever speaks his Word (the Son) in the power and hearing of the Holy Spirit.

The Father, his eternal Word, and the Spirit are also *coinherent*. We touched on this earlier when introducing the term *perichoresis*. The Father is in the Word, and the Word is in the Father, and the Spirit is in the Father and the Son, and so on. We can also refer to this as *indwelling*. The persons of the Godhead mutually indwell one another, and so by extension the Speaker (Father), his Word (Son), and his Breath (Spirit) indwell one another.

> The Father's wisdom is expressed in the Word. This expression in the Word shows that the Father dwells in the Son. The Father's thought is in the Son. In addition, the Father's Word is in the Father even before he expresses it to the world. That implies that the Son dwells in the Father. And the Spirit, as the breath of God, works in power in conformity with the character of the Word. The Spirit is in the Son and the Son is in the Spirit. The Spirit carries out the purpose of the Father, and manifests the power of the Father, which implies that the Father dwells in the Spirit and the Spirit in the Father.[9]

This is the linguistic, consciousness analogy for God: Speaker, Speech, and Breath.

Because we are created in God's image, we also speak words in the power of our breath. Thus, the consciousness analogy is simply another observation we can make in light of the union between Genesis 1 and John 1. "In the Trinity, the language in John 1:1 represents the Father as the speaker, the Son as the speech (the Word), and the Holy Spirit as the breath. This triad in divine speech is clearly analogous to what happens in human speech. We have a human speaker, his speech, and the breath or other medium that carries the speech to its destination."[10] Every day we image God the moment we open our mouths. In fact, in a sense, we even image the divine Speaker, Word, and Breath with regards to coinherence or indwelling.[11] Our words dwell in us, as does the breath we use to produce them.

Our imaging of God in the consciousness analogy (speaker, speech, and breath) is quite profound and should draw us to awe and worship. Of course, because of the difference between the Creator and his creatures, there are differences between us in this analogy. Though it may seem that I have driven this point into the ground, we must constantly remind ourselves that God is qualitatively different from us. (Much theology goes awry precisely

9. Poythress, *In the Beginning Was the Word*, 21.

10. Poythress, 31.

11. Poythress, 32.

because this qualitative distinction is disregarded or forgotten.) An example of this qualitative difference is the fact that we do not have the ability to create things with our speech; that is a power only God has. But even here, because we are made in his image, there are creaturely derivatives that point back to this creative capacity of God's speech. For example, we forge or create relationships with our words. Every time we meet a stranger, we have the opportunity to use the God-given power of language to begin forming a relationship with that person. We can use language, too, when building upon our existing relationships with our family members and friends. Human language has been endowed by God with a creative or shaping power that images God's all-powerful speech on a creaturely level.

The second sense in which we image God in our use of language is what I will call the *interpersonal analogy.* In a previous chapter, we discussed how God is a self-communicative being. He is one God in three persons who eternally express accolades of love and glory to each other. In an analogous way, we express ourselves to other human persons. As Bavinck put it, we long to express, reveal, and give ourselves to others. However, because of the effects of sin on our lives, "love and glory" are seldom the words that capture our interpersonal communication. Now, it is true that we should only be "glorifying" God, not other people, so that word does not apply to creaturely communication. But we are repeatedly called upon to honor our father and mother (Exod 20:12; Deut 5:16; Matt 15:4) and to honor one another (Rom 12:10; 1 Cor 12:26; Phil 2:29; 1 Tim 5:3; 1 Pet 2:17; 3:7), and honor is a derivative of glory.[12] In addition, there are many passages in the New Testament that call us to love one another (John 13:34, 35; 15:12, 17; Rom 12:10; 13:8; Gal 5:13; Eph 4:2; 1 Thess 3:12; 4:9; Heb 10:24; 1 Pet 1:22; 4:8; 1 John 3:11, 23; 4:7, 11). Foundational to this interpersonal human love, however, is the love we are to have for God himself, as Moses wrote in Deuteronomy, "You shall love the LORD your God with all your heart and with all your soul and with all your might" (Deut 6:5).

Let us pause here to make a very important point: *our love for God grounds our love for others.* In other words, the interpersonal love we have for God is meant to inspire interpersonal love for other creatures made in his glorious image. The interpersonal love we have for God is rooted in the interpersonal love that is expressed among the persons of the Godhead. So, there is a relationship between God's love for himself, our love for God, and our love for others (figure 7).

12. Note, however, that any honor or praise we receive is merited strictly by God's grace, who created us with "glory and honor" (Ps 8:5).

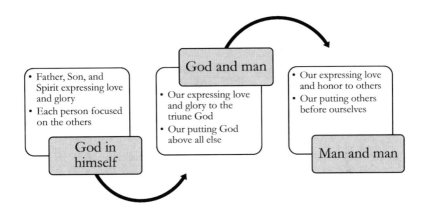

Figure 7: Model for Interpersonal Love

Having said that, we struggle to love God and to love others because of the effects of sin in our lives. In a later chapter, we will discuss what I call the "linguistic nature" of sin—how our sinful behavior is a disruption and distortion of the communion behavior we were always meant to practice in faithfulness.

The interpersonal analogy of communication in God is also represented in the New Testament, where each of the divine persons is given speaking or hearing roles. As Kevin Vanhoozer writes, "the gospels assign speaking parts to each of the three divine persons."[13] The Father speaks (Matt 3:17; 17:5; Mark 1:11); the Son obviously speaks throughout the gospels; and the Spirit speaks through believers (Matt 10:20). The Son also hears (John 12:49–50), as does the Spirit (John 16:13). In obvious ways, we image God in how we speak to and hear other human persons.

Now, with these two senses of linguistic imaging—the consciousness and interpersonal analogies—let us return to God's creation of Adam. Adam and Eve were each marked with the consciousness analogy of language as image bearers. We see this first in Adam's linguistic action of naming the animals in Gen 2:19–20. This action marks Adam as an image bearer of the God who speaks (consciousness analogy). This extends even to the nature of Adam's speech with regards to its *meaning*, *control*, and *presence*. These attributes of Adam's speech image the ultimate meaning, control, and presence of God's speech.

> God repeatedly speaks. And the words he speaks have *meaning*. Each of God's utterances in Genesis 1 has specific meaning, and each specifies what will come forth. Sometimes the utterances include specifications as to how the newly created thing is to function.

> Second, God's words exert *control*. God's word controls the world that he creates. The immensity of his power is clearly exhibited in the immensity of the effects that his word has. As Psalm 148:5 summarizes it, "He commanded and they were created." God's word exhibits his own omnipotence.

> Third, the word of God manifests the *presence* of God. The presence of God is made strikingly evident by the fact that God's word has the attributes of God. It has divine power, or omnipotence, as is evident from its power to bring forth created things that match its specification. It has divine wisdom, as is evident from the wisdom displayed in the completed creation. It has

13. Vanhoozer, *Remythologizing Theology*, 246.

divine goodness, as is evident from the goodness of the created product (Gen 1:31). God's word shows us God.[14]

These three elements are coinherent and bound up with one another, since the Father (as the source of all meaning), the Son (the controlling power and wisdom of God who upholds the world; Heb 1:3; Col 1:17), and the Spirit (the living, breathing presence of God) are coinherent. Analogously, Adam's words have meaning, control, and presence.[15] This is evident in his naming of the creatures. By using names to differentiate between animals, Adam expresses meaning. He also calls our attention to the unique identity of each animal (using the particle perspective and the element of contrast, which we already examined). Adam simultaneously exercises control, a control that reflects God's own linguistic control in naming elements of creation (e.g., the day and night; Gen 1:5). In doing this, Adam draws our attention to the wave perspective and the element of variation. The creatures that Adam names move about in God's world in waves of activity, and the pronunciation of their names involves variation in the voice and pronunciation of human creatures. The animals that Adam names are also themselves variants, particular manifestations of themselves in the unfolding of time. Lastly, Adam is present with his words because the names that he chose reflect his personal decisions as a unique human being. Adam's naming here also draws our attention to the field perspective and the element of distribution, for Adam as a "very good" image bearer is in relationship with Eve and with God, and he has a context (distribution) in the created order, in time and space. Thus, as an image bearer of the speaking God, Adam's use of language, his communion behavior, reflects the meaning, control, and presence that are rooted in God's trinitarian nature. His communion behavior also evokes the particle, wave, and field perspectives as well as the elements of contrast, variation, and distribution—all of which are rooted in the Trinity!

And consider this: Adam's very speech (as part of creation) is grounded in the Trinity and sustained by the Word of God, which upholds all things. In other words, Adam's communion behavior rests upon and reflects the divine communion behavior that brought him into being! At this point, I hope the subtitle for the book is clear. *This* is why language (communion behavior) is at the center of everything.

Adam and Eve were also marked with the interpersonal analogy of language as they converse with God and with one another (Gen 1:28–30; 2:23; 3:9–13).

---

14. Poythress, *In the Beginning Was the Word*, 26.

15. Poythress, 30.

Both analogies of communion behavior—our ability to speak and our ability to commune with the tripersonal God and his creatures—constitute the core of the image of God in man. Language (communion behavior) is the ground of God's image, from which all of our other good imaging behaviors or attributes emerge. As the Westminster Confession of Faith says, we image God in knowledge, righteousness, and holiness, but those behaviors are only ever manifested in communicative settings of one sort or another—either in the consciousness or interpersonal analogies of language.

Our knowledge forms and develops in the context of our engagement with the world, which we already noted is communicative, expressing God's glory and handiwork. And because knowledge pertains to the personal world that the triune God has created, the world that continues to speak to us about him, our knowledge is ultimately *personal*, not propositional. In other words, knowledge does not ultimately have to do with facts and functions; it has to do with facts and functions in the exhaustively personal and purposeful atmosphere in which we have been placed by the self-communicating God. So, we image God in our knowledge, but that knowledge lives in a communicative context—either in the world that communicates to us about God or in personal relationships that this personal God has ordained, relationships which image the personal communion of God himself. What I mean to say is that language—communion behavior—is the playground for human knowledge. Whatever we know, we know in relation to other persons who are made in the image of God, and in relation to the God who is three persons in one essence. We perform the action of *knowing* in the profoundly communicative world of the trinitarian God. Human knowledge thus grows out of communication between God and his people and between people themselves.

Righteousness, too, is grounded in language, for righteousness has to do with moral uprightness. Much of the time, moral uprightness takes shape in interpersonal relationships. The command not to covet or steal is an interpersonal command. Do not covet or steal *from this or that person*. Or, when righteousness does not take shape in interpersonal relationships among humans, it does so in our personal relationship with God, a relationship that is based upon God's communication with us both in the world he has made and in his inspired word. Again, whenever we are righteous, we are righteous in personal, communicative contexts. So, language is the playground for personal righteousness. Whenever we are righteous by God's grace, we are so because of and through communion behavior.

Holiness is grounded in language as well. Holiness refers to our being set apart. We are first of all set apart from the rest of creation precisely because of language, because of our ability to speak and commune with others.

Communion behavior is what makes humanity the crown jewel of God's creation. Thereafter we were meant to continue to live in holiness as those who love and honor other persons. So, whenever we are holy, we are holy in communicative contexts—in our speech with others, or in our decision to refrain from taking part in certain activities, which is a response to God's speech in Scripture. Language, again, is the playground for human holiness. Whenever we are holy, we are holy because of and through communion behavior.

In all of this, I mean to draw our attention to the profound gift of language as the core of the image of God in us. So wonderfully have we been made, so perfectly spoken into being, that we speak *back* and shine light on the glorious communion of the Trinity. To answer the question we posed at the beginning of the chapter—who are we?—I would say, *we are creatures who speak, creatures who are meant for communion with God and with other creatures.*

But, what does all of this have to do with our personal lives? Are not the previous chapters mainly theoretical? Have we not just been dealing in ideas? Far from it: in discussing or thinking about language, we meddle in the marrow of our humanity, and that has very practical implications for us. The second half of the book is meant to show us just how practical and powerful these implications are for us each day, in the context of the unfolding story of Scripture.

What That Means for You and Me

5

Relying on the Trinity for Our Understanding of Reality and Language

IN THE PREVIOUS CHAPTERS, we examined what language is more broadly—how language is related to God, how it is related to his creation, and how it is related to his image bearers. The second part of this book is about practical issues, which I have woven into the narrative of Scripture: creation, the fall, redemption, and consummation. In these chapters, we will be concerned with the daily blessings and bruises we receive through language, as well as the blessings and bruises we give to others. But before we get to discussing some of these issues, we must begin by reaffirming our perspective on language and reality with regards to God's communion behavior. We have done a bit of this already, but it is time to give it more explicit attention as the foundation for how we see God, the world, and ourselves. I end the book by listing some principles for living each day in what I earlier called "the worded world," a world which has language at its center.

COMMUNION BEHAVIOR AS A PERSPECTIVE ON REALITY

We have learned that the Trinity created all things through language, i.e., through divine communion behavior. This is expressed in the nature of the world as we know it, for every fiber of creation confesses God's glory, lordship, and character. The world has been "worded" or spoken by God. *That* is the biblical perspective on reality.

This means several things for our general perception of the world. First, it means that everything is intimately personal. As Van Til once wrote, "Our surroundings are shot through with personality because all things are related to the infinitely personal God."[1] Now, we already know the answer as to why reality is infinitely personal: It was brought into being by the infinitely personal communion behavior of the infinitely personal God. The Father, Son, and Spirit know and love one another with infinite intimacy. They are ever in communion with one another. Thus, the world that God has made through communion behavior is a reflection of God's intimate and infinite fellowship with himself in three persons. There is nothing in creation that does not relate to or reflect the tripersonal God of the Bible.

Second, every part of reality has a purpose that has been specified by God.[2] In fact, God's specified purpose, delivered through communion behavior according to his sovereign plan, is what makes everything in reality what it is.

> Creation and providence take place by God's speaking. For example, "God said, 'Let there be light,' and there was light" (Gen 1:3). God's speech specifies everything. He specifies that certain things will exist: light, the expanse of heavens, the sea, the dry land, the plants, and so on. He also specifies *how* they will exist. The plants will grow on the land. They will reproduce "according to their own kinds" (Gen 1:12). Providentially, he specifies the coming of snow and ice and their melting.
>
> He sends out *his command* to the earth;
>
> *His word* runs swiftly.
>
> He gives snow like wool;
>
> He scatters frost like ashes.
>
> He hurls down crystals of ice like crumbs;
>
> Who can stand before his cold?
>
> He sends out *his word*, and melts them;
>
> He makes his wind blow and the waters flow. (Ps 147:15–18)

1. Van Til, *A Survey of Christian Epistemology*, 78.

2. I am here drawing on Poythress's work in *Redeeming Philosophy*. This includes his vocabulary choice of "specify" to refer to what God has created, which in his book is treated under the category of metaphysics.

God specifies everything: "he upholds the universe by the *word of his power*" (Heb 1:3).[3]

This is a teaching vital to Christians in our time, for there is a long-held and unchallenged assumption that parts of philosophical speculation in human history, particularly what secular philosophers have said about what things *are* (i.e., metaphysics), can and should be embraced. We must address this briefly, despite the difficulty of the subject matter. I already said that this part of the book is meant to be practical, so I can assure you that there are practical implications of what I am about to say.

Much of Western philosophy is built upon Aristotle.[4] Aristotle often talked about what things are in terms of *substance* and *accidents*.

> A *substance* is an individual thing: a rock, a tree, a table, an animal, a person. With one exception . . . all substances contain both form and matter. In general, the *matter* is what something is made of: the ingredients of bread, the clay of the statue. The *form* is the *whatness* of a thing, the qualities that make the thing what it is: bread, tree, statue, person. The matter is the *thisness*. The matter is what distinguishes one piece of bread from another, one brick from another, one person from another.[5]

An *accident* for Aristotle was a feature that something took on that was not essential to its substance.[6] For instance, I have a mug with the symbol for Westminster Theological Seminary embossed on the front. The substance of my mug is what makes it what it is: a container for hot liquid. It has both form and matter. The accidents include its specific height and weight, the shape of the handle, and the symbol for the seminary.

Now, you do not have to understand all of what Aristotle means here to see some of the unbiblical assumptions. Metaphysics is tough terrain to climb. But there is one thing I hope you can notice. What influence does Scripture have on Aristotle's thought here? Where, in Scripture, do we find evidence (direct or indirect) for the elements of reality as comprised of impersonal substances and accidents that have no professed relation to God? Nowhere. The basic categories that Aristotle is working with—categories that many well-intending Christians have adopted over the centuries—are not drawn from the pages of Scripture. In fact, Aristotle himself was so removed from biblical truth that he went so far as to say that friendship

---

3. Poythress, *Redeeming Philosophy*, 105–6.

4. Poythress, *Logic*, 27.

5. Frame, *A History of Western Philosophy and Theology*, 70–71.

6. Frame, 113, 150n59.

between God and man was impossible.[7] I have a fundamental problem with taking my categories for existence and the nature of reality from a person who thinks that way. Such categories powerfully shape our perception of reality. They form the bedrock of our worldview.

In contrast with this, our view of reality as specified by God's communion behavior is clearly biblical. As we saw, it shows up on the very first page of the Bible and runs all the way through the book of Revelation. As Christians, we should be taking our cues from Scripture concerning the nature of reality—God, the world, and other people. In this case, we should be understanding reality in terms of God's deeply personal speech or communion behavior, not in terms of impersonal substances and accidents.

Now, I want to be sensitive here. There are great and godly men and women in the history of the church who have used secular philosophy with the goal of bringing it into submission to God's truth. In my view, that is a worthy end but a risky method. Rather than moving from secular philosophy to Scripture, we should be moving from Scripture to secular philosophy, using the clear and powerful word of God to burn away the dross of sinful thought. To that end, I would encourage us to perceive reality in light of God's communion behavior. The existence and purpose of a given object or person in our world is *spoken* or *specified* by God according to his sovereign plan. That is what I would call a *biblical metaphysic*.

However, this view of reality—as intimately personal and purposeful—seems foreign to us, doesn't it? When you walk outside and look around, does the world seem personal? Is it not easier to perceive it as a collection of impersonal objects (substances and accidents) that God *might* use for his specific purposes? I would say that such a view of reality is tainted by sin, and we all struggle with it. We tend to think the world is fundamentally *impersonal* rather than fundamentally *personal*. Part of the reason for this, I believe, is that we do not regularly remember that when we walk around outside, we are walking in a worded world, a world that is being upheld by the personal Word of God's power (Heb 1:3). This world speaks of God, but sin has made the beauty and purposes of the personal God somewhat of a foreign language. We do not typically walk outside and interpret the grass or rolling hills or a house as testaments to the character of the God who spoke things into being and is holding everything together through his divine Word (Col 1:17). Sin has blinded us to the communion behavior of God, to the centrality of language and communication to all of life. And it

---

7. *Nicomachean Ethics* 8.7, "When one party is removed to a great distance, as God is, the possibility of friendship ceases."

is language—God's creative, redemptive, and sustaining speech—that is at the center of all things.

Because sin has affected us by drawing us out of fellowship with God, we see the world as an impersonal place. As we grow in communion with him, conforming to the image of Christ in the power of the Holy Spirit, our perception should change. God's word should illuminate our minds and show us what we were blind to before. As the psalmist wrote, it is the Lord who "opens the eyes of the blind" (Ps 146:8; cf. Isa 42:7). How does he do this? *Through his word.*

When Isaiah called the ancient Israelites to repent, he said, "Hear, you deaf, and look, you blind, that you may see!" (Isa 42:18). Isaiah was not talking about physical sight; he was talking about perception of the world, a perception for Israel that was distorted by sin and could only be restored by the God of grace, who proclaims his salvation through language. Through Isaiah, God repeatedly called his people to repentance and submission to his word, but they resisted. He called them to *hear*, but they stopped up their ears. As a result, they were enslaved to a sinful view of the world.

> 19 Who is blind but my servant,
>
> or deaf as my messenger whom I send?
>
> Who is blind as my dedicated one,
>
> or blind as the servant of the LORD?
>
> 20 He sees many things, but does not observe them;
>
> his ears are open, but he does not hear.
>
> 21 The LORD was pleased, for his righteousness' sake,
>
> to magnify his law and make it glorious.
>
> 22 But this is a people plundered and looted;
>
> they are all of them trapped in holes
>
> and hidden in prisons. (Isa 42:19–22)

The ancient Israelites would not see the flesh-and-blood savior who called them out of darkness and into God's marvelous light (1 Pet 2:9), but they would be offered the same salvation in promises and types, which was the case for all the Old Testament saints. The Westminster Confession of Faith summarizes this truth by stating that the benefits of Christ were communicated to God's people in the Old Testament through "promises, types, and sacrifices, wherein He was revealed, and signified to be the seed of the woman which should bruise the serpent's head" (WCF 8.6). Hearing and receiving the words of God in his promises is what had the potential to help the Israelites change their perception of reality and their behavior within it.

This is as true for us today as it was for the ancient Israelites, but now we have the full gospel in the person and work of Christ proclaimed to us in Scripture, in words. Apart from God's glorious words of revelation, we are *blind*. We do not see the world aright. It takes constant reminding—through the prayerful reading of Scripture and the preached word of God—for us to see the world this way. Every day we must battle an ultimately godless worldview that creeps in to suggest that the world around us is *not* personal, that the Trinity has *not* spoken all things into being, that God is *not* present with us and drawing us into deeper communion with himself through Christ. We must battle this worldview because it is inimical to the truth of Scripture. God *has* spoken all things into being; he *has* specified their purpose according to his singular and sovereign plan; he *is* with us (in fact, he is *in* us); reality *is* intimately personal because it reflects the infinitely personal God, who beckoned it into being by communion behavior—a behavior that we image every day of our lives.

THE WORLD IS NOT A NEUTRAL PLAYGROUND

Related to this point, we must constantly remind ourselves that reality is not a "neutral playground." In other words, reality—your front yard, the sidewalk, the post office down the street, New York City, Ireland, the Atlantic ocean, etc.—is not a blank slate on which persons are gathered and sustained for a few fleeting moments before they pass away into nothingness. The world is God's (Ps 24:1). He spoke it. He upholds it. He is glorified in every part of it. Everything is permeated by *his* spoken purposes. This goes hand in hand with the truth that everything is steeped in God's communion behavior and thus speaks about him. We live, move, and have our being in the reality that God has created and controls by his speech (Acts 17:28). We do not live in an abandoned atmosphere void of God's personal presence. We dwell, as it were, in a divine conversation that God willed to speak, for all that has come about in creation and redemption has come about by his good pleasure, even as he works in and through us (Phil 2:13). God did not have to speak all things into existence; he *chose to*.

This is all the more remarkable when we consider our unique place in creation. You and I are *precious* to the trinitarian God—unfathomably precious. He willed to speak us into existence—despite what he foreknew would be the incomparable cost to himself, the death of his incarnate Son. We do not marvel enough at this: Because God is all-knowing, he knew in eternity past that we would fall. Yet he still created. Why? Out of love—heavy, profound, pervasive love.

And what's more, God held out this love to us in Christ *even as we were hostile towards him* (Rom 5:8). Think about that for a moment.[8] The Son of God was upholding the world even as it raged against him. The spit and breath of every hostile and accusatory word uttered by the Pharisees; the threads of rope and shards of glass that struck his back; the splintering wood that dug into his skin; the sharp, cold nails that broke through his hands—all of it was held together by *this* Word of God. As the Son of God, Christ was holding the world together even as it poured out its energy to tear him apart. Is that not love beyond all measure, beyond all comprehension? We are fiercely loved by one who suffered so much at the hands of those who cared so little.

The biblical teaching that God's love is beyond all measure complements the truth that God is ever present with his people. As Jesus told the disciples before his departure, "I am with you always, to the end of the age" (Matt 28:20). There is no place where God is not, no crack or crevice in the world or in the thoughts of men that can shut him out.

Because of this, we must always reject the broader secular assumption that the world is somehow *neutral*, that all people are seeking hope and assurance amidst a place that is, at best, ambiguous about the existence of God, or, at worst, void of his presence. We are not all starting out in a godless reality and then straining our necks to find him around every dark corner. The world is inundated with God's presence, so much so that the Apostle Paul says that there is *no one* who does not know of him. He writes, "what can be known about God is plain to [ungodly and unrighteous people], because God has shown it to them. For his invisible attributes, namely, his eternal power and divine nature, have been clearly perceived, ever since the creation of the world, in the things that have been made. So they are without excuse" (Rom 1:19–20). Note the final parts of that passage: "in the things that have been made." *Everything that has been made is revelatory of the eternal power and divine nature of God.* Is this not what we have been saying all along—that God's communion behavior has marked the world so that it speaks of him everywhere? And because it speaks of him everywhere, no one has an excuse to deny God's existence. There will be no one who dies and stands before God rightfully claiming that there was not enough

---

8. I owe some of these reflections to a sermon by Dave Cummings, delivered on Sunday, January 28, 2017.

evidence—that the world was neutral and God did not reveal himself clearly enough in a godless atmosphere. No—nothing would be more appropriate than for God to say to such persons, "I was everywhere. I spoke everything, and it all speaks *of me.*"

Always remember that there is no one walking the earth who has a valid excuse for not knowing God. The God who created, governs, and judges all things is known to all, but people suppress that knowledge in rebellion (Rom 1:18). True, they do not all have *saving* knowledge of God. They do not know the person of Christ by the regenerating power of the Holy Spirit. Rather, they have what we might call *culpable* knowledge of God. They have enough knowledge of God to know that he exists, that he has revealed himself, and that they are responsible for responding to that revelation.

The communion behavior of the triune God thus brings us to see the world as intimately personal and thoroughly revelatory of God. This is the world we live in. We might remind ourselves of this each morning as we rise and set our feet down on the floorboards that God is holding together by his Word, asking ourselves what they are saying of God—and what everything else around us is saying about him, for reality cannot help but speak of him who spoke it. *Amen. Help me, Lord.*

COMMUNION BEHAVIOR AS A PERSPECTIVE ON LANGUAGE

In addition to reshaping our perspective on reality, God's communion behavior also serves more narrowly as a perspective on human language. It does this in two senses.

First, the concept of communion behavior keeps before us the imprint of the Trinity on human communication. Earlier we discussed two sets of triads: the particle, wave, and field observer perspectives, and the elements of contrast, variation, and distribution. Another triad within human language that we have not yet mentioned is the triad of grammar, phonology, and reference.[9] A simple example illustrates this.

> *I gave thanks to the Father through Christ, by the power of the Holy Spirit.*

This sentence can be broken down in terms of its grammatical structures. There is a subject and verb (*I gave*), a direct and indirect object (*thanks, the Father*), and two prepositional phrases that modify the action of the sentence (*through Christ, by the power of the Holy Spirit*). The grammar helps

9. Pike, *Linguistic Concepts*, 70–106.

me understand what is in focus (often the subject in English sentences) and what action is being carried out, for whom, and to what purpose. We can learn a great deal about the meaning of this sentence simply from analyzing the grammar and syntax (word order).

At the same time, this sentence can be analyzed in light of its phonological features. For instance, we could choose to stress any one of the words in this sentence. Each variation in the pronunciation would nuance the meaning in some sense, though it would not fundamentally alter it.

> **I** gave thanks to the Father through Christ, by the power of the Holy Spirit.

> I **GAVE** thanks to the Father through Christ, by the power of the Holy Spirit.

> I gave **THANKS** to the Father through Christ, by the power of the Holy Spirit.

> I gave thanks **TO** the Father through Christ, by the power of the Holy Spirit.

> I gave thanks to **THE** Father through Christ, by the power of the Holy Spirit.

> I gave thanks to the **FATHER** through Christ, by the power of the Holy Spirit.

> I gave thanks to the Father **THROUGH** Christ, by the power of the Holy Spirit.

> I gave thanks to the Father through **CHRIST**, by the power of the Holy Spirit.

> I gave thanks to the Father through Christ, **BY** the power of the Holy Spirit.

> I gave thanks to the Father through Christ, by **THE** power of the Holy Spirit.

> I gave thanks to the Father through Christ, by the **POWER** of the Holy Spirit.

> I gave thanks to the Father through Christ, by the power **OF** the Holy Spirit.

> I gave thanks to the Father through Christ, by the power of **THE** Holy Spirit.

I gave thanks to the Father through Christ, by the power of the
HOLY Spirit.

I gave thanks to the Father through Christ, by the power of the
Holy **SPIRIT**.

I could do the same thing with phrases from the sentence. Different
pronunciations might be appropriate in different contexts. Thus, the phonological options in terms of prominence (which word I choose to stress) is
one reflection of the great depth of meaning embedded in a simple sentence
such as this one.

And yet this sentence also can be analyzed in terms of its real-world
referents or meaning. What does it mean to "give thanks"? Is thankfulness
an inner disposition, or an external response, or both? Does "to the Father"
imply that the Father has a location, or am I simply saying that the Father is
the recipient of my thankfulness. What exactly is meant by the prepositions
"through" and "by" in the second part of the sentence? Is Christ an instrument, a medium of some sort? What about the Spirit? Are all three divine
persons in this sentence meant to be understood in a certain way? The referents and the meaning of the words provide another avenue for analysis
and understanding.

Still, we need grammar, phonology, *and* reference to understand parts
of this sentence in its depth and context. Take away the grammar, and nothing is left. The same applies if we take away the phonology or the reference.
All three together are found in this one utterance.

What might be apparent to some readers is that each of the triads we
have discussed functions in a way that mirrors perichoresis or coinherence.[10] Each of them focuses on the same substance (an object or a chunk
of verbal language), and yet each of them is distinct. Kenneth Pike would
say that each of them is a "restructuring" of the same substance. This is
analogous (though not directly correspondent with) the sense in which the
persons of the Trinity are distinct and yet one. There are, as we have mentioned repeatedly, three persons in one divine essence. So, the structure of
communication can help us to appreciate that

> God has impressed his trinitarian character on language. When-
> ever we use language, we rely on what he has given us. We also
> rely on the mutual indwelling of the persons of the Trinity. Be-
> cause of this indwelling, our use of language holds together. In
> the use of language, we live in the presence of God who through

10. Poythress, *In the Beginning Was the Word*, 56–59, 156–158, 263–264.

the Spirit gives us life and through the Spirit empowers our use of language.[11]

Second, communion behavior—given its broader nature—helps us understand that language cannot be neatly or structurally separated from the rest of human behavior. Our communication with God and with others is not in a box that is insulated from other things that we do. That is one of the reasons why I have consistently referred to language as "behavior" and not as a "faculty" or "instrument" or "medium." "Behavior" is a term that represents all of what we do. I am here following in the footsteps of Kenneth Pike, who wrote that

> Language is behavior, i.e., a phase of human activity which must not be treated in essence as structurally divorced from the structure of nonverbal human activity. The activity of man constitutes a structural whole, in such a way that it cannot be subdivided into neat 'parts' or 'levels' or 'compartments' with language in a behavioral compartment insulated in character, content, and organization from other behavior. Verbal and nonverbal activity is a unified whole . . .[12]

Leave aside some of the technical terms of Pike's definition. What he is saying here is that we cannot compartmentalize communication from the rest of what we do. Our activity is a "unified whole." For this reason, I have chosen to define language as *communion behavior* since the adjective "communion" aptly describes what sort of end our communication serves, and yet the phrase does not thereby isolate language from the rest of what we do.

I believe that there is a theological precedent for this—for human behavior being understood as a unified whole—but I want to be careful in articulating it.

Orthodox theologians throughout history have consistently upheld what they call the doctrine of divine simplicity. There are no parts in God. He is numerically and essentially one. This means that all of his attributes and characteristics are identical with his essence.[13] He is not simply one whom we can describe as "righteous." He *is* righteousness. The same goes for his love, holiness, and so on (figure 8).

---

11. Poythress, 22.

12. Pike, *Language in Relation to a Unified Theory of the Structure of Human Behavior*, 26. See also Waterhouse, *The History and Development of Tagmemics*, 15.

13. There are, however, attributes that God has voluntarily taken to himself by virtue of his "new relation" with creation. See Vos, *Theology Proper*, 177–78.

Figure 8: The Simplicity of God

The doctrine of divine simplicity means that,

> The characteristics of God are not "parts" of God that come together to make him what he is, but are rather identical with his essence, and thus with him. The simplicity of God not only affirms that whatever God essentially is, he is necessarily, but it says even more than that. The simplicity of God holds that God's essential attributes are not characteristics or properties that exist (in the same way that he exists) in any way "outside" of God, such that his having such characteristics or properties entails his participation in something other than himself. God just is his essential characteristics, and his characteristics are identical to him.[14]

This is what theologians mean when they refer to God as *simple.* Simplicity is also referred to as an *incommunicable attribute* of God. In other words, as creatures we cannot image this divine attribute; it is not something that God has "communicated" to us. For this reason, Bavinck writes that simplicity is only something we can discuss in God's case.

> In the case of creatures all this is very different. In their case there is a difference between existing, being, living, knowing, willing, acting, and so on. "All that is compounded is created." No creature can be completely simple, for every creature is finite. God, however, is infinite and all that is in him is infinite. All his attributes are divine, hence infinite and one with his being. For that reason he is and can only be all-sufficient, fully blessed, and glorious within himself.[15]

As creatures, we not only have physical parts, but also are not identical with our attributes. We are, as Bavinck put it, "compounded." In fact, we have quite a checkered past in even modeling the attributes that we are called to "put on" in Christ-like submission by the power of the Spirit—compassion, kindness, humility, meekness, patience, love (Col 3:12–14). Indeed, when it comes to being identical with our attributes, the chasm between God and his creatures is wondrously deep and wide. We are not like God in his simplicity. Let that much be clear.

However, though we cannot image God in his simplicity, that does not preclude us from talking about some sort of unity in our lives. We are not simple, but through God's providence, he has connected all the parts of our lives to his one plan of redemption. So we can certainly talk about the

---

14. Oliphint, "Simplicity, Triunity, and the Incomprehensibility of God," 221–22.

15. Bavinck, *God and Creation*, 176.

divinely governed and sustaining unity in our lives. All of our behavior is *structurally integrated* because every part of us is involved with the process of redemption. God has created all things through communion behavior, and he controls and sustains all things through that communion behavior—*all things.* That means all of our "parts," attributes, and behaviors are unified by God's singular plan to redeem us, having chosen us in Christ before the foundation of the world (Eph 1:4).

This should remind us of a figure introduced in an earlier chapter (figure 1), showing how human language is integrated with the rest of our behaviors. Our lives are unified wholes because God is orchestrating every detail according to his singular purpose: to redeem his chosen people. Every synapse, every muscle movement, every decision, every judgment, every passion, every hope is interwoven into God's singular plan. His plan reaches into every part of us. This is further evidenced by the fact that we are called to respond to and engage with God not simply in terms of our language, or in terms of our external behavior, but in terms of *all that we are.*

Remember Deuteronomy 6:5, "You shall love the LORD your God with all your heart and with all your soul and with all your might." Jesus echoes this in Matthew 22:37, adding the human mind to the list: "You shall love the LORD your God with all your heart and with all your soul and with all your mind." Yes, even the mind is part of our loving response to God. That is why Jesus critiques those who would claim to be righteous in their actions alone. The life of the mind is riddled with corruption, and that is a critical part of our salvation. It is not enough to avoid committing physical adultery. For Jesus, a man is still guilty if he "looks at a woman with lustful intent," for he "has already committed adultery with her in his heart" (Matt 5:28). Behaviors must be matched by thoughts of the same order. Thus, when Paul calls upon the Colossians to set their *minds* on things above (Col 3:2), he is simultaneously calling them to act in a corresponding manner. This is because God's loving offer of salvation is holistically effective. "We are commanded to love God with everything that we are."[16]

All of us—that is what love for the triune God demands. As John Owen admonished his readers so many years ago concerning the love of God, we must embrace the Father's love in his offer of salvation (through his Son and by the Spirit) holistically. So, once you receive salvation, Owen tells his readers, "let thy mind know it, and assent that it is so; and thy will embrace it, in its being so; and all thy affections be filled with it. Set thy whole heart to it."[17] Indeed, he might as well have said, "Set thy whole *life* to it."

16. Oliphint, *The Majesty of Mystery*, 11.

17. *The Works of John Owen*, 2:34.

Now, I say all of this because Scripture is clear that our lives are unified wholes. We respond to salvation as unified persons—all of our faculties, behaviors, and thoughts. Salvation for God's creatures is holistic. It covers and demands *all*. And if this is the case, which few would debate, then why should we adopt an atomistic approach to language, an approach that separates language from the rest of what we think and do? Why not follow through with this holism—established by God's one plan of salvation—by taking up a view of language that integrates it with the rest of human behavior?

In other words, I am making a theological argument for communion behavior as our biblical understanding of language, precisely because communion behavior encourages us to see the interrelationships between verbal communication and the rest of what we do. And we *must* come to see ourselves holistically, as much as that is possible for finite creatures. The concept of communion behavior allows us to do this well because it directs our attention, it focuses on the particular end of certain behaviors, *without* excluding our other nonverbal behavior.

Carrying with us, then, communion behavior as a perspective on reality and language, we can move forward to survey what practical implications this has for our use of language in light of the four major stages of what theologians refer to as "redemptive history": creation, fall, redemption, and consummation. My reason for proceeding in this way is that it presents us with four practical questions that we can consider concerning our use of language.

- What was language created to do (what purposes did it serve)?
- How has our use of language been corrupted and broken by sin?
- How has God worked to restore our use of language through Christ?
- What is the ultimate goal to which language points us?

6

Creation and the Purpose of Language

IF WE WANT TO know what language was created to do, what purposes God intended it to serve, we naturally begin with Genesis 1–2. We have already spent some time in this passage, but our focus in this chapter will be slightly different from what is was previously. Here we are primarily interested in what these first two chapters of Scripture tell us about God's initial purposes for human language—for our communion behavior.

LANGUAGE FOR COMMUNION

Since we have thus far defined language as communion behavior, there is a sense in which any expression of God towards his creatures is an act of communion. In an analogous sense, any expression of one person towards another is an act of creaturely communion. The triune God, by condescending to our level and communicating his will for Adam and Eve (and for us), is drawing humanity closer to himself. In endowing us with the capacity to communicate, to use language, God has opened the way for us to communicate with him and with each other, and communication in one way or another always leads toward communion. So, perhaps the primary purpose of language is, in fact, communion with God and others. This should come as no surprise, and it has been affirmed by others of our time. Kevin Vanhoozer, for instance, writes that "language is a God-given capacity that enables human beings to relate to God, the world, and to one another. Specifically, language involves a kind of relating with God, the world, and others that yields personal knowledge. Language, that is, should be seen as the

84

most important means and medium of communication and communion."[1] Vern Poythress reminds us that "one of the purposes of language—in fact, a central, predominant purpose—is to be a vehicle for personal communication and communion between God and human beings."[2] The very fact that God speaks to Adam in Genesis 1:28 already points us to the truth that the primary purpose of language is communion—between God and humanity and between people made in God's image. Because we have already discussed this at some length, I would like us to consider more specifically what that purposeful communion looks like.

LANGUAGE FOR COVENANT

First of all, this purpose for language—to commune with God and others—does not occur in a vacuum. Language takes place in a *covenantal context*. Note the words that God first speaks to Adam.

> 28 And God blessed them. And God said to them, "Be fruitful and multiply and fill the earth and subdue it, and have dominion over the fish of the sea and over the birds of the heavens and over every living thing that moves on the earth." 29 And God said, "Behold, I have given you every plant yielding seed that is on the face of all the earth, and every tree with seed in its fruit. You shall have them for food. 30 And to every beast of the earth and to every bird of the heavens and to everything that creeps on the earth, everything that has the breath of life, I have given every green plant for food." And it was so. (Gen 1:28–30)

> 15 The LORD God took the man and put him in the garden of Eden to work it and keep it. 16 And the LORD God commanded the man, saying, "You may surely eat of every tree of the garden, 17 but of the tree of the knowledge of good and evil you shall not eat, for in the day that you eat of it you shall surely die." (Gen 2:15–17)

God speaks to Adam and thus communes with him, but this communion takes place in a *covenant*. In other words, there are prescriptions for Adam to follow if he is to remain in perfect relationship with his creator. There are also prohibitions. Positively, God tells Adam and Eve to multiply, to have dominion over all that God has created, to steward it. Adam and Eve are meant to be royal representatives of God on earth—shepherding all

---

1. Vanhoozer, *Is There a Meaning in This Text?*, 205.
2. Poythress, *In the Beginning Was the Word*, 38.

that God had created through his communion behavior. Adam was to dwell in the Garden of Eden, "to work it and keep it." Negatively, God tells Adam (and, by extension, Eve) that he must not eat of the tree of the knowledge of good and evil. He also tells Adam what will happen if he does so: he will certainly die. All of this makes up the covenantal context of language. Our communion with God, in other words, is a covenantal communion; it takes place on God's terms, not ours. Our communion with God is a submissive communion.

For this reason, Oliphint writes, "Language is employed, by God initially (Gen 1:28–30; 2:16–17) and then by humans, as a way of expressing the connection with God and with the world that is given to human beings in creation. In other words, the *purpose* of language is *covenantal*. It is to be employed to give expression to God's relationship to us, first of all, and then our relationship to God and the world."[3] Or, in Vanhoozer's words, "The design plan of language is to serve as the medium of covenantal relations with God, with others, with the world."[4]

Now, we might be tempted to think that this covenantal context of language makes language somehow less personal. For many people today, the word "covenant" conjures up thoughts of a cold and pragmatic resolution between two nations or political parties. Does the notion of covenant sap the personal vigor from language? Is it somehow foreign or peripheral to its personal, communion-centered purposes?

I would argue the exact opposite. Though the term "covenant" can take on impersonal connotations for some people today, it is actually a deeply personal expression of God's love for us. To hold a conversation with someone is one thing; to make a covenant with someone is entirely different. A covenant is *binding*; it is an expression of unflinching commitment. This is amazing when we consider that the triune God—who spoke all things into existence—came down to our level and made a covenant *with us*. Scott Oliphint refers to this as God's *covenantal condescension*.

> The Bible, from beginning to end, is replete with instances of God's covenantal condescension. The Bible itself is a product of that condescension. Covenantal condescension is a necessary aspect of his binding himself to his creation. Once he (freely) chose to create, he would need also to "stoop down" in order to relate himself to his creation. This "stoop" in no way modified or diminished his aseity. Rather, it gave us, his human creatures, a revelational way to understand his majestic character. It revealed

---

3. Oliphint, *Reasons for Faith*, 119.
4. Vanhoozer, *Is There a Meaning in This Text?*, 206.

that character to us, and it required us to see his condescension for what it really was—his merciful determination that we have fellowship with him.[5]

Fellowship with the tripersonal God—that is why God came down to our level and voluntarily bound himself in covenant with us. The covenantal nature of language, in other words, is a deeply personal expression of God's love for his creatures, for you and me.

LANGUAGE IN COVENANT: TRUSTING AND GOVERNING (NAMING)

Now, in this covenantal context—a context in which God binds himself to us but also gives us authoritative commands and directions—how did God intend for us to use language, before sin entered the world? Certainly, the answer to this question can and should draw on later revelation in Scripture, but let us for the moment keep our eyes fixed on Genesis 1–2 (we will consider other passages in the following chapters). In this context, it seems clear that we were to use language passively or receptively by *trusting* in God's word above all else (Gen 2:16–17). Actively, we were to use language in *governing* the rest of creation by naming it and thus distinguishing its various elements (Gen 2:19–20). Let us deal with each of these in more detail.

First, given the covenantal context in which Adam and Eve found themselves, their *trust* in God's word, his verbal revelation, was paramount. The groundwork for this trust is laid by God's providing food for them. "And God said, 'Behold, I have given you every plant yielding seed that is on the face of all the earth, and every tree with seed in its fruit. You shall have them for food'" (Gen 1:29). God's good providence showed Adam God's love—his desire to care for and sustain his image bearers. Of course, this also established Adam and Eve's dependence on God. They relied on his providence for physical nourishment. This dependence on a good God lays the foundation for Adam and Eve's trust in him. God has shown his goodness to them, so they have reason to trust his words.

This is supported also by God's command not to eat of the tree of the knowledge of good and evil (Gen 2:16–17). God knew that harm—indeed, death itself—would come to his creatures if they ate from this tree, so he gave them clear and explicit directions to follow so that they would avoid this and remain in loving communion with him.

---

5. Oliphint, *Covenantal Apologetics*, 62.

God's providence of food and his verbal directions as to how Adam and Eve should live in the garden reflect God's goodness. This goodness gave Adam and Eve every reason to trust in God's words. In sum, God's communion behavior, which had brought the world into being and faithfully sustained it, also revealed his love and care for his creatures. Adam and Eve *knew* that their God was good and loving. They knew that he wanted not only to sustain them, but to protect them from harm. It is this clear knowledge that would have served as a stepping stool for their trust in God. Whenever God spoke to them, their covenantal response was meant to be *trust*. They were to trust God's words because those words were rooted in his love and care for them. Deception and cunning were alien to God's relationship with his creatures, which is what makes the serpent's words so cutting (Gen 3:1–5), but we will get to this in the next chapter.

In a derivative sense, Adam and Eve were meant to trust each other's words. Today, many secular scholars (and some Christian ones) tell us that we should interpret language with a "hermeneutic of suspicion." This is just an academic way of saying, "Don't trust what you hear or read. Always begin with doubt." This idea is completely foreign to the context of Genesis 1–2. At that point in the history of God's world, there was no reason to distrust the words of another creature. God's words reflected his goodness and love, and people were made in his image. Thus, derivatively, their words were meant to reflect goodness and love for others. Adam and Eve's words to each other were meant to be received with *trust*.

Now, before moving on to discuss Adam and Eve's governing through language (naming), we must make a very important observation: There was and is a hierarchy of trust in the world. By that I mean Adam and Eve were to trust God's authoritative words above any words of a creature. This does not imply that creatures were bound to deceive and maltreat one another. It simply means that God, as our Lord and maker, reserved the highest place of authority, control, and presence.[6] God alone is Lord; God alone is all-powerful; God alone is ever present with his people. These attributes of God were expressed through his communion behavior: God's speech created, sustained, and evoked his presence with his creation. Because of this, his image bearers were to hold him in the highest regard; they were to trust his words, his verbal communion behavior, above all else. Their trust in another creature's words would only be permissible if it aligned with those of God. This is what I mean when I say that there was a hierarchy of trust. In fact, we can even sense how this trust was rooted in God himself. The Father, Son,

---

6. I am here drawing on John Frame's triad of authority, control, and presence. See Frame, *Doctrine of the Knowledge of God*, 15–18, 62–63.

and Holy Spirit eternally and perfectly trust one another, because they are fully *in* one another (perichoresis). This divine trust within God, however, cannot be replicated on the creaturely level (figure 9).

H	**Divine, eternal trust amongst the Father, Son, and Holy Spirit**
i	
e	
r	Creaturely trust in the speech (communion behavior) of God
a	
c	Creaturely trust in the speech (communion behavior) of one another
h	
y	

Figure 9: Hierarchy of Trust

This hierarchy of trust is critical to keep in mind when we come to the next chapter and discuss the linguistic nature of sin.

Second, given the covenantal context in which Adam and Eve found themselves, they were meant to *govern* creation by *naming* it. It may not seem obvious how naming is a form of governing, so let me explain.

Adam's naming of the animals in Genesis 2:19–20 is a creaturely representation of God's authoritative speech. In fact, it is a creaturely representation of God's authority, control, and presence. We touched on this in the previous chapter. Adam's speech is marked by meaning (which is related to God's authority, since God is the source of all meaning), control, and presence. As Poythress writes,

> Man's speech shows meaning, control, and presence. In this respect it images the meaning, control, and presence of God's speech. Naming the animals clearly expresses meaning, in distinguishing different kinds of animals from one another and in expressing the commonality belonging to a group of animals of the same kind.
>
> The making of a name is also an act expressing control over language. "And whatever the man called every living creature, that was its name" (Gen 2:19). The man established a name for the creature, and from then on that was its name. The man thereby controlled the future of language. In addition, the man exerted control over the animals themselves. In Hebrew culture, naming was not equally everyone's privilege. The power to name belonged to the one who had authority to do it. God's naming of created things in Genesis 1 expressed his authority and sovereignty over those things. Likewise, Adam's naming the animals went together with the fact that he had been given dominion over them (Gen 1:28).
>
> Finally, does Adam's naming express presence? God is omnipresent, and therefore present in every event on earth. But is there also a derivative presence, a presence of Adam as a person in the speeches that he makes? Clearly there is. The speeches express his desires, his thoughts, and his purposes. He intends to name the animals, as an act of his person. And in the lingual act of naming, he expresses that personal intention. It is Adam acting, not a robot that happens to have the shape of Adam. So Adam's act of naming expresses his personality. Adam is present in his speech.[7]

---

7. Poythress, *In the Beginning Was the Word*, 30.

There is much here that we could unpack, but since I believe that Poythress's message is clearly expressed, let me deepen our awareness of one of the points he makes, which will tie in with an earlier discussion we had.

It can be difficult to understand concretely how Adam's naming establishes *meaning*. In fact, the question "What does 'meaning' mean?" is far more complex than it might seem. Poythress writes that Adam's naming establishes meaning "in distinguishing different kinds of animals from one another and in expressing the commonality belonging to a group of animals of the same kind." Yet we can still push here and ask, "But what *is* meaning?" This question is an ocean in itself, and here is not the place to begin navigating the currents of semantics. For our purposes, we might for the moment think of meaning as *something of shared value between the trinitarian God and his image bearers*. Adam's naming of the animals has value to him as it expresses his creaturely control and presence. It has value to God in the sense that God respects the names that Adam has given (Gen 2:19), and by accepting those names, God is respecting Adam's personality and the creaturely control he has bestowed upon him.

This sense of meaning, established through naming, also reflects the Trinity in terms of the triads we discussed earlier. First, Adam's naming of the animals can be viewed from the particle, wave, and field observer perspectives. From the particle perspective, each of the names that Adam gives to the various creatures marks those creatures as distinct entities within the created realm. Each animal is attached to a particular sound (a name), and the stability of the creature's name reflects the stability of its place and purpose in God's creation. From the wave perspective, each name is a sequence of sounds flowing into one another. The name of each animal would always occur in a particular context—a phrase, clause, or sentence. The beginning and ending sounds of the name would thus blend fluidly with previous and subsequent sounds, and yet the distinct sounds or phonemes of the name would distinguish it from the other surrounding words. The surrounding words can be understood as margins of a wave, and the distinct sounds would constitute the crest of the wave—what sets it apart as a wave in the context of an ocean of relative silence. From the field perspective, each name would have a context or place in relation to all of the other names. Each name would refer to an animal that is similar to and different from other animals, and the entire species or group of animals serves as the context for identifying particular ones. All of the animals would be ultimately set against the background of earth, out of which they were raised up by the creative power of God (Gen 1:24). Each name, from the field perspective, is a thread in the web of God's animate creation.

Second, Adam's names have elements of contrast, variation, and distribution. Each name, negatively, contrasts with other names and, positively, is marked as unique. An example from contemporary English might make this clearer. *Bear* contrasts with *tiger* in the string of sounds that comprises each word. The "B" in bear is what linguists call a voiced consonant. The vocal chords vibrate when the sound is being articulated. The "t," on the other hand, is unvoiced; the vocal chords are not vibrating when the sound is articulated. The two names also differ in the focal vowel sounds: *air* vs. *eye*. These contrasts serve to identify the names as different. Each name would also have limitless variations in pronunciation. No puff of breath is exactly the same; no articulation of sound is identical. Like snowflakes, sounds are unique. So, every time the words *bear* and *tiger* are pronounced, even by the same person, their precise articulation differs ever so slightly. The names also show variation when different speakers from different regions pronounce them. Someone from the Boston area might say *bay-uh* or *t-eye-guh*. This variation in pronunciation would still direct us to the same referent; it would just indicate something of the speaker's origin. Lastly, each name would be distributed in certain meaningful contexts or situations. For example, names of animals that live in the same environment often occur together (*worm, beetle, ant*), as do names of animals that have the same sort of diet. We expect to hear the names of certain animals when someone is talking about carnivores or herbivores, for instance. The name *tiger* would be distributed in such a context.

Third, the names that Adam comes up with are also embedded in the grammatical, phonological, and referential hierarchies. Each of the names would have been a noun or noun-like, marking a particular thing. The name would thus have a grammatical place in Adam's language, just as animals' names have a grammatical place or role in our sentences. As already noted, each name would have a unique pronunciation or sound, and each name could be stressed in a given sentence or expression. Lastly, each name had a clear referent that Adam established. Adam was in charge of linking a particular string of sounds with an element (an animal) in the real world.

These triads in relation to the names that Adam created show us how naming reflects the Trinity in senses we have already explored. Particle, wave, and field; contrast, variation, and distribution; and grammar, phonology, and reference bear striking resemblance to the persons of the Godhead. In this sense, *naming* is a trinitarian, image-bearing activity. It has meaning because it does something on a creaturely level that is rooted in the trinitarian God. It thus has value for God, derived from God, and shared by his image bearers. That is how names have meaning.

Now, the meaning of the names that Adam provides for the animals is an act of governance, for it controls elements of the created realm by showing how each thing has a distinct place and function in God's plan (particle, contrast, grammar), is part of a dynamic and diverse atmosphere (wave, variation, phonology), and is interrelated with everything else in God's created world (field, distribution, reference). Adam's naming, then, was not just a fun, linguistic game. It was part of God's commission for Adam to have dominion over creation.

In summary, in the covenantal context of creation, Adam was meant to use language passively or receptively by *trusting* in God's Word above all else (Gen 2:16–17), and, derivatively, by speaking true words that elicited the trust of others. Actively, he was to use language in *governing* the rest of creation by *naming* it. Both of these functions of language before the fall imaged the communion behavior of God, whose words demand ultimate allegiance (trust) and who establishes and names all that he has made. Certainly, there are more functions to language than trust and governance through naming, but these are the functions highlighted thus far in Scripture, in Gen 1–2. We will come across other functions of language in the chapters ahead.

IMPLICATIONS FOR US

In the paragraphs above, we have highlighted some of the initial purposes for language in creation, but before ending the chapter, we should ask, "What does Adam and Eve's covenantal use of language have to do with us in the twenty-first century?" I will end each of the next few chapters with a question like this, drawing our attention from the abstract to the concrete. However, we must be careful not to make a one-to-one correspondence between what a given text, in this case our text about creation, meant in its original context and what it is saying to us today. Our process of interpretation should move from (1) the original context of the passage to (2) the place that this passage has in the story of redemptive history (especially with regards to how Christ fulfills the passage, since all of Scripture is about him) to (3) an understanding of what God is saying to us now through that passage.[8] This process of interpretation prevents us from reading into a text what we would like to see and ensures that Christ is always the center of Scripture.[9] We can follow this process before drawing out implications for us that will affect our use of language each day.

8. Poythress, *God-Centered Biblical Interpretation*, 116.

9. Also consider what is commonly referred to as Clowney's Triangle, where we move from the truth symbolized in the text to the history of revelation that culminates

First, the original context of the passage is the creation account, *prior to* the entrance of sin into the world (Gen 3). Sin would have a riveting effect on our use of language, but Genesis 1–2 is focused on the covenantal context of creation before the serpent slithered onto the scene. This passage is also in the context of what we call the *creation mandate*, which includes God's call for us to multiply, rule over the earth, and subdue it.

As for the second step, we know that Genesis 1–2 is only the beginning of the story. Adam and Eve fail to trust God's words above all else; they break covenant with him, and so all created reality plunges into the depths of dissonance, decay, and spiritual destitution. God answers this situation with amazing mercy and grace, promising to one day crush the head of the serpent through the seed of the woman (Gen 3:15). From that point on, humanity would walk a long road of redemption paved by the very grace and patience of the Trinity. On one side of that road grow the weeds and bramble of rebellion, deceit, and corruption; on the other side grow the sovereign mercy and grace of God, who would one day send his own Son in the power of the Holy Spirit to reconcile the world to himself (Col 1:20). Christ has indeed come and paid the immeasurably costly price for our salvation. Redemption has come to us through Christ, by the power of the Spirit, whom God also sent on our behalf (John 14:26). Yet, though redemption has come and will move forward as God has planned, it is not yet completed or *consummated*. Christ will return and the whole world will be judged, and one day all those whom the Spirit has moved to put their faith in Christ will dwell in uninterrupted fellowship with the Trinity—one day.

That brings us to the third step. Given the place of this passage in redemptive history, we can ask what God is saying to us through Genesis 1–2 today. There are a few take-aways for us.

Trust in God's word is still paramount. If this was the case before the entrance of sin into the world, how much more so is it the case today? Adam and Eve were to trust in God's words above all else, and they lived in a world that was free of sin.[10] They had one, crystal clear, personal divine voice that called for their trust. This was challenged only when the seditious serpent proposed that they take *his* words over those of God. Today, though

in Christ, and then end up with an understanding of the connection between the original symbolized truth and God's climatic revelation in Jesus Christ, the governing revelation for our lives. See Poythress, *Reading the Word of God in the Presence of God*, 249–50. On Christ as the center of Scripture, see Gaffin Jr., "Systematic Theology and Hermeneutics."

10. I recognize that the presence of the serpent (Satan incarnate) in the Garden of Eden is a profound mystery—one that has not been resolved by any theologian in history, to my knowledge. So, I mean here that the world was at least free of sin *experientially*. That is, its creatures had not experienced sin for themselves.

redemption has come in the Spirit-driven power of Christ and cannot ultimately be hindered (even by Satan himself), we have a thousand sinful voices daily calling out for our trust: commercials, magazine articles, song lyrics, non-Christian acquaintances and friends, and so on. Every instance of language (of creaturely communion behavior) calls out for trust. But amidst the cacophony of sound, we must continue to read Scripture and hear God's own voice above every other. We are still called to trust in *his* words above all else. Only God's words are true—inerrant, infallible, honest, merciful, gracious, clear. That is why we must daily pick up the Bible and read. Every day we must hear the one voice—the only voice that covenantally requires our trust. Yet, this trust for us is a *trinitarian trust*, that is, it is a trust in the truth of God's word brought to life *by* the Holy Spirit (John 16:13) *in* the name of Christ (John 20:31) to the glory of God the Father (Phil 2:11).

If we keep this in mind, we can put ourselves in a situation to respond to the voice of God in Scripture even amidst an onslaught of deceitful and distracting worldly voices. Recall the hierarchy of trust. You may find it helpful to choose a day and do the following exercise (figure 10). First, read Scripture and write down how God is calling you to trust his words for that day. Pray that the Spirit would illuminate you to see Christ in that passage and how he has reconciled you with the Father and given you a permanent place in God's family. Second, as you go through the day, write down all of the other voices that are calling for your trust. I think you will be amazed by what you find. There are *so* many voices calling for our allegiance—on the radio, in personal conversations, in blog posts, and magazine adds. Becoming more aware of them will help you to see how remarkably different the voice of God in Scripture is, and how we are all daily called to hear that voice and respond, through the Holy Spirit, in Christ-like humility.

H
i
e
r
a
c
h
y

Divine, eternal trust amongst the Father, Son, and Holy Spirit

How is God calling you to trust him in a particular passage?

What other voices are calling for your trust today? How do they want you to respond to them, and how does this compare with God's words to you?

Figure 10: Hierarchy of Trust Exercise

Naming still has great power and reflects meaning, control, and presence.
Remember that in Genesis 1–2 naming was a form of governing, a way of
carrying out God's divine mandate to rule the earth and subdue it. Indeed,
one of the basic features of communion behavior (language) is its naming
and labeling capacity. Adam named the creatures that God had created, but
the action of naming parts of reality continued long after that. Creatures
were given names, but so were places, practices, events, and ideas. Our naming—in all of its manifestations—is a derivative of Adam's original naming
activity. Adam's naming was meant to establish God-centered meaning,
reflect his maker's sovereign control, and evoke the triune God's personal
presence in the world. It would do this *through* Adam's own unique personhood (his creaturely authority, control, and presence). Yet, sin affected each
of these purposes. After Genesis 3, our naming would often be careless and
graceless, would reflect our rebellion against God's control, and would suggest that we live in a place that is void of God's presence.

In Christ, all naming and labeling is being restored. All that is to be
redeemed takes refuge in his *name* by bowing before him (Phil 2:9). This
includes us as God's image bearers, but it also includes the rest of creation
(Rev 21:5). Christ is making all things new *through* himself, for "all things
were created through him and for him" (Col 1:16; Rom 11:36). Nothing—
not even our naming and labeling capacity—is redeemed apart from Christ.
In the Father's providential plan for redemption, all names find meaning,
submit to the governing Word (the Son), and evoke the glory of the ever-
present Spirit.

Naming and labeling—in all of its dimensions—is thus a deeply theological activity. It images the Trinity, who has named his creation, and who
has called all of his creatures to the one name of his Son, Jesus Christ, the
name above all names (Phil 2:9), whose living-giving Spirit (1 Cor 15:45)
is responsible for *our* names being written in the book of life (Luke 10:20;
Phil 4:3; Rev 3:5; 13:8; 21:27). All of our naming, then, if it is to be true and
covenantally faithful, has meaning, control, and presence *only* through the
Spirit, in the Son, and for the Father. Just as our trust is trinitarian, so our
naming must be trinitarian.

Let us bring this to bear on our current situation. In a sense, we are a
"naming culture." We like to label things, and we often overlook what power
those names and labels can have. We use names to categorize, distinguish,
and describe parts of the world around us, yet we often do so without even
thinking about the amazing grace of the Trinity. Our naming of the world
around us cannot take place as if God were not present, as if he did not send
his Son in the power of the Spirit to renew all things (Rev 21:5). Rather, our
naming must account for the grace of the trinitarian God. It must, in some

sense, reflect God's meaning, control, and presence. What's more, we must be conscious of the original governing power God bestowed on Adam's naming of the animals. Naming is an attempt to govern, not a superficial labeling exercise. It affects not just how we see the world (in light of God's meaning, control, and presence) but how we respond to it.

Consider some of the naming activities we carry out each day and how these names are linked to responses.[11] Do we respond to such names in light of God's meaning, control, and presence, and in light of our creaturely calling to image that meaning, control, and presence? If we do not, we might be responding in a way that is tacitly anti-trinitarian—responding to names and labels as if the world were void of the grace and redemption ordained by the Father in sending his Son and Spirit to raise to life those who were dead in sins and trespasses (Eph 2:1).

NAMING ACTIVITY	POTENTIAL RESPONSE ELICITED
Character descriptions	
Cold, unfriendly, dishonest	Resist, avoid, distrust
Warm, friendly, honest	Engage, interact, trust
Medical and psychological diagnoses	
Cancer	Fear, anxiety, anger, denial
Anxiety disorder[12]	Panic, confusion, frustration, hopelessness
Behavior Evaluations	
Selfish	Avoid, judge, criticize
Honest	Respect, admire
Sacrificial	Respect, admire
Compassionate	Respect, admire

Figure 11: Common Naming Activities

11. I am aware that these naming activities are of a different nature than Adam's. Adam was giving identifying labels to God's creatures, labels that would remain stable. Some of the names in the chart here are not stable, i.e., they can change over time, as a person's character develops or situation changes.

12. To see an example of anxiety addressed from a Trinitarian perspective, see Pierce Taylor Hibbs, "Panic and the Personal God," Journal of Biblical Counseling 29, no. 3 (2015): 36–41.

I am not here saying that all of our labels must be explicitly trinitarian. It would be difficult to understand what that would even look like practically. (How could we name the phenomenon of "cancer" in a way that reflects the Father, Son, and Holy Spirit's work of redemption? Should we even attempt to do so?) What I am saying is that our *reception of* and *response to* the names and labels of our culture must come from a trinitarian context.[13] In other words, we should be receiving and using names or labels today in a way that accounts for the awe-inspiring, gracious work of the Trinity in restoring all things and in fulfilling Adam's original commission to name elements of reality, and we should do so in a way that respects how ultimate meaning, control, and presence reside in God alone (figure 12).

13. I am thinking here of Kenneth Pike's claim that meaning is grounded in a native participant's (language speaker's) response. See Pike, *Language*, 598.

Naming Activity	Trinitarian-Shaped Response
Character descriptions	
Cold, unfriendly, dishonest	Approach, engage, encourage: for the Trinity has approached, engaged with, and encouraged sinners who were once at enmity with him (Rom 5:8; Eph 2:3).
Warm, friendly, honest	Thank (God), hold communion with, trust biblically: for people are warm towards other only by God's grace (cf. 1 Cor 15:10), the Trinity is the hearth of communion, Christ has made us friends of God (John 15:15; James 2:23), and the speaking God calls us to measure all truth according to his Word.
Medical and psychological diagnoses	
Cancer	Trust, hope, strength: for the Triune God works all things together for the good of those who love him (Rom 8:28), offers us the eternal hope of glory by indwelling us (Col 1:27; John 14:23; 1 John 4:4), and we are strongest when we are weakest (2 Cor 12:9–10; Phil 4:13).
Anxiety disorder	Perseverance, purpose, hope: for in Christ God has won victory for us and fights our battles (John 16:33; 1 Cor 15:57; cf. Exod 14:14), God will carry out his purposes in our sufferings (cf. Heb 2:10), and God promises to grant us peace beyond understanding when we come to him in prayer (Phil 4:7).
Behavior Evaluations	
Selfish	Empathize, exhort, encourage: for we were once enemies of God and children of wrath (Eph 2:3), but now in Christ and by the Spirit called to walk in the good works that God has prepared for us (Eph 2:10; Col 1:10), and the Father, Son, and Spirit comfort us in all of our afflictions (2 Cor 1:3–4).
Sacrificial	Praise (God), imitate: for God's ultimate sacrifice of his Son—raised by the Spirit to draw all people to himself—is a glorious truth (John 12:32; Rom 11:33–36), and God calls us to conform in every way to the image of his Son (Rom 8:29).

Figure 12: Trinitarian Responses to Naming

The example responses in figure 12 reflect our response to the Trinity in his meaning, control, and presence. Our responses to the names and labels that we have given to different parts of creation—to places, character traits, medical phenomena, behavior patterns—should be colored by the Trinity and his communion behavior, which not only created all things, but is *re-creating* all things. Remember our quotation from Bavinck earlier: "By the word God creates, preserves, and governs all things, and by the word he also renews and re-creates the world."[14]

In sum, naming (both our naming and our responses to names) is being redeemed by the triune God. In Genesis 1–2, naming had a divinely-endowed governing power, giving the world meaning, exercising creaturely control, and evoking personal presence. Today, as all naming is being redeemed by the Trinity, bowing to the name that is above all names (Phil 2:10), we must both name and respond to names in a trinitarian context. We must respect the power of naming as a trinitarian activity that has great potential both to hurt and to heal.

However, as has already been indicated, the trust and governing capacities of language have been used corruptly by sinful creatures. In fact, sin itself began as a corruption of language, and it is for that reason that all sin can be seen as *linguistic*. This brings us to the next chapter.

14. Bavinck, *God and Creation*, 273.

7

The Fall in Language: Sin as Linguistic

IMMEDIATELY FOLLOWING THE PASSAGE of Scripture where we learn about God's purposes for human language (Gen 1–2), we encounter the passage exposing Satan's antithetical purposes for it. Genesis 3 is a relatively short chapter in Scripture, but it is incredibly concentrated. Here, we learn a great deal about the fall *in* language, if we can put it that way, and the nature of sin.

THE FALL IN LANGUAGE

We have already hinted at how *everything* takes place in a linguistic environment. The triune God created all things through his communion behavior, and all of reality is marked by this in that it "speaks" to us about the God who made it. As God's image bearers, humans are communicative at their core. Language, we noted, is the beating heart of the image of God.

Language is so central to the fabric of reality, so pervasively woven into all that has been created, that it makes perfect sense for an attack on God and his creatures to come through language. That is precisely what happens in Genesis 3. Language—the medium of communion, covenant, and godly governance—is bent and brandished by Satan for purposes of disunion, rebellion, and chaos. This what I have in mind when I use the phrase "the fall *in* language." Language is the context, the arena, for our fall. And, as we will see in a later chapter, language is the context for our redemption through Christ.

THE SERPENT'S DISTORTION OF GOD'S WORD

What exactly happened in Genesis 3? We mentioned earlier that there was a hierarchy of trust set up through God's words. We were meant to trust his words above the words of any creature. This did not mean that creaturely words were unreliable or ambiguous; it simply reflected the Lordship of the Trinity in communication and communion. The Father, Son, and Holy Spirit command the highest covenantal allegiance *from* us and promise the deepest interpersonal communion *to* us. Creaturely communion and communication (the two concepts are intertwined) are at a lower level of the hierarchy of trust. All creaturely words must be measured against the words of God himself.

Knowing that, we might say that Adam and Eve's temptation in Genesis 3 was *a covenantal temptation.* It was a temptation that tested their allegiance to the covenantal Trinity. Yet, in light of what we have seen regarding language, the temptation set before Adam and Eve was at heart a *linguistic temptation,* a temptation in language. Let us revisit the passage before I explain what I mean by this.

> Now the serpent was more crafty than any other beast of the field that the LORD God had made. He said to the woman, "Did God actually say, 'You shall not eat of any tree in the garden'?" 2 And the woman said to the serpent, "We may eat of the fruit of the trees in the garden, 3 but God said, 'You shall not eat of the fruit of the tree that is in the midst of the garden, neither shall you touch it, lest you die.'" 4 But the serpent said to the woman, "You will not surely die. 5 For God knows that when you eat of it your eyes will be opened, and you will be like God, knowing good and evil." 6 So when the woman saw that the tree was good for food, and that it was a delight to the eyes, and that the tree was to be desired to make one wise, she took of its fruit and ate, and she also gave some to her husband who was with her, and he ate. 7 Then the eyes of both were opened, and they knew that they were naked. And they sewed fig leaves together and made themselves loincloths. (Gen 3:1–7)

What a dark passage this is, and bitter! There is much we can glean from a careful reading of these verses, but I will try to focus us on a few points to explain how this episode with the serpent is what I called a "linguistic temptation."

Note first of all the craftiness of the serpent. The Hebrew word that is translated here as "crafty" is *orūm*, and it means something like "shrewd." In English, there are many senses for this word, and several of them might apply here: "penetrating near the truth," "causing trouble," or "marked by artfulness or trickiness."[1] As we will see momentarily, what the serpent does in his speech can be captured by each of these descriptions. What's more, the serpent is identified not simply as crafty, but as the *most* crafty. Why is he the craftiest beast of the field? The answer, I believe, lies in his use of language.[2]

First, the serpent begins with a question. This is more than an arbitrary choice of rhetoric. Presenting Eve with a question is a way of disguising his intent, which would later be revealed more explicitly. We do this all the time in conversation, though not necessarily with sinful intent. For instance, when we are in the car, I can ask my wife, "Do you think this is the best way to get to the YMCA?" My hint is that I believe this is *not* the best way to get to the YMCA, but I can present my opinion less abrasively if I embed it in a question (and, of course, I'm open to the possibility that my wife will defend her decision and that I may be wrong).

But the serpent goes well beyond embedding his opinion in a question. Look at what he does: "Did God actually say, 'You shall not eat of *any* tree in the garden'?" (emphasis added). *Any* tree? Did God say that? When reading this passage, we might forget to turn back a page and look at God's words to Adam (or even to look back to the middle of chapter 2): "And God said, 'Behold, I have given you *every* plant yielding seed that is on the face of all the earth, and *every* tree with seed in its fruit'" (Gen 1:29; emphasis added). One word makes all the difference: *every* is changed to *any*, and a negative (*not*) is added. God emphasized the positive and only after that did he tell them the negative, as we read in 2:16–17. The meaning is now the exact opposite of that which God originally communicated (figure 13).

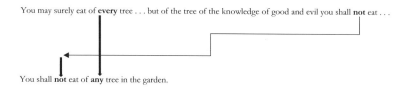

You may surely eat of **every** tree . . . but of the tree of the knowledge of good and evil you shall **not** eat . . .

You shall **not** eat of **any** tree in the garden.

Figure 13: The Serpent's Crafty Question

1. *Webster's Third New International Dictionary, Unabridged*, s.v. "shrewd," accessed February 16, 2017, http://unabridged.merriam-webster.com.

2. I am here relying on the exegetical work by Vos, *Biblical Theology*, 34–36, which is also highlighted by Beale in *The Temple and the Church's Mission*, 396.

This is the subtly of the serpent. In one slithery move, he replaces a word, transposes a negative, and puts the life of the human race on the line.

Notice how the serpent's use of language reflects the earlier English senses of the word "shrewd." First, his statement is an attempt to *penetrate near the truth*. It is not the truth, surely, but he aims to present his question so as to come as close to the truth as possible. Remember this: The most dangerous lies are the ones that come closest to the truth. Tall tales are easy to cast aside, but perverted paraphrases nestle themselves far more easily in the human heart. Second, his words are *marked by artfulness and trickiness*. Make no mistake, the serpent was artful and tricky in his question. What appeared to be an innocent inquiry was a death threat in disguise. Were the devil incarnate today in human form, he would not be a babbling buffoon. He would be a high cultured, eloquent rhetorician, parading before the masses with words sweeter than honey. That is what marks the devil, manifested in the serpent. Third, the serpent *causes trouble*. That is perhaps the greatest understatement of all time. The serpent did not just cause trouble, he *was* trouble. As we learn later in Scripture, the devil *is* the father of lies (John 8:44). He is trouble in the sense that his entire existence is dedicated to driving God's covenantal creatures off the beaten path of God's word, God's verbal communion behavior. The devil wants dissonance, not communion. His attack on Adam and Eve was a calculated effort to use the very medium of God's covenant with his creatures to tear them away from him. And he succeeded—at least, it looked that way.

Now, once the serpent has Eve lured by his deception and she begins to doubt the goodness of God, the fall has already begun. Geerhardus Vos notes that even in Eve's initial response to the serpent—"but God said, 'You shall not eat of the fruit of the tree that is in the midst of the garden, neither shall you touch it, lest you die'" (Gen 3:2–3)—she betrays a sense of disunion and distrust. She follows the words of the serpent, not in their *matter* but in their *manner*. Specifically, the serpent used negative exaggeration to distort God's original wording; Eve follows this mannerism by using another negative exaggeration: "neither shall you touch it." Vos writes, "In this unwarranted introduction of the denial of the privilege of 'touching' the woman betrays a feeling, as though after all God's measures may have been too harsh."[3]

The serpent here seizes the opportunity to lead Eve further astray. He casts off his disguised language and claims outright that God is a liar: "You will not surely die" (Gen 3:4). There is a stabbing sense of irony here—in fact, this is the first and most insolent use of irony in all of history. The

3. Vos, *Biblical Theology*, 35.

only liar in existence has stood before one of God's covenantal creatures and managed to convince her that her *good* God is actually the liar. That is villainy at its worst: to turn the tables on one who is wholly good (God) and manipulate his image bearers into thinking the opposite. Vos writes that the serpent here "seeks to awaken in the woman doubt in the pronounced form of distrust of the word of God recognized as such."[4] Distrust in God's word—does that not resonate with what we have said about the covenantal purposes of language, that God's image bearers were to trust his words above the words of any creature? Adam and Eve together (for Adam accepted Eve's later offering of forbidden fruit and, at the least, failed to use God's words to guide his own eating of the fruit) took the words of the serpent—a creature—over the words of the true and triune God. They violated the hierarchy of linguistic trust.

It is important to remember that Adam is guilty of the same sin that Eve committed. He broke the hierarchy of linguistic trust by either taking the words of Eve (again, a creature of God) over those of God or by failing to use God's words to guide his action (eating the fruit). Even if Eve did not speak to Adam about the fruit, but merely offered him some, Adam should have had the covenantal sense to ask, "Where did you get this from?" Before he took the fruit and ate, he was covenantally bound to determine if eating *this* fruit aligned with God's words.

So, what broke the world was a violation of the linguistically established order. By communion behavior God had created all things; by communion behavior he holds it together; by communion behavior he set the covenantal bounds of the divine-human relationship. The violation of God's communion behavior, the distrust of his holy and true words, is what sent fractures through the prism of reality. All came together in language; all broke apart in language.

This is what I have in mind when I say that the fall was *in* language. Our fall into sin did not occur in a vacuum. It cannot be isolated to non-verbal human actions (e.g., the actual eating of the forbidden fruit). No—it happened in the context of communion behavior. It happened *in* language.

THE NATURE OF SIN AS LINGUISTIC

This naturally leads us to a discussion of the nature of sin as linguistic: a breaking of communion behavior. This understanding of sin may seem new, but it is essentially in line with traditional Reformed positions. Geerhardus Vos, for instance, writes that the essence of sin is "that man (1) divorces

4. Vos, 35.

himself and his relationships from God; (2) places them as a separate center in opposition to God; (3) makes them act against God."[5] Notice how each of the elements in Vos's list is tied to the notion of communion (and hence of communion behavior): (1) in divorcing themselves and their relationships from God, Adam and Eve break communion with him and violate the hierarchy of trust that is established through God's communion behavior; (2) rather than being in fellowship with the triune God and believing whole-heartedly that this God loves them and is for them, Adam and Eve put themselves in a separate circle in opposition to him, expressed by their doubt of his words and their allegiance to creaturely words; (3) their violation of the hierarchy of trust leads them to act in defiance of God's verbal command not to eat the fruit from the forbidden tree.

While Vos's language is entirely appropriate and biblical, we can also situate the same truth in terms of the concepts we have been developing in this book: sin is a violation and subsequent distorted use of communion behavior (language). That is to say, sin is linguistic in nature; it is bound essentially to the breech of God's covenantal communion behavior. Put in more common terms, sin is at root the doubting, distrust, and rejection of the words of God. Sin is a violation of the covenantal relationship that God has established through communion behavior.

DISUNION, REBELLION, AND CHAOS

In the previous chapter, we saw that language fosters communion, serves God and others in the context of trust, and is part of God's divine mandate for his image bearers to govern the world through naming. In Genesis 3, we see the opposite take place: language (ironically, *communion* behavior) is used to create disunion, serves as a medium for rebellion, and brings about chaos in the created realm.

Disunion. The serpent's words sow seeds of doubt in Eve's heart. Adam and Eve then violate the hierarchy of trust and reap the bitter benefits of broken fellowship with the God who spoke them into being. In questioning the motives of an utterly good and loving God, Adam and Eve grow apart from him—so much so that they run in fear: "And they heard the sound of the Lord God walking in the garden in the cool of the day, and the man and his wife hid themselves from the presence of the Lord God among the trees of the garden" (Gen 3:8). What follows in the subsequent verse is a remarkable display of God's grace, perhaps the first instance of redemption-oriented language: "But the Lord God called to the man and

5. Vos, *Anthropology*, 51.

said to him, 'Where are you?'" (Gen 3:9). God is all-knowing. He has pristine awareness of where Adam and Eve are. He spoke them into his spoken world and upheld them (along with the rest of the world) by the Word of his power (Heb 1:3). He does not need to ask where they are. What's more, God is under no obligation to speak to creatures who thought the worst of him and distrusted the only one whose words cannot be broken. Certainly, God's eternal silence would have been warranted; he had made a clear and gracious covenant with his creatures through communion behavior. They had broken that covenant by rejecting his words and choosing those of a slippery serpent. Silence on God's part was his justified covenantal response.

And yet he spoke to them! This speech of God is grace—unprovoked, unmerited, uncalled for grace. And God calls his creatures from behind the bushes with the very same rhetorical structure that the serpent had used to lure them into dissonance and death: a question, *where are you?* The softness of his speech is heart-wrenching, as if the triune God were saying, "Where, my beloved listeners, have you gone? I have come to commune with you." But the communion had been ruptured, as God knew, of course. This is brought out in Adam and Eve's response to God's query. Communion is self-revealing, self-giving, the offering of one person to another in loving fellowship. Adam and Eve *hid* (Gen 3:10). They behaved in what would become the textbook response of creatures in rebellion against God. They hid from him, and thus expressed disunion from their covenant Lord.

Rebellion. This disunion is the campsite for rebellion. Only enemies dwell in opposing camps. Allies reside together. The fact that Adam and Eve attempted to remove themselves from God's presence (though this is futile) is a prelude to the long and ugly history of mankind raging against the Lord of love. The removal of Adam and Eve from the Garden of Eden—the place where God dwelled with his image bearers and spoke to them—marked the established distance between covenant breakers and the God who was faithful to his covenant. In Genesis 3:15, God would make a new covenant, a covenant of grace, and would one day come to fulfill both sides of it by giving his only Son as a ransom for sinners.

Chaos. The chaos that came about in God's world after the linguistic sin of Adam and Eve is rooted in God's curses.

> To the woman he said, "I will surely multiply your pain in childbearing; in pain you shall bring forth children. Your desire shall be contrary to your husband, but he shall rule over you." 17 And to Adam he said, "Because you have listened to the voice of your wife and have eaten of the tree of which I commanded you, 'You shall not eat of it,' cursed is the ground because of you; in pain

you shall eat of it all the days of your life; 18 thorns and thistles it shall bring forth for you; and you shall eat the plants of the field. 19 By the sweat of your face you shall eat bread, till you return to the ground, for out of it you were taken; for you are dust, and to dust you shall return." (Gen 3:16–19)

This chaos or disorder that comes as a result of God's curses is what we might call *controlled chaos.* God is still all-powerful and in complete control over all things. He still upholds the world by the Word of his power. After the fall, this truth of God's utter control is now conjoined with the bitter discord of sin and its ravaging effects on a world brought into being through communion behavior.

Notice here that it is only through the medium of language that the harmful effects of the fall are brought to bear on the world. This underscores the point that has been implied in much of the book so far: *nothing comes to pass apart from God's communion behavior.* The speech of God creates; the speech of God sustains; the speech of God blesses and curses. God is Lord of all *through his language.* His speech specifies all that comes to pass.

The chaos of a fractured creation is really the mark of a world separated from the God of communion. Through his covenantal communion behavior, God supported all that he had made. After the fall, the world that is at every point dependent on God's speech suffered covenantal curses: the blinding pain of childbirth, warring interpersonal desires, thorns and thistles, sweat . . . and death. All of these effects come about by the choice of creatures to break communion with the God who communes with himself in three persons. Disunion and rebellion lead to disorder and death. Put differently, the chasm that opened between God and his creatures was also a chasm that would separate the world as it now is—in all of its brokenness, hostility, confusion, and loss—from the world as it should be, a world in communion with the God whose communion behavior gave birth to its being.

DISTRUST AND DISTORTED GOVERNANCE

Corresponding to the curses that God pronounced is the distrust and distortion that enters human language.

The breaking of trust. Trust flourishes in covenantal communion. The hierarchy of trust that we referenced earlier represents how trust was a built-in feature of language, both between God and humans and amongst humans themselves, provided that interpersonal human communication was still submissive to God's verbal communication. Before the fall, trust was as common and as vital as the air we breathe. Only by having that air polluted would we come to a painful realization of how much we rely on it for communication.

The breaking of trust in language can be understood on two levels: the divine-human level and the human-human level. On the divine-human level, Adam and Eve would struggle to live in a world that was struck by the curse of sin. Doubt was around every corner, rather than the trusting fellowship they had before the fall. They would now have to struggle to believe in the words of God. They would doubt the truth of his promises, as their children would do all too frequently. In fact, their children would be born into doubt—a horrible heritage! They would doubt the promises that God had made (Num 14:11; 20:12; Deut 1:32; 9:23; 2 Kgs 17:14; Ps 78:32; 106:24) even though God never broke a promise (Josh 21:45; cf. Titus 1:2); they would doubt God's presence with them (Exod 17:7), even though he is everywhere with his people and with his words (Ps 139:7–12);[6] they would doubt God's power (Ps 78:22), even though his eternal power and divine nature are displayed in every corner of the universe (Rom 1:20); they would doubt his love, even though he *is* love (1 John 4:8) and would give himself for them in the person of his Son (Rom 8:35–39; Eph 3:14–19).

They would also doubt one another. On the human-human level, this would be more pervasive. If after the entrance of sin we have difficulty trusting the true and triune God of love, how much more so do we distrust corrupt creatures! Indeed, for many of us today, our default response to verbal statements is doubt, and we have even been taught that this is somehow a virtue, as if skepticism were an ultimate good. Surely, skepticism has its uses, and we should be testing the words of others against the clear and true word of God. But skepticism as an end itself is cynicism. The fact that some people hold skepticism to be a virtue is evidence of just how far we have come from being creatures in communion with God and with each other.

In short, the lie of the serpent has broken the trust between God and his creatures and between creatures themselves (figure 14). This has put a rift between persons and the triune God and between persons themselves (represented by the bolded black lines).

---

6. "God is immanent. He is present in the whole world. He is also especially present, with his offer of redemption in Christ, as we read Scripture. Much modern thinking assumes or alleges that God (if there is a God) is absent when we read Scripture. But he is not, and it makes a difference. We meet God, not merely a text that substitutes for God." Poythress, *Reading the Word of God in the Presence of God*, 30.

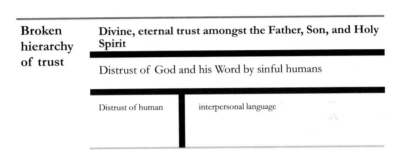

Figure 14: Broken Hierarchy of Trust

The Distortion of Governance. The broken trust on the divine-human and human-human levels is not the only way in which sin has wreaked havoc on God's good creation. There is also now a distortion of governance. This, again, comes on two levels: the divine-human and human-human.

On the divine-human level, there is distortion of governance on our part in the sense that we have the audacity to live as if we were our own gods. This is expressed in theological circles as *autonomy*. What do I mean by this? To many theologians, "autonomy" is somewhat of a dirty word. Here are a few ways in which they have defined it.

- "Intellectual autonomy is the view that human beings have the right to seek knowledge of God's world without being subject to God's revelation. It first appears in the history of human thought in Genesis 3's narrative of the fall, in which Adam and Eve make their decision to disobey God's personal word to them. In their decision, they affirm their right to think autonomously, even to the point of contradicting God himself."[7]

- "In a word, the unbeliever lives as if he were *autonomous*, subject only to his own law. Nobody can really be autonomous, because we are all subject to God's control, authority, and presence."[8]

- "The sinner seeks to be *autonomous*. He will, therefore, seek to set himself up as a judge over that which presents itself to him as revelation."[9]

- "The revelation of a self-sufficient God can have no meaning for a mind that thinks of itself as ultimately autonomous."[10]

- "If we do not serve God, we will end up serving something, whether that is one of the false gods in ancient Israel, or the god of material success, or human pride, or simply autonomy."[11]

In short, autonomy is willful rebellion against a sovereign God; to act autonomously is to act as if God does not exist, or as if he has not revealed

7. Frame, *The Doctrine of the Word of God*, 15–16.
8. Frame, *A History of Western Philosophy and Theology*, 22.
9. Van Til, *Introduction to Systematic Theology*, 225–26.
10. Van Til, *The Defense of the Faith*, 112.
11. Poythress, *In the Beginning Was the Word*, 107.

himself, or if he has revealed himself, people are not required to submit to the authority of that revelation, that is, the authority of God's verbal communion behavior.

We must start by reminding ourselves that the triune God is the only one who is autonomous. He alone is self-sufficient, and, as Bavinck put it, "an infinite fullness of blessed life" in three persons.[12] He governs himself and, through himself (through his communion behavior), governs all things. This is the plain truth of who God is, and it will never change.

However, that did not stop Adam and Eve (or any of us, for that matter) from challenging God's autonomy by claiming that they could govern themselves *apart from* God's verbal communion behavior. In choosing to act on the words of the serpent, Adam and Eve simultaneously claimed autonomy for themselves. They claimed, in other words, that they did not need God (the only truly autonomous being) or his communion behavior in order to interpret the world and act on those interpretations. Their governing behavior, which was meant to image the Father, Son, and Holy Spirit, became *rebellious* governing behavior. Rather than trying to govern and steward God's creation in accordance with God's words, they attempted to act in isolation from him and his revelation, which is impossible anyway, since they themselves are part of that revelation as image bearers!

It is worth pausing here to note that autonomy is embedded deep in the human heart. It is, as it were, the spiritual black plague that has no cure but Christ. In our innermost sinful being, there is a wicked call for self-governance, and this must be daily defeated through a surrender to Christ's Lordship—through prayer and a meditation on Scripture, God's governing and authoritative verbal communion behavior.

The distortion of governance can be seen in many facets of the fallen world today: physical and spiritual abuse replace servant-like stewardship; working and keeping the land has often been more of an attempt to destroy and ravage it for profit; marriage, an interpersonal covenant meant to reflect God's unity and plurality, has been riddled with divorce, the harsh opposite of communion. But because we earlier discussed creaturely governance as it relates to naming, we might focus on the distortion of governing in that area.

Since Adam and Eve were barred from God's intimate presence in the Garden of Eden, all of their naming would be done at a distance from God, in a sense. Certainly, they could not go anywhere to escape God's presence, but their relationship with the ever-present God would be constantly disturbed. In other words, though they would not ever be absent from God's

12. Bavinck, *God and Creation*, 308–09.

presence, they would act *as if* they were, in the sense that they would ignore his sovereign Lordship in everything they did. In terms of autonomy, Adam and Eve (and their descendants) would vainly attempt to behave autonomously, in isolation from the ever-present God. This is always vain since, as Frame noted above, "Nobody can really be autonomous, because we are all subject to God's control, authority, and presence."[13]

This vain attempt at autonomy would infiltrate every part of human behavior, especially communion behavior (language). Here I am thinking specifically of verbal communion behavior: spoken language.

As we saw in the previous chapter, an important part of our communion behavior was its naming or labeling capacity as this was an extension of our creaturely dominion. Our naming, like Adam's, was meant to reflect our own limited meaning, control, and presence and be a testament to the Trinity's ultimate meaning, control, and presence. In this sense, the naming element of our language was to be a witness to the God who communes with himself and who used his own communion behavior to create a world that would be in covenant with him. The result of sin, however, was to mar that paradigm. In short, sin has led us to use and receive names as if they had meaning apart from God, as if we could successfully rebel against God's control, and in feigned isolation from his presence.

Meaning apart from the meaningful Trinity? Let me start by stating what may seem obvious: there is *no meaning* apart from the exhaustively meaningful God of the Bible, the God who gives meaning to all things in relation to his plan of creation and redemption. God, in a profound sense, *is* meaning. The Father, Son, and Holy Spirit—one being in three persons—is the root of all personal values (love, joy, peace, hope, fellowship), and what is meaning if not the shared values of persons?

However, sin has pulled the proverbial wool over our eyes. It has blinded us to this most obvious truth. And the result is that we go about naming and labeling as if such names and labels have lasting meaning apart from the Trinity, as if we could even pronounce the word "meaning" apart from the creative and sustaining communion behavior of the triune God! In a spiritual sense, this is the epitome of madness. It is as if we were to walk into someone's living room, sit down on sofas, and have a casual conversation about how there is no such thing as oxygen. Our very existence is dependent on oxygen, which allows us to have the conversation in the first place. The definition of insanity is to deny or reject something that we must stand upon *as we deny or reject it*. The world's definition for madness is a malady of mankind—a broken mind, a chemical imbalance, a psychiatric

---

13. Frame, *A History of Western Philosophy and Theology*, 22.

disorder. In contrast, Scripture's definition for madness is rooted in a denial or rejection of the majesty of the triune God, for we cannot escape him. As we have seen, every speck and spark of reality "speaks" of him.

Along these lines, Paul quoted an ancient poet from Crete to remind his audience that God himself is our total environment: "In him we live and move and have our being" (Acts 17:28). *In* the God who communes with himself in three persons, *in* the God whose communion behavior created and sustains the world—*in* this God we live and move and exist. There is no way we can get outside of the Trinity—not with our actions, not with our thoughts, and certainly not with our communion behavior, which images God at every turn.

So, when it comes to our names and labels, it is nothing short of ludicrous to think that they have meaning apart from (or at least without reference to) God—as if God were not involved in *directing*, *guiding*, and *judging* the names and labels we create and use each day, not only in terms of our intended meaning, but also in terms of the damage that ensues.

Let me go a little deeper here, at the risk of getting too philosophical. Meaning, which I understand to be the values of the Trinity as revealed in God's written communion behavior (Scripture), only exists if it is rooted in the eternal plan of God, made known to us in the Bible. Anything that we might think of as outside the plan of God would, in fact, be meaning*less*. Given this biblical reality, people can really only *pretend* that their names and labels exist apart from God's ultimate meaning, but this is an exercise in futility. It is what we might call *autonomous naming*, a form of rebelling against God with our language. Nothing has meaning apart from the God who speaks (the only being who is autonomous). Thus, any creaturely meaning we attribute to something through a name must account for the plan of God. And when we ignore that plan—as it is presented in Scripture—we vainly attempt to ignore the all-controlling meaning that God has instilled in every fiber of reality. Put differently, we can name and label elements of reality around us, but if we do not consider how these names and labels square with God's revealed plan, we may be uttering mishomers—names and labels that do not reflect who God is and what he is doing in the world.

Let's look at an example. Imagine if my non-Christian friend were to say that another one of our mutual non-Christian friends, call him Tom, is *honest*. Recall that describing a person's character (figures 11 and 12) is one of the ways in which we continue the tradition of naming parts of creation, following in Adam's footsteps. Most of us make these sorts of character descriptions almost every day. Usually, we mean something like, "Tom regularly and consistently tells the truth; he does not hide things from others."

Now, on a superficial level, this may indeed be the case. Perhaps in our interactions with him, Tom attempts to tell the truth consistently and does not withhold anything that seems significant. The question I would ask in light of our previous discussion is this: In offering this character description, how have we accounted for or been shaped by the spoken plan of God in Scripture? The answer, I believe, is that we have *not* accounted for or been shaped by God's spoken plan—at least not consciously. This may seem trivial, but notice what this does: it asserts that we can name parts of creation (expressing meaning) without giving a second thought to God's meaning as revealed in the Bible. Does that not strike you as odd? Are we not in danger of treating God's plan—the Father's choosing and redeeming of his people through Christ by the power of his Holy Spirit—as functionally irrelevant to our use of language? Attempting to name and label parts of the world around us—objects, ideas, people, places—without giving so much as a head nod to the God who speaks is very strange. And, in fact, I argue that it produces potentially harmful results.

Think of Tom's situation this way: there is no such thing as bare honesty. There is no "general" character trait of honesty that we can pick out and apply to a given person. *Every person is in covenant relationship with the Trinity.* They are, as Van Til would say, covenant breakers or covenant keepers. That means that when we give a name or label to someone like Tom, we must account for Tom's covenantal status. Strictly speaking, Tom is truly honest only insofar as his covenantal commitments (professed faith in the triune God) align with Christ-like, Spirit-inspired covenantal behaviors (including language). Because in this case Tom is a non-Christian, we might give him the attribute of *honesty* in casual conversation. Yet Tom is, in fact, *dishonest* in the most profound way. Because Paul tells us in Romans 1 that all people know God and are covenantally responsible to him, if Tom says he does not believe in God, then in Paul's words he is "suppressing the truth in unrighteousness" (Rom 1:18). On the deepest level of his creaturely identity, Tom is *dishonest*, so why be content with saying that he is honest in a superficial way, a way that ignores who God is and what he is doing in the world around us? In casually calling Tom *honest*, we may be practicing the world's trend of *autonomous naming*. We may be naming and labeling parts of creation *as if* God's presence and plan had little to no effect on whatever we are considering.

With this example, I want to be sensitive. I do not want to come across as saying, "Every non-Christian is a bold-faced liar!" My purpose in this example is not to call down judgment on non-Christians. But I do want to recognize the biblical truth that unbelief, according to Paul, is self-deception; unbelief is a suppressing of the truth. So we should exercise more caution and care before giving someone a name or label. As Christians, we simply *must* bring who God is and what he is doing to bear on everything that we do—even something as seemingly menial as a character description.

This approach to naming and labeling has implications for how we respond and react to the language of others as well. Let me give another example, this time a Christian one. I once overheard a student praising a professor for a book he had just written. "This is so helpful!" she said. By implication, she was also telling the professor that *he* was so helpful. The professor responded in a way that struck me. He said, "Well . . . praise the Lord!" Praise the Lord? Not, "I'm glad it was helpful" or "Thank you—I worked very hard on it"?

As I thought about the professor's response, I realized that he reacted in a way that revealed his belief. For this professor, God was in control of all things; God had called him to the teaching profession, had blessed his thinking and revealed the truth to him, had given him the ability and the stamina to write clearly and effectively. It was *the Lord* who was ultimately responsible for this book that the student was so excited about. So, his response was to redirect attention from himself to the God who gives great gifts: Praise the Lord!

This brings up an important point—our reactions to names and labels reveal much about the spiritual maturity of our souls. Christians love to compliment one another, and so do non-Christians. But because of what we know about who God is and what he is doing, we are called to walk the world with a mirror: reflecting the kind words of others toward the Trinity (figure 15), rather than allowing such words to inflate our egos.

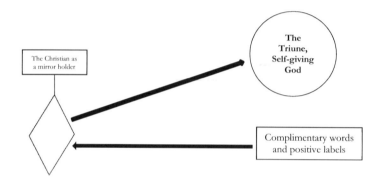

Figure 15: Christian Response to Compliments

This is just one example in which our use of names and labels can take into account the triune God—both who he is and what he is doing (his plan). And we know both of those things only through our reception of his written communion behavior: the Bible. Let me say it once more: There is no true meaning in our names and labels apart from the exhaustively meaningful Trinity and his purposes for us. As Van Til once wrote, "There is purpose *within* the universe because the triune God has a purpose *for* the universe. Every purpose within the universe must, in the last analysis, be referred to God. Without this reference to God, no purpose within the universe has meaning."[14] We might also say, "without this reference to God, no name or label within the universe has meaning."

In sum, our attempts to use names and labels without any regard for God's exhaustively purposeful plan is what we have called *autonomous naming*, and this sort of naming is sapped of the true meaning our words are meant to evoke in an environment that has been created, sustained, and redeemed through God's communion behavior. The meaning of our names and labels, both in our production and reception of them, must take into account the exhaustively meaningful plan of the triune God.

Control apart from the all-controlling Trinity? A similar principle holds for the control exercised by our names and labels. Recall that our use of names and labels is a form of governance, a way of controlling the world around us, or, better yet, a way of faithfully stewarding it. In giving the animals names, Adam was exercising his God-given control over creation as an image bearing steward.

Just as there is no meaning apart from the spoken plan of the triune God, so there is no real control apart from God's revealed plan. In other words, there is no control outside of the communion behavior of the Trinity. We can manipulate and cast down others with our names and labels, but nothing is going to stop the progression of God's all-controlling plan of redemption. One day, every knee *will* bow and every tongue confess Christ's Lordship (Phil 2:10; Rom 4:11). And as history is moving towards that point, God is aware of every decision and behavior of his creatures to either steward the created order with our names and labels according to the Lordship of his Son, and to build up our fellow image bearers with grace-giving, Spirit-led speech, or tear apart the created order and speak words that assault the grace and peace that Christ has brought into the world.

Again, let's look at an example. Medical diagnoses are another common part of governance through naming. Let us consider the word *cancer*. This is especially relevant to many of us today because cancer has affected so

14. Van Til, *Christian Theistic Evidences*, 161.

many. My father, for instance, died when he was only 47 from a cancerous brain tumor. Because of the devastation this phenomenon has caused, the word *cancer* is chilling to many of us. It sounds like a cold and definitive death sentence. And I say with a heavy heart, it *is* a death sentence for millions of people each year.

But let us go back to this idea of control being rooted in God's all-controlling plan. When we hear the name *cancer*, do we account for the power and control of the triune God? Do we put this label in the context of God's all-powerful Word sustaining every part of reality—even the doctor's lips as he utters the diagnosis? For many of us, the answer is no. When I first learned that my father was in fact going to die from the cancer he had, my response was fear and trembling. My knees started to give way, and it became hard to swallow.

Cancer, along with every other physical malady, is not purposeless or outside the control of the Father, Son, and Holy Spirit. God uses *everything* for the good of those who love him (Rom 8:28)—and that includes cancer, fibromyalgia, and leukemia as much as it does tooth aches and head colds. Cancer, from this perspective, is not a death sentence; it is an intimidating opportunity for us to conform to the image of Christ through suffering with hope (Rom 8:17; Phil 3:10; 1 Thess 4:13; 2 Thess 2:16; 1 Tim 4:10). So, we *could* define cancer like everyone else in the world does, acknowledging only its physical effects on the human body. Along with the rest of the hopeless world, we could say that cancer is "a mass of tissue cells possessed of potentially unlimited growth that serves no useful function in the body, robs the host of nutrients necessary for survival, expands locally by invasion and systemically by transmission of cells along lymphatic and blood pathways, and unless recognized early and removed kills the host."[15] *Or* we could account for the all-controlling plan of God and define cancer as "a devastating effect of the fall that wreaks havoc on the mind and body and yet is used by the Father for his purposes of strengthening, sanctifying, and conforming us to the image of his Son by the power of the Holy Spirit, who is a guarantee of the eternal hope we have. Cancer is either an instrument of redemption in the hands of an almighty God or a door that leads to eternal communion with him." Do you see the difference? Christians should receive and use this label (cancer) in a way that acknowledges the all-powerful creative and redemptive communion behavior of God. We do not use language as the rest of the world does; we use it with a biblical awareness of the trinitarian hope to which we have been called (Eph 1:18).

15. *Webster's Third New International Dictionary, Unabridged*, s.v. "cancer," accessed February 24, 2017, http://unabridged.merriam-webster.com.

Another way of framing this would be to say that the control of naming and labeling—the governance of language—ultimately resides in God. It is his redemptive speech—the Word of God in the flesh—who controls and upholds all things. The Word of God is Christ, the name that governs the destiny of creation. Any controlling use of names and labels submits to the highest name, the all controlling Word of the Father who indwells us by the Spirit. Apart from the all-controlling, ever-shaping communion behavior of God in the person of Christ, our names and labels have no control, no power, no governance.

As alluded to at the outset of this section, through the persons of the Son and the Holy Spirit, our Father is directing, guiding, and judging the names and labels we use. He is *always* in control. The question for us is, will we speak and hear names and labels in submission to that control, with an awareness of who God is and what he has done, or will we continue to ignore this?

Personal presence apart from the tripersonal God? Just as there is no meaning and no control apart from the self-communing Trinity, so there is no human personal presence outside of the context of divine personal presence. As we saw in earlier chapters, by creating all things through his communion behavior God marked the whole world with his presence, and everything "speaks" about him in some way. As Paul said in Acts 17:28, "In him we live and move and have our being." We live in the context of the exhaustively meaningful, all-controlling, ever-present Trinity. We are never in a room by ourselves.

Just as God's words evoke his personal presence, so our use of names and labels was meant to reflect our creaturely presence in a way that pointed back to God. Adam's naming of the animals in Genesis 2 reflected his personality—his unique choices in ascribing certain sounds to certain creatures. Yet this was not meant to reflect Adam in isolation. His names for the animals pointed to a deeper divine presence in the God who spoke Adam into being and gave him linguistic dominion over the other parts of creation. Adam's names thus reflected his own personality in one sense and testified to the divine personality of the triune God in another sense.

Sin, however, has distorted this. It is difficult for people to see *us* in our words, let alone the God who spoke us into being. The personal presence that God has built into naming and labeling is often forgotten in our use of language. In some ways, we operate as if our naming and labeling only sometimes reflects our personal presence. We act as if we have to use words in a special way in order for others to see or hear us in them. For instance, I can write my wife a love note and leave it on her desk, and she will undoubtedly feel my personal presence there. I have a letter from my father that he wrote to me when I was eight, right before he underwent his first major brain surgery. Every word in that letter seems steeped in his presence. When I read the letter, I hear his voice. In situations such as these it may be relatively easy for us to sense the personal presence that accompanies our words. But if I write down items to pick up at the store and my wife reads that list, she will not feel my personal presence, will she? If I give an article or essay that I have written a certain title, readers will not necessarily sense my personal presence in the title, will they? They will not sense *me* in the name of the essay. They will just extract information, right?

Sin has blinded us to the truth that all names and labels, in one way or another, reflect the personal presence of the one who has given them. What's more, names and labels must point back to God in terms of his covenantal relationship to creation. In other words, a particular name or label might be wicked and sinful, but it still points back to God in the sense that it directs our attention to the good and righteous covenantal standards that he has delivered to us in his Word. The point is that there is no such thing, really, as (1) an impersonal use of words or (2) a use of words that can be barred from God's presence. That is to say, a speaker's or writer's personal presence is always in a name or label because it is *that person* who has given or repeated the name or label. No name floats through the atmosphere unattached to a person. *People* are always the ones using names and labels, and every person emits his or her personal presence with the use of names and labels. In addition, every name and label emits the personal presence of God, who judges all of our words as either covenantally faithful or covenantally rebellious. As Jesus said, "on the day of judgment people will give account for every careless word they speak" (Matt 12:36).

Once again, an example may help. As I write this, I am staring out the windows of a lake house in northern Pennsylvania. It is still early in the morning. The trees and bushes by the lake are a charcoal color, and behind them the cloudy sky is a dirty white-gray, glowing softly as the sun begins to rise. The trees are all swaying in the strong wind, waving their little fingers in circles, their trunks rocking back and forth. For a moment, I imagine that everything is under water, moving in the current of the wind. When my family wakes up, I will probably say, "It's windy." Those spoken words will obviously reflect my personal presence with them because they can hear me utter the sentence. However, you as a reader can only process the words on the page. Is my personal presence reflected in something as banal as a statement about the weather? And does my label of the weather say anything about God's presence?

I would say so. First, my written words reflect that I am endowed, like you, with an ability to mark the world with *my* presence.[16] Writing—on a paper or electronic page—shows that I am here, and that I can impress myself on the world in some way. And when you read the words I write, you are not simply processing sounds internally and piecing together clauses and ideas. You are reading *me*. You are reading a message that I, and no other, has placed in the world. Certainly, many people (even many of my own family members today) have spoken or written the sentence, "It's windy." But none of those people is me, and none of them was in the exact time and place that I was when I thought of those words and wrote them on this page. This is the case with all of our words, for no word enters the world in isolation from a person. Language always begins with persons, and it always traces back to them. So, yes, my banal statement about the weather reflects my personal presence.

Second, my sentence actually reveals a great deal about God's presence. I am not, after all, merely making a statement about the weather; I am making a statement about the weather *in God's world*. All of reality, remember, "speaks" of God, and the wind is no exception. The wind speaks of God's sovereignty over the atmosphere, and it tells us of his power and his covenantal faithfulness. God made a wind blow over the earth after the flood in order to reveal the land (Gen 8:1). In this sense, wind is part of God's fulfillment of the promise he made to Noah and his family to protect them from the flood (Gen 6:18). Later in Genesis, God used an eastern wind to bring locusts to Egypt (Exod 10:13), expressing judgment over Israel's abusive host and, once again, affirming his faithfulness to his promises. And the eastern wind again appeared later in the narrative to part the waters for the people to walk through the Red Sea on dry land (Exod 14:21). All throughout Scripture, God brings the wind out from its storehouses (Ps 135:7) and uses it to do his bidding; its power is submissive to him. It is his messenger (Ps 104:4).

What's more, the wind has a mysterious resemblance to breath, particularly the breath of God. We discussed in another chapter how the Father speaks the Son (the Word) in the power of his breath (the Holy Spirit). The Spirit, the divine breath of the Father, is also in the Son. Jesus, in fact, even gives the Spirit to his disciples in John's Gospel by *breathing* on them.

> 19 On the evening of that day, the first day of the week, the doors
> being locked where the disciples were for fear of the Jews, Jesus
> came and stood among them and said to them, "Peace be with

---

16. For more on the nature of writing as evoking our personal presence, see Hibbs, "We Who Work with Words."

you." 20 When he had said this, he showed them his hands and his side. Then the disciples were glad when they saw the Lord. 21 Jesus said to them again, "Peace be with you. As the Father has sent me, even so I am sending you." 22 And when he had said this, he breathed on them and said to them, "Receive the Holy Spirit. (John 20:19–22)

Earlier in the Gospel, Jesus related the Holy Spirit to the wind. When confronted by Nicodemus about his divine identity and the kingdom of God,

> Jesus answered, "Truly, truly, I say to you, unless one is born of water and the Spirit, he cannot enter the kingdom of God. 6 That which is born of the flesh is flesh, and that which is born of the Spirit is spirit. 7 Do not marvel that I said to you, 'You must be born again.' 8 The wind blows where it wishes, and you hear its sound, but you do not know where it comes from or where it goes. So it is with everyone who is born of the Spirit." (John 3:5–8)

People who are born of the Spirit—people who have been chosen by God himself to be convinced of and convicted by his truth—have the Spirit working in them, but the Spirit moves mysteriously, like the wind. We can sense the presence of the wind when it is among us, just as I could observe the wind blowing through the trees at the lake house, but we do not know where it comes from or where it is going. Jesus thus uses the wind to portray the movement of the Holy Spirit. So, the wind in some ways reflects the nature of the Holy Spirit, particularly his movement.

In striking ways, the wind draws our attention to the Trinity. Its association with breath helps us to remember the Holy Spirit as the breath and life-giving power of God (Gen 2:7; Job 33:4). Its unique movement reminds us that the Holy Spirit is a divine person, distinct from the Father and the Son and yet one with them, working with the eternal Word of the Father to both create and redeem all things. Banal statements about the weather, as it turns out, have far more to them than we might think. Just as all linguistic expressions do in one way or another, they reflect the presence of the triune God. There is no use of naming and labeling that can occur apart from the presence of God, and so all of our names and labels can and should be used in light of this amazing truth.

What I hope to have done in this section is to affirm that our use of names and labels—both productively and receptively—must account for and reflect the meaning, control, and presence of the triune God.

LYING: THE HEART OF SIN AS LINGUISTIC

Now, I would like to draw all of our observations together by reminding us that all of the names and labels that we use in pretended isolation from the triune God were brought about by the linguistic action of the serpent: his lie. It was the lie of a snake that, in part, led to our sinful state.[17] It was a lie that brought about our apparent ruin.

Because of this, I believe that lying—deceit—serves as an illuminating perspective on the nature of sin. We earlier noted how sin is linguistic; it occurs in an environment that was created and sustained by God's communion behavior. It also occurs in the covenantal context of creation, which God continues to uphold by way of divine speech. And if sin is linguistic, then it seems that deceit is at the heart of sin. That is why truth is so important.

Later New Testament revelation tells us that truth is not merely a principle to be upheld but a person to be communed with (John 14:6). In this sense, "it is appropriate to see the Son, the Word, the second person of the Trinity, as the final, archetypal truth of God. The truth that we receive comes to us through him."[18] And because the Son is the truth of God and the Word of the Father, he is "the source for the particular words that God speaks to convey truth to us."[19] So, when Adam and Eve rejected the words of God in Genesis 3, they were in a sense rejecting God himself—the second person of the Trinity, through whom God's creaturely words were spoken. Thus, the fall is not a story about the violation of truth as a principle; on a deeper level, it is a story about *personal* violation—the breaking of trust and truth that had a profoundly personal origin in the Son of God himself.

The serpent, in this situation, was a *counterfeiter*. He tricked Eve and her husband into distrusting the authentic, original truth by presenting them with an imitation. "He offers something close to the truth, but it is a counterfeit. Like a counterfeit twenty-dollar bill, it has to look genuine in order to trick people. But a careful inspection discloses that it is fake."[20] This is Satan's MO; his evil lies not broadly in malice or ill will. It lies in lying.

Satan's actions throughout human history, just as everything else, are marked by contrast, variation, and distribution. The contrastive and identifying feature of his work and words is always *deceit*. This takes on a plethora

---

17. This is not to say that we are not responsible for sin. We are *fully* responsible, but the serpent certainly has an important role to play in the fall.

18. Poythress, *In the Beginning Was the Word*, 290.

19. Poythress, 290.

20. Poythress., 113.

of variations in all of our lives, and his actions and words are distributed in particularly evil contexts. But Satan is always and everywhere a *liar*.

Jesus draws our attention to this in John's Gospel when he criticizes those who reject him and his message.

> I know that you are offspring of Abraham; yet you seek to kill me because my word finds no place in you. 38 I speak of what I have seen with my Father, and you do what you have heard from your father." 39 They answered him, "Abraham is our father." Jesus said to them, "If you were Abraham's children, you would be doing the works Abraham did, 40 but now you seek to kill me, a man who has told you the truth that I heard from God. This is not what Abraham did. 41 You are doing the works your father did." They said to him, "We were not born of sexual immorality. We have one Father—even God." 42 Jesus said to them, "If God were your Father, you would love me, for I came from God and I am here. I came not of my own accord, but he sent me. 43 Why do you not understand what I say? It is because you cannot bear to hear my word. 44 You are of your father the devil, and your will is to do your father's desires. He was a murderer from the beginning, and does not stand in the truth, because there is no truth in him. When he lies, he speaks out of his own character, for he is a liar and the father of lies. (John 8:37–44)

A liar and the father of lies—that is Satan's identity. When he spoke through the serpent in the Garden of Eden, he was working out of his own character. Lying and deceit opened the door to a sin-stained world. It is helpful, then, to consider how deceit may be the root of all our sinful uses of language.

DERIVATIONS OF DECEPTION

Sin started with deceitful speech, and we can see an element of deceit in all of our sinful uses of language.

To deceive or lie is to misguide and mislead. In his masterpiece *Gulliver's Travels*, satirist Jonathan Swift defined a lie as "a thing which was not."[21] When we think about it, all of our sinful uses of language give off the scent of deception.

Lying. Of course, much of our corrupt use of language bleeds through in our lying to others. This takes at least two forms, sometimes mixed: what

---

21. Jonathan Swift, *Gulliver's Travels* (New York: Peebles Press International, 1975), 258.

we might call *positive deception* and *negative deception* Positive deception occurs when we deliver words to another and present false or misleading information. If a friend asks me if I have prayed for a particular need that he communicated, and I tell him that I have when I haven't, then my deception is positive. I am offering him words that do not correspond to the truth. I have said, in Swift's words, "a thing which was not." Negative deception is when we withhold the truth for some personal gain or malicious intent. Using Swift's language, we might say it is "not speaking a thing which is." For example, what if I were to find one of my wife's old chapsticks lying on the counter top? I might throw it away, and then my wife might ask me what I remembered seeing on the counter top earlier that day. I could say, "Just some junk mail and a few pieces of fruit." Not telling her that I found the old chapstick and threw it away is an instance of negative deception. I am withholding the truth from her out a selfish desire for her not to be mad at me for throwing away something she still valued. Both sorts of deception are corruptions of language. Both are an affront to the truth, to the divine person of the Godhead who himself *is* truth.

When we practice positive or negative deception, we are following in the slithery path of the serpent. The serpent practiced both positive and negative deception. Positively, he directly opposed God's words when he said, "You will not surely die" (Gen 3:4). Negatively, he spoke in half-truths, withholding certain things from Adam and Eve. He told Eve that when she ate the fruit of the tree of the knowledge of good and evil, her eyes would be opened (3:5). This was partially true, for when Eve ate the fruit and gave some to Adam and he ate, their eyes *were* opened, but they were not like God, as the serpent had promised. Instead, they only saw that they were naked (Gen 3:7), which brought them shame and encouraged them to make clothes for themselves to cover up their nakedness. This was an act of disunion, for love is an open self-giving, not a concealment. In covering themselves, Adam and Eve were illustrating an implication of breaking covenant with the God of communion.

Exaggerating. Our exaggerations are also rooted in deception, for they seek to distort the truth for selfish gain. The serpent did this with his initial question to Eve, "Did God actually say, 'You shall not eat of any tree in the garden'?" (Gen 3:1) As we saw, Eve was led astray from the truth by the serpent's distortion of God's original words. Exaggeration deceives by going beyond the bounds of truth—stretching it so that it *resembles* the original but does not *represent* it faithfully. The distorted resemblance then becomes a spark that ignites a fire of distortion. The serpent's exaggeration led to Eve's own exaggeration: "but God said, 'You shall not eat of the fruit of the tree that is in the midst of the garden, neither shall you touch it . . .'" (Gen 3:4).

Exaggeration leads to a breaking of communion between God and persons and between persons themselves, for it feeds off of the truth like a parasite in order to reap the benefits of its host for selfish enjoyment. It uses deception, in other words, to break communion.

Mocking. Mocking others is similarly an act of deception, since when we make fun of others, we are not representing them truthfully, as God sees them. Mocking is a means of belittling and diminishing others, making them feel lesser. Yet, in the frequently referenced Bible verse, "For God so loved the world, that he gave his only Son . . ." (John 3:16), we see how precious God's creatures are to him, and God's love serves his creatures in such a way that it makes them feel greater. He gave his only Son out of love for *every* person. That is love unparalleled. Now, Scripture is clear that not every person will respond to this love in faith, but that does not negate the truth that all persons are treasured by God as his image bearers. Mocking others is, at heart, a kind of deception whereby persons are told that they are *not* so treasurable. In fact, says the mocker, perhaps they are of little or no value. Mockery, like the other distorted and sinful uses of language, leads to disunion—the forging of a chasm between God and his loved ones, and between people who are meant to love one another (John 13:34–35).

Abusing. Closely related to mocking others is abusing them with language. To abuse others verbally is to cut them down with words, which were meant to foster communion between persons.[22] Abusive language can take many forms: name-calling, declarations of hate, threats of violence. All abusive language is linked to deception in a way that we might not notice. We often associate truth with propositions or information. But truth cannot be isolated from love. They are bound up with each other ultimately because they are bound up in God himself. The second person of the Trinity is truth (John 14:6), but God is also love (1 John 4:8). The Holy Spirit is the bond of love between the Son (divine truth) and the Father (the source of divine meaning). The Father loves the Son and shows him all that he does (John 5:20), and the Son loves the Father and willingly descends to reconcile God's people to himself. The Spirit is involved in this mission of truth and love, since the Spirit searches the depths of God and reveals God's love in the gospel to his people (1 Cor 2:10). Thus, divine love and divine truth are married to each other in the being of God and cannot be separated in creation. They are bound together in God himself, and they are bound together in the gospel. So, we cannot violate the truth without being unloving, and we cannot be unloving without violating the truth. Likewise, we cannot reject the Son who is truth without rejecting the Father's love (Luke 10:16), and

22. Hibbs, "Words for Communion," 5–8.

we cannot reject the Father's love apart from rejecting the truth of his Son. In light of this relationship, abusing others with our words is simultaneously an assault on truth *and* love. This is what brings deception into the picture. Abusing others with words is deceptive (an assault against the Son) because it is unloving (a rejection of the Father), and it is unloving (a rejection of the Father) because it is deceptive (an assault against the Son).

Judging. Using judgmental language is deceptive for similar but slightly different reasons. Judgmental language, though it is directed at others, is an attempt at *self-elevation*, an attempt to put ourselves above others. But this runs contrary to the truth of the gospel. In Phillipians, Paul tells his readers to follow the model of Christ,

> Do nothing from selfish ambition or conceit, but in humility count others more significant than yourselves. 4 Let each of you look not only to his own interests, but also to the interests of others. 5 Have this mind among yourselves, which is yours in Christ Jesus, 6 who, though he was in the form of God, did not count equality with God a thing to be grasped, 7 but emptied himself, by taking the form of a servant, being born in the likeness of men. 8 And being found in human form, he humbled himself by becoming obedient to the point of death, even death on a cross. (Phil 2:3–8)

In judging others, we do the exact opposite of what Christ did for us. We elevate ourselves above others out of selfish ambition or conceit.[23] This is also deceptive in the sense that it suggests to others a hierarchy of human worth, as if some persons were more valuable to God than others. This is simply not the case, for "all have sinned and fall short of the glory of God" (Rom 3:23). All people are in desperate (not moderate, but desperate) need of redemption and adoption through God's Son by the power of the Spirit. There is no hierarchy of human worth in God's eyes, but our judgment of others suggests that there is, and this is deceptive on a deep level. It violates the truth that all are equally in need of salvation.

Boasting. Boasting is similarly self-elevating, and it detracts from the glory of God. In this latter sense, boasting is deceptive. It promotes what cannot be true: we are not more glorious than God himself, and we are not responsible for any good gifts that we have been given. In fact, all our lives are a gift from God, and any good thing we receive or do must be attributed to him (1 Tim 6:13; cf. Matt 7:11).

---

23. I am not dealing here with righteous judgment, that is, our calling attention to the violation of God's standards as provided in Scripture. Rather, I am talking about selfish claims to higher status and worth in God's eyes.

One of my favorite Bible verses is a pair of questions that Paul asks the Corinthians, the first of which is rhetorical: "What do you have that you did not receive? If then you received it, why do you boast as if you did not receive it?" (1 Cor 4:7) The Christian life is a life that acknowledges the pervasiveness of divine gift-giving. And because of this pervasiveness, we are called to reverence, worship, and thankfulness. We are to give "thanks always and for everything to God the Father in the name of our Lord Jesus Christ, submitting to one another out of reverence for Christ" (Eph 5:20–21; cf. Col 1:12; 3:17; 1 Thess 5:18; Rev 11:17). In the context of such a calling, any attempt to bring attention to our abilities or gifts deceptively portrays the power of the gospel. The gospel, after all, is not what *we* can do for God through the Spirit and in the name of Christ; rather, it is what the Father has done in us through his Son by the power of the Holy Ghost. Christians must expose the deceit of the former statement and the truth of the latter one.

Suppressing (rebelling). The next corrupted use of language is deeply related to the gospel and gets at the heart of unbelief. As a parent of toddlers, I experience nearly every day how blatant rebellion can be. Responding to shouts of "No!" and screaming denials are part of shepherding young children. Yet, often I see myself in the rebellious behavior of my kids. There are times when I tell them something that is unequivocally true. When trying to persuade my three-year-old that we should go outside to play, I have said, "It's nice outside." Sometimes I get the angry retort: "No! It's *not* nice outside!!" I have learned in these situations not to repeat the truth endlessly (though I *really* want to sometimes). Shouting matches with toddlers never end well. But in these encounters with my children I am reminded of my own spiritual rejection of God's plain truth. At dozens of places throughout the New Testament, God tells us that his Son has been sent to suffer and die for sinners, and that he has been raised from the dead. How often, even as a professing Christian, my rebellious heart shouts, "No! That's *not* true!! It can't be true. It's not logical—no!"

The same occurs when I read God's promises in Scripture, which seem too good to be true. "I am with you always, to the end of the age" (Matt 28:20). "No—I don't feel that way! No!" "I will not leave you as orphans; I will come to you. Yet a little while and the world will see me no more, but you will see me. Because I live, you also will live" (John 14:18–19). "No, no, no—that can't be true. We *won't* live forever with you!" It's embarrassing, isn't it? These internal thoughts reveal the heart in disconcerting ways. They show my rebellion, my tirades of unbelief against a God who is loving and cannot lie.

While these thoughts are often internal for many Christians, they are external for non-Christians. Paul tells us in Romans 1 that all people know God. They do not simply have a vague sense of deity or encounters with some nebulous emotional high. They know *God*. They know that he is true, and yet they use language—the trinitarian gift of God—to suppress this truth. They rail against their own salvation with hostile discourse and denunciations. Or, they rebel more quietly, refusing to lift their heads and set their eyes on a heavenly Father who is *always* before them.

The rejection of the gospel, the suppression of God's truth in rebellion, is also linked to deception, for disbelief is an act of *self-deception*. It is a process by which people tell themselves over and over again that the God of the Bible is the strange hero of an outdated fairytale. They interpret all of their experiences as testimony to this lie. And as days and months roll into years, they can become embedded deeper and deeper in a fiction foreign to the truth of Scripture. That language can be used deceptively in our own hearts to deny the plain truth of the Bible is perhaps one of the saddest travesties in our communicative history. As we will see in the next chapter, this is a crisis that only God himself can take on. And he *has* taken it on in the person and work of his Son and in that of the Holy Spirit.

Not caring. This may be the most dangerous corruption of language in our time. For many of us, it is not that we abuse others or spend a great deal of time mocking and boasting. We do our fair share of that, certainly, but most of the time we are simply apathetic or ignorant. We do not care about how we use language or what language tells us about who God is and what he is doing. We simply live *in* language, as it were, without paying any attention to it. This is a lethal act of self-deception, similar to that of suppressing the truth. By not caring about how we use words or what language reveals about the nature of reality and the God who rules it, we surrender the most fundamental truth: we live in a worded world, spoken into being by the self-communing God, sustained and governed by the Father's divine Word and the power of the Spirit, everywhere revealing the triune God. Language is central to who God is, to who we are, to what the world is like, and to how redemption will be brought to completion. Living in ignorance of this truth does great damage to our faith.

IMPLICATIONS FOR US

I will stop here, leaving the rest of the discussion for the following chapters. For now, let us consider some practical implications for us that have risen to the surface in this chapter.

There are quite a few implications for us here, many of which foreshadow where we are moving in the pages ahead. So, let me draw our attention to just three implications that should have a significant effect on our use of language every day: covenantal communion, truthfulness, and deceit.

Covenantal communion. Most of us are not in the habit of using language primarily in terms of its covenantal nature and its purpose of drawing persons into deeper communion with the tripersonal God and with one another. We might think of language more as a tool for information exchange or a means of social development. Language does serve these purposes, so our habits are not unfounded. But as I hope to have made clear by now, that is not the ultimate purpose or use for language. We must go much deeper.

All language occurs within a covenantal and communion-directed context, which makes us responsible for our communication and the results that it leads to. We noted this earlier in Kevin Vanhoozer's words, where he describes discourse—meaningful units of communication—as covenantal:

> The design plan of language is to serve as the medium of covenantal relations with God, with others, with the world. There are two dimensions to this covenant of discourse: the inter-subjective bond between speakers and the objective bond between language and reality. First, language is the medium in which we relate to others. Speakers have a responsibility for their linguistic actions, for example, to be true to their word, as in a promise. Language is not a code that bespeaks the subject, but a covenant that bestows dignity and responsibility on the agent of language. Far from relieving speakers from responsibility, then, the institution of language actually grounds and enables it. Second, language is the medium in which we relate to and seek to understand the world.[24]

And it makes perfect sense that we would use language to understand the world if God's language (communion behavior) is what created the world and continues to sustain and govern it. Language is the key to understanding God, ourselves, and the world that he has spoken into being. It is also true that, because we are image bearing creatures born into covenantal relationship with God, we always use language in the context of covenant.

The first level of this covenantal context is our relationship with the triune God. Each of us is born into covenant; we have no choice in that. Everyone simply enters the world as a creature in covenant with God. All that we do is done in either covenant faithfulness or covenant rebellion. For Christians, our covenantal faithfulness is perfectly fulfilled by God himself in the person and work of Jesus Christ. He represents us fully. Thus, when Christians stumble and sin, God looks at us and sees his incarnate

24. Vanhoozer, *Is There a Meaning in This Text?*, 206.

Son, whose blood has atoned for all of our covenantal rebellion—past, present, and future. But this does not give us license to use language or any other phase of human behavior thoughtlessly. Just the opposite, in fact: as Vanhoozer notes, this establishes our responsibility. In other words, the covenant between the triune God and his people has not been repealed by Christ; it has been ratified by the Father, restored by the Son, and upheld by the continuing work of the Spirit. We still live in the context of covenant. We still use language—communion behavior—in the context of covenant and are responsible for our communication. The second level of this context is our relationships with other people, since interpersonal relationships have always been a part of God's covenant with his people. (For instance, note how many of the Ten Commandments set guidelines for interpersonal relationships.)

This has a few clear implications for our use of language everyday—on both of the levels noted above. On the divine-human level, it underscores the importance of *prayer.* Prayer cannot be pawned off as a merely religious exercise. Prayer is, in fact, at the root of our relationship with God, for by prayer we use communion behavior to commune with the God who dwells in self-communion! Prayer is not only rooted in the trinitarian nature and work of God, since we pray by the power of the Holy Spirit, in the name of Christ our mediator, to the Father our loving Lord;[25] it also is an activity that showcases the centrality of language as the core of God's image in us. God speaks, and he loves for us to speak back to him in prayer. Prayer cannot continue to serve as a Christian's spiritual wish list—something we read off in the early morning and then forget about, aside from mealtimes and traumatic moments in life. *Prayer is meant to be a biblically nurtured and consistently sustained conversation between the triune God and his creatures.* Our communication with God, and our growing spiritual communion with him, is not intermittent or limited to requests. It is constant and full. But do you and I pray this way? Do we go to God in prayer only to make requests, or do we go to him when we want to rejoice, to think, to grieve, to laugh? Is our prayer life a continual conversation, rooted in our reading of Scripture, God's clear and authoritative word to us? If it is not, we are missing out on one of the most basic means to commune with God and to understand the power of language in our relationship with him. One of the ways you might put this into practice is to begin the conversation (though, in a sense, God began it the moment you were born). Stop acting as if you have to go into a private corner to talk to the God of the universe. He is not tucked away in a cloister; he is all around you. In fact, he is *in* you. As we noted earlier, if you

25. Trueman, "The Trinity and Prayer," 201–04.

are *in* Christ and keep his word, then the Father, Son, and Spirit make their abode in your soul. So, it is not awkward to speak to God as if he were right beside you, since he is in fact *inside* of you. It is actually more awkward *not* to speak to God continually. God is in you—listening, shaping, directing, guiding—so why not speak to him? Why not have a conversation with the Trinity that never ends? After all, that is the glory to which we are looking forward in eternity. It is to our spiritual benefit if we start and continue that conversation right now. The world may think you are crazy for talking to God all the time, but the world is backwards and upside down. Constant prayer—constant communion with the Trinity—should be the norm for Christian life, not the exception.

On the human level of our covenantal context, we might begin our interactions with others (family members, friends, acquaintances, strangers) by remembering that *communion* is the ultimate goal of language. We use language to draw close to others, so how might we start this process in everyday conversation? One approach we could take is to *begin with sympathy and long for unity.* Sympathy, rather than prejudice and judgment, is the road to union. When we sympathize with others, we simultaneously recognize the distance between us and attempt to bridge that distance with communion behavior. For example, consider an interest that someone close to you may have, an interest which is foreign to you. My younger brother is interested in fashion photography. I am not immediately drawn to this, so I could avoid conversations with him that center on this topic. *Or* I could begin from a position of sympathy, asking myself what he might see in this: the beauty of form and aesthetics, the capturing of time in space, the changing outward expressions of human values. I do not have to adopt my brother's interests in order to speak with him and learn more about what his passion is and why he is drawn to it. But if I approach my conversations with him from a place of sympathy, it will be far easier to appreciate his enthusiasm and to encourage him. And, provided his interest is not violating biblical standards, is not this loving enthusiasm and encouragement a hallmark of communion behavior?

In my sympathy, there is a deep desire for unity that is also an obvious part of what it means to commune with others. Not all of my brothers currently see eye-to-eye with me in terms of my Christian faith, but that does not stop me from longing to be united to them by the power of the Spirit. Deep in my heart is a longing for union with him, and even deeper is a longing for their union with the Trinity. Beginning our conversations with sympathy and a longing for union will thus help us to keep our priorities straight in everyday conversations, directing us to the ultimate end that language serves: communion with God and with each other.

Truthfulness. As with the previous section, this implication has two levels: the divine-human and the human-human levels. On the divine-human level, we are called upon to receive the truth of God's speech in Scripture with unswerving loyalty. That was what our first parents were called to do, and, as we will see in the next chapter, that is what Christ did with his heavenly Father. In a day when many basic biblical teachings about human identity are being questioned (e.g., human sexuality, gender roles), we must remember the ancient covenantal call to trust the truth of God's words in Scripture. This will not be popular, and we must be willing to pay a price for it—a price that might ultimately be decided by those who reject the Christian faith. But it is critical to remember here that our commitment to the truth of Scripture is not merely propositional; it is *personal*, for the truth of God's words is rooted in the second person of the Trinity, who *is* truth. Rejecting the truth of God's Scripture or compromising with secular culture on positions that the Bible clearly opposes is tantamount to rejecting God himself in the person of the Son. When we uphold the truth of Scripture, we simultaneously uphold the truth of the gospel in the person of Christ, who is God's ultimate Word of reconciliation to us.

This requires that we be rooted or steeped in Scripture, going to it daily for insight, discernment, passion, and direction. If the word of God is the sword of the Spirit (Eph 6:17), we cannot wield it unless we wear it on our person, keeping it with us every day, always ready to remove it from its sheath and cut through the thickets of sinful thought. That much is clear.

In terms of our relationships with other persons, we must never downplay the weight that truth has in our conversations—truth from Scripture, but also truth in our communication. It *matters* that we tell the truth, for doing so is a reflection of our covenantal communion with the God of truth. Telling the truth is an expression of allegiance, not a bare moral decision. In speaking truthfully, we show our loyalty to God. In speaking deceitfully, we show divided allegiance between God and Satan, the father of lies.

Deceit. This brings up the final implication: do not underestimate the power of deceit within language. Frequently, the media draws our attention to more obvious manifestations of our corrupt human nature—acts of terrorism, hate crimes, the spread of drug dependence, and so on. There is a dire need for our prayers here, but there is also a brooding spirit of deceit in human language that is far more lethal than we realize. It was not physical power or fear or substance abuse that brought about the fall of mankind; it was linguistic deceit. Satan's weapon of choice was words. He chose them carefully, and he crafted his message with cunning. Deception appears to be the root of evil in Genesis 3. This highlights once again the importance of clinging to God's words, which alone are true and trustworthy. It also helps us to remain vigilant in a culture with so many messages, so many words streaming on the television and on the web. We can and should sift those words with the truth of Scripture. As the writer of Proverbs pointed out, "When words are many, transgression is not lacking" (Prov 10:19). There is deceit and trickery in the messages all around us. The only sure way to avoid being duped by a world bent on its own destruction is to prayerfully rely on the truth of God's words in the power of the Holy Spirit. As Jesus said in John's Gospel, "the Helper, the Holy Spirit, whom the Father will send in my name, he will teach you all things and bring to your remembrance all that I have said to you" (John 14:26). The Spirit will always be faithful in bringing to our remembrance the truth of what Christ has said. In that divine gift of grace, we are protected from the deceitful words of a fallen world.

It is now time to see how the fall of language was restored by divine language—by the Word of God himself. In Christ, we find redemption and restoration for every facet of human language. We find, in other words, the redemption of our communion behavior.

8

Redemption: The Word Entering the World

WE HAVE MENTIONED SEVERAL times how the world we live in is a *worded world*. It is a world brought into being and sustained by God's speech, by God's communion behavior. The loving, linguistically-established communion between the triune God and his creatures, however, was horrifically disrupted (though, by God's grace, not destroyed). A liar slithered into the Garden of Eden and encouraged Adam and Eve to fracture the harmony between them and God (and, indirectly, between themselves). He encouraged them to break the hierarchy of trust, choosing the words of a creature over those of their Creator.

The fall would set in motion a long and painful history of deafness, distrust, and rebellion on the part of God's people. As we turn the pages of the Old Testament, we find reference after reference to God's covenantal language—his offerings of promises, guidance, and direction that are met with disbelief, stubbornness, and wayward living.[1]

In the time of the patriarchs, for instance, God made promises to bless Abraham and to multiply his offspring (Gen 12:1–3). Yet Abraham responded not with trust in God's words but with an attempt to use deceit to control his own destiny. When he and his wife went to sojourn in Egypt, he instructed her to lie about her own identity in order to protect him

---

1. I will not in this chapter survey all the redemptive highlights in Old Testament history and how they point ahead to Christ. That work has already been done well by others. For starters, I would direct readers to Edmund P. Clowney's *The Unfolding Mystery: Discovering Christ in the Old Testament*.

(12:11–14). There were glimmers of hope in Abraham's life, such as when he believed in God's covenantal promise later in the story (Gen 15:6).[2] But this was an exception, not the norm. In the following chapter, Abraham repeats Adam's sin by taking the words of a creature—this time, his wife—over those of God. God had promised to bless Abraham with offspring, but his advanced age suggested that this could not happen. Sarai (later renamed Sarah) took matters into her own hands, and Abraham made no protest. "And Sarai said to Abram, 'Behold now, the LORD has prevented me from bearing children. Go in to my servant; it may be that I shall obtain children by her.' And Abram listened to the voice of Sarai" (Gen 16:2–3). Notice here that verse 3 is not merely the end of a small piece of narrative. Abraham listening to the voice of Sarai reveals that he is *not* listening to the voice of God, who had promised him offspring through his barren wife. Yet, God would still graciously provide and be true to his words: "The LORD visited Sarah as he had said, and the LORD did to Sarah as he had promised. And Sarah conceived and bore Abraham a son in his old age at the time of which God had spoken to him" (Gen 21:1–3).

Abraham's pattern of behavior would be echoed in the lives of his children. During that great story of God's deliverance—the Exodus of his people from slavery in Egypt—we find repeated examples of people distrusting God's covenantal words and acting in rebellion. Recall how many times God's people complained in the desert, doubting God's promised protection and his leading of them to the land of Canaan (e.g., Exod 12:11–12; 16:2–3; 17:1–3). In a beautiful reaffirmation of his covenantal faithfulness, God reminds them, "If you will *diligently listen to the voice of the Lord your God*, and do that which is right in his eyes, and *give ear to his commandments* and keep all his statutes, I will put none of the diseases on you that I put on the Egyptians, for I am the LORD, your healer" (Exod 15:26; emphasis added). *Listening* and *giving ear* to God's words was always the path set before his creatures. Ever since God had spoken Adam into being, he had presented the same, simple covenantal requirement to his creatures: listen to his voice; listen to his speech; listen to his verbal communion behavior.

We know, of course, that God's people throughout the Old Testament had a listening problem. They continually either distrusted God's words or openly rebelled against them. This was especially obvious during the reign of the kings and the time of the prophets. The kings were meant to be godly stewards of the people, pointing them toward the God who had spoken and continued to guide and protect them in holiness. But the kings of Israel

---

2. We know from later biblical revelation that this belief of Abraham was the work of the Holy Spirit in him, for God alone is responsible for the redeeming faith of his people, a faith in God's words.

and Judah were far from holy. They led the people away from God, and so God sent prophets to reaffirm the words of their covenant Lord. A prime example is Isaiah. Notice how he opens his message to Judah by focusing on the worded world.

> Hear, O heavens, and give ear, O earth;
> for the LORD has spoken:
> "Children have I reared and brought up,
> but they have rebelled against me.
> The ox knows its owner,
> and the donkey its master's crib,
> but Israel does not know,
> my people do not understand." (Isa 1:1–3)

Isaiah calls the worded world to witness. The heavens and the earth (and all that is within them), which God had brought into being and sustained through communion behavior, was the prophet's audience. Isaiah was calling all of creation to hear the message—the judgment-laden verbal communion behavior—of the speaking God: God's children have distrusted his words and rebelled against him so consistently that they no longer know or understand him.

We often miss here the connection that the prophet is making between language and knowledge or understanding. _Knowledge and understanding only come through language._ More specifically, knowledge and understanding only come through _God's covenantal language._ Apart from God's words, there is no knowledge or understanding. This is echoed later in the New Testament, when Paul tells his readers that in God's Word, the divine incarnate Son (John 1:1), "are hidden all the treasures of wisdom and knowledge" (Col 2:3)—_all_ the treasures, not "some" or "most." The prophetic words that Isaiah spoke—just as was the case with all of God's words to his people in the Old Testament—were creaturely derivatives of the one eternal Word. God's Son is the original, eternal Word, and so "all words, all discourses spoken in time, are derivative from this original."[3] By implication, Isaiah was pointing his audience to the speech of God, and the ultimate speech of God is the eternal Son, the Word of the Father.

The people of God are contrasted with the natural world—a world that is apparently _less_ confused than the image bearers who are called to hear God's words and know him. "The ox knows its owner, and the donkey its master's crib, but Israel does not know, my people do not understand."

---

3. Poythress, _In the Beginning Was the Word_, 256.

The people do not know God or have understanding because they have not received and kept his words. They have strayed from the linguistic path he set before them in his commandments. The result of ignoring God's words is a lack of knowledge and understanding—and not just generally, but a lack of knowledge and understanding *about God*. And because God himself is our light (Ps 36:9; Isa 60:19; John 1:9; 8:12; 9:5; 12:46), a lack of knowledge about him is darkness.

When God's people reject his language, they reject *him*, for he is the speaker; and when they reject him, they walk a road to darkness and death. Into this darkness—a darkness that spans centuries, a darkness that would make a spark seem like the sun—came our redemption: the Word himself.

THE DAWNING OF LINGUISTIC LIGHT IN THE DARKNESS

At the incarnation, the eternal Word of the Father came into his worded world. God spoke *himself* into creation. Let me say it again: The Father spoke the Word—his Son—by the power of the Holy Spirit, into the world that he had made through his Son and Spirit. This is the dawning of eternal linguistic light. Over the years, I have been so moved by this breathtaking redemption of God that I decided to put my thoughts into verse. The poem below pales in comparison to the great Christian poetry that has been written throughout the ages, but it at least expresses something of my awe.

> *Speech of God*
>
> We dwelt in darkness; you live in light.
>
> In grace, your lips drew near to us upon a silent night.
>
> Eternal lungs filled with your Spirit
>
> Breathed your Word through a virgin's womb that all might hear it.
>
> The lowing cattle, the rustling hens
>
> Saw the speech of God and shuttered their quiet amens.
>
> And the shepherds huddled in the cold
>
> Lingering to marvel at a Word both new and old.
>
> The lowest around the highest stood,
>
> Knowing full well that this holy, quiet night was good:
>
> There animals and men in concourse

Settled into straw bed sleep before divine discourse.

God's sending, or we might say "speaking," of his Son (the eternal Word) into the world parallels and yet far exceeds God's speech at creation. Van Til remarked that at the beginning God spoke *into* nothing.[4] What he meant by this is that there was no "nothing" before God created. As odd as it sounds, "nothing" is still "something." The nothing that was the context for God's creation was itself created by God. This is how we should properly understand what theologians refer to as creation *ex nihilo*, "out of nothing." "Nothing" is not the source of creation; God is. So, we can deduce that "nothing" did not exist until God chose to create *into* it. Another way of putting this is to say that God spoke his creative words into the context of nothingness. Note how this contrasts with the context of God's redemptive speech: in sending the eternal Word to the world, God spoke himself *into the context of a human being,* the virgin Mary. This is richly personal redemption: spoken by a personal God, through a personal vessel, to redeem a personal world—a world created and sustained by personal, trinitarian communion behavior.

In the incarnation, we see that God works from the inside out.[5] He redeems us not by calling us to conform to external behavioral patterns but by entering the very bloodstream of humanity, and yet not compromising his divinity in the process. This is the profound mystery of the incarnation. At no point in his earthly life, death, or resurrection did the eternal Son, the Word of the Father, cease to be God. Oliphint writes,

> . . . . This is the wonder and majesty of the gospel! *God Himself* has come. He has come, not only to be with us, but He has come as *one of us.* He is not simply with us when we suffer; *He Himself* suffered in our place.

> Through all of this—His conception, birth, life, death, resurrection, and ascension—at no time did Christ cease to be fully God as the Son of God. It is *God Himself,* therefore, who has accomplished all that was needed for our salvation. That accomplishment came at a great price—the ultimate price. And the price was paid *to God, by God.* No wonder, then, that no other religion

---

4. Van Til, *Defense of the Faith,* 50n18.

5. I sometimes use an analogy from western medicine. When we are sick, we sometimes take pills that release certain elements in the bloodstream and combat various harmful cells and viruses that are causing pain and discomfort. Medicine, in this sense, works from the inside out. In an analogous way, the gospel is something that must be received by the heart (Matt 13:19) before it can be displayed in our behavior. In an ultimate sense, God redeemed us from the inside by taking on a human nature. He voluntarily entered into authentic human life in order to redeem it from the inside out.

in the history of the world has conceived of such a thing. It is, in a very real sense, beyond imagining. It is utterly mysterious, even while it is the bedrock and primary Christian truth that every true Christian confesses.[6]

What I would emphasize here, in addition to Oliphint's highlighting of such a profound mystery, is that the eternal Word of the Father was sent or spoken *in the context of a person*. God is *that* involved; he is *that* loving. If creation into nothing brings us to awe, re-creation in the virgin birth should bring us to tears. Christ is the sweetest Word we can hear, the most beautiful sound of the Father—indeed, the eternal speech of God come in the flesh.

BRINGING COMMUNION, RESTORING TRUST, RE-NAMING THE WORLD IN HIMSELF

Now, what does this mean for us in light of what we have learned about the fall *in* language? To start, it means that just as the fall was *in* language, so redemption would be *in* language. The fall in language came through the crooked words of a serpent and the distrust of God's creatures; redemption in language would come through the eternal Word of truth, God's own Son, who would restore the hierarchy of linguistic trust between God and his image bearers. In sum, the fall in language broke our communion with the triune God, fractured our trust in God's language, and encouraged us to name and label parts of creation autonomously. In contrast, redemption in language restores our communion with the Trinity, our trust in God's words, and our dependence upon the God of language in our naming and labeling. And, as we will see in the later part of this chapter, the redemption of language goes far beyond naming and labeling, just as human language involves much more than this. Indeed, the redemption of language involves every communicative act a person can carry out. That is to say, redemption in language is a holistic redemption of communion behavior.

Bringing communion. Let us start by exploring how God's redemption in language restores our communion with God and with each other. Christ, as the ultimate redeeming Word of God, came to do what Adam and his progeny failed to do. We have already seen how Adam and Eve were called to trust God's words, and that trust was a prerequisite to their intimacy— first with God and then with each other. Trust is what allows for communion. Thus, when Adam and Eve broke the hierarchy of linguistic trust, they simultaneously opened a chasm between themselves and the God who *is*

---

6. Oliphint, *The Majesty of Mystery*, 72.

exhaustive interpersonal trust amongst the Father, Son, and Holy Spirit. They set themselves in opposition to this God and would begin a long and painful history of striving to trust the only words that are worthy of trust— the words of God, which he spoke throughout history and which are now preserved for us in Scripture. They would struggle every day to take God at his word, and they would most often fail. In fact, their habit of distrust grew so severe that they would eventually block their spiritual ears and be *unable* to hear God's words. This inability, we find later in Scripture, is actually a form of judgment by the self-communicating God. Judgment for the God of language, in other words, comes in the form of *communicative impairment* with regards to divine revelation.

A prime example is the message of judgement in Isaiah 6, which is echoed later in the New Testament by Jesus himself. Isaiah proclaimed God's judgment upon Judah and Jerusalem—a judgment God had himself communicated to Isaiah in a vision (Isa 6:1–7). Notice what this judgment entails:

> 8 And I heard the voice of the Lord saying, "Whom shall I send, and who will go for us?" Then I said, "Here I am! Send me." 9 And he said, "Go, and say to this people: "'Keep on hearing, but do not understand; keep on seeing, but do not perceive.' 10 Make the heart of this people dull, and their ears heavy, and blind their eyes; lest they see with their eyes, and hear with their ears, and understand with their hearts, and turn and be healed." (Isa 6:8–10)

Focus especially on the absence of *hearing* and the people's *heavy ears*, and consider that this judgment is linked to the people's practice of idolatry. As G. K. Beale put it, "the blindness and deafness of Israel in verses 9–10 is a description of idol worshipers being judged by being made to reflect the very idols that they worship." But do not lose the linguistic element of this judgment. God's message through Isaiah is both cutting and clear: "Ignore the words of the communicating God and you will become like an non-communicating idol. You will have your linguistic ability, which is at the heart of what it means to be an image-bearer of the God who speaks, impaired." This is linguistic judgement—it attacks the people's communicative ability, and thus prevents them from having communion with the triune God! If we cannot communicate with God and receive from him the message of redemption, then we cannot commune with him.

---

7. Beale, *A New Testament Biblical Theology*, 364–65. As he puts it so eloquently, "what you revere you resemble, either for ruin or restoration" (368–69).

Of course, God has a sharp sense of irony here. His judgment comes in the form of communicative impairment, and yet this judgment must itself be communicated through words! The very pronouncement of the judgment in language is a signal that it has already begun to take place. *A failure to heed God's word leads to a failure to hear God's word, and a failure to hear God's word precludes personal communion with him.* That, as we have seen all along, is the devastating effect of the fall *in* language.

Jesus, the Word of the Father come in the flesh, would draw his disciples' attention to this in the Parable of the Sower (Matt 13). After telling this parable to the people, Jesus answers the question of his disciples: why are you speaking in parables? Consider Jesus's response:

> 11 And he answered them, "To you it has been given to know the secrets of the kingdom of heaven, but to them it has not been given. 12 For to the one who has, more will be given, and he will have an abundance, but from the one who has not, even what he has will be taken away. 13 This is why I speak to them in parables, because seeing they do not see, and hearing they do not hear, nor do they understand. 14 Indeed, in their case the prophecy of Isaiah is fulfilled that says: "'You will indeed hear but never understand, and you will indeed see but never perceive.' 15 For this people's heart has grown dull, and with their ears they can barely hear, and their eyes they have closed, lest they should see with their eyes and hear with their ears and understand with their heart and turn, and I would heal them.' 16 But blessed are your eyes, for they see, and your ears, for they hear. 17 For truly, I say to you, many prophets and righteous people longed to see what you see, and did not see it, and to hear what you hear, and did not hear it. (Matt 13:11–17)

This is a hard teaching: As a judgment for linguistic rebellion (rejecting the words of God), the Lord closes the eyes and ears of those who might receive his verbally transmitted, redemptive revelation. Notice the profound parallel to Isaiah's ironic judgment, but here even more pronounced. In the prophet's day, God's message of judgment came in words that the people would not hear. In Jesus's day, God's message of judgement came in the Word that they would not accept (cf. Matt 13:57; Mark 6:4; Luke 4:24; John 1:11). This showcases the vitality of language, of God's words—and, by extension, God's eternal Word: the person of the Son. Salvation is a matter of *hearing* and accepting the eternal Word of the Father, just as covenantal obedience was a matter of *hearing* and accepting the temporal words that God spoke in history.

The point in all of this is that communion with God—deep, relational intimacy—is established through God's speech, which we have defined as his communion behavior. In light of this, the ultimate judgment by the communicative God is not physical pain or even death. The ultimate judgment is a block in communication, a deafness to his speech. The ultimate redemption is thus an opening in communication and the restoration of communion. And here is the profound truth of the gospel: this opening in communication between us and God would not come through a message, but through a man. It would come not through a proposition, as though sin were primarily intellectual; it would come through a person, for sin is a matter of the heart, and the heart governs our personhood.

Here is the greatest evidence that language is not, at root, a tool for information transfer, a system for idea exchange. Language is all about *persons*. Its purpose is to join persons in communion on the levels we noted earlier: the divine-human level and the human-human level. So, God's restoration of his people through divine language, through the eternal Word, accords not only with who we are as communicative creatures but with who God is, the self-communing Trinity. He longs to commune with us—a longing of unparalleled grace—and in his good pleasure, he speaks *himself*. The Word became incarnate for the sake of our communion with the Trinity.

It is instructive to consider just how this communion is effected, for language is at the center of salvation, particularly with Scripture's focus on the *name* of Christ. We have already seen the importance of naming, but here naming takes on a whole new dimension. In Adam's day, he was tasked with naming the animals: speech left his mouth and labeled elements of the world around him. In Jesus, divine speech leaves God's mouth but draws us back to him in the one name of Christ (figure 16).

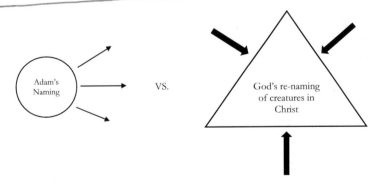

Figure 16: Adam's Creative Naming vs. God's Redemptive Re-Naming

There is a sort of reversal in the direction of naming, if we might put it that way. With Adam, multiple names go *out* (proceeding from his person) and establish distinction; in the one name of Christ, we go *back* to God in unbroken unity.[8]

It is very important here to remember that salvation comes through the person and work of Christ, but this salvation is inextricably bound up with his *name*. As we mentioned earlier in this chapter, at the incarnation God speaks himself into the worded world. He takes on a name in the land of the living (Ps 27:13). This name is absolutely essential, for it harkens back to the naming that Adam carried out in Genesis 2. The names of God's creatures represent their entire existence. When people mention your name, they are referencing all of who you are—past and present. A name is not simply a label; it is a marker for persons, a symbol for life lived. Jesus's name thus references his person and work. His *name* is what saves. His *name* is what brings communion.

If this idea seems novel, just consider some of the New Testament passages that reference the *name* of Jesus with regards to our salvation.

- "She will bear a son, and you shall call his name Jesus, for he will save his people from their sins" (Matt 1:21).

- "But these [signs] are written so that you may believe that Jesus is the Christ, the Son of God, and that by believing you may have life in his name" (John 20:31).

- "And Peter said to them, 'Repent and be baptized every one of you in the name of Jesus Christ for the forgiveness of your sins, and you will receive the gift of the Holy Spirit'" (Acts 2:38).

- "But when they believed Philip as he preached good news about the kingdom of God and the name of Jesus Christ, they were baptized, both men and women" (Acts 8:12).

- "But you were washed, you were sanctified, you were justified in the name of the Lord Jesus Christ and by the Spirit of our God." (1 Cor 6:11).

- "And this is his commandment, that we believe in the name of his Son Jesus Christ and love one another, just as he has commanded us" (1 John 3:23).

8. As the next chapter will discuss, the consummation of language is complete communion between God and his creatures. We will be one with each other and with God (John 17:21).

It is the name—the name of Jesus Christ—that bears our salvation. The name is a reference to all that Christ has done and is doing. That name . . . that name is beautiful. It is "the supreme name of God."[9]

The name of Jesus Christ does many things for God's people. Charles Wesley wrote a wonderful hymn in the eighteenth century, now familiar to most of us: "Oh for a Thousand Tongues to Sing" (a fitting title for a song that worships the speaking God). One of the stanzas reads:

> Jesus! the name that charms our fears,
>
> That bids our sorrows cease;
>
> 'Tis music in the sinner's ears,
>
> 'Tis life, and health, and peace.

Wesley's word choice makes me smile. Note here the undoing of the fall in language. The serpent had charmed our trust and given us fear. The name of Jesus charms our fears and calls us back to trust. In fact, he instills trust in us by his life-giving Spirit.

And the Spirit has a critical role to play in our being brought into the one name of Christ, for the Spirit is he who imparts redeeming life to creatures in the Son. This is really a redemptive development of what happened at the dawn of creation. Recall our earlier discussion about creation coming about through God's communion behavior: the Word and the Spirit worked together for creation. The Father breathed out his creative Word in the power of the Holy Ghost. In redemption, he breaths out the eternal Word into human flesh so that we might be redeemed from the inside out. So, God's communion behavior creates (the Father speaking through the Word in the power of the Spirit), and God's communion behavior saves (the Father sending or "speaking" the Son in the life-giving power of the Spirit). More to the point, it does this through the name of Jesus Christ, a name which has been given by the Father himself through divine revelation (Matt 1:21; Luke 1:31).

And here is where the mystery of the Trinity comes to the fore. We might understand the name of Jesus Christ in isolation from the Father and Spirit. But the name of Christ cannot be understood apart from the other persons of the Trinity. The name Jesus Christ references the entire life of the incarnate Son, but it also references the divinity of Christ, for the one person of Christ has a divine and human nature. The name of Jesus Christ thus denotes God. And while Jesus as God the Son is distinct from God the Father and God the Spirit, he is not separated from them. In a sense, the

---

9. Poythress, *In the Beginning Was the Word*, 293.

Father, Son, and Spirit all share the same name (cf. Matt 28:18–19), if by that we mean its reference to the divine nature.

In fact, God's naming of himself—as the Father, Son, and Holy Spirit—reflects some of the linguistic features we noted in an earlier chapter.

> We can . . . see the relevance of naming to God's trinitarian character. The Father is God; the Son is God; and the Holy Spirit is God. As God, they have the same character, that is, the same "name." The baptismal language in Matthew 28:18–19 speaks of the "name" in the singular: "Go therefore and make disciples of all nations, baptizing them in the name of the Father and of the Son and of the Holy Spirit, . . ." It is true, of course, that in the literal sense we have distinctive names for each person of the Trinity—"Father," "Son," "Spirit." But they share a common character as God. In fact, when Paul speaks of calling "on the name of the Lord" in Romans 10:13, he quotes a verse from Joel 2:32 that has the tetragrammaton, Lord, and applies that holy name to the Son.

> We see, then, that the "name" of God or character of God covers all three persons of the Trinity. We have a particular, key example here of the three interlocking aspects: contrastive-identificational features, variation, and context (distribution). The contrastive-identificational features are the attributes of God, such as lordship, being merciful and gracious, and so on. The variation is the variation among the persons of the Trinity. The features of God's character apply to each person. The context is the context of God's works of creation and redemption, about which whole passages speak. And these contexts in their relationships reflect the original, archetypal relationships among the persons of the Trinity. Each person is not only a particular instance of God and of the character of God, but is such in relation to the other persons.[10]

This God—the God who names himself as Father, Son, and Spirit—created and redeemed all things through divine speech—through the eternal Word that would come in the flesh. In the Word of the Father and the power of the Spirit we were created; in that same Word and Spirit we are re-created, in the *name* of Jesus Christ.

Thus, in the name of Christ, our communion is restored with the triune God. The door to communion is opened by a name which is, in a very deep sense, a trinitarian name. This does nothing to take away from the

---

10. Poythress, 278.

distinctness of Christ or of "Jesus Christ" being the name above all names (Phil 2:9). It simply accents the truth that *all* of God was involved in our redemption. That redemption, we have noted, is our communion with the Trinity. In the name of Jesus Christ—which references his entire person and work as well as the distinct persons of the Father and Spirit to whom he is eternally bound in loving fellowship—the door to communion with the Trinity is opened.

Restoring trust. Perhaps one of the greatest benefits to this communion is the restoration of what we earlier called the hierarchy of trust. Let me start by reintroducing a modified version of an earlier figure.

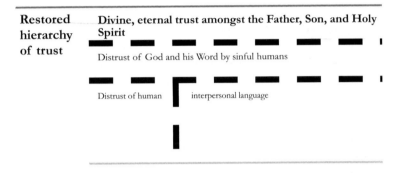

Figure 17: Restored (But Not Yet Consummated) Hierarchy of Trust

I have titled this figure the "Restored (but not yet Consummated) Hierarchy of Trust" because, as we will see in the next chapter, our trust with the loving Trinity is not yet at its fullest fruition. We know this by experience, since we still struggle to trust God's words and often distrust the words of others. In the sense of the figure above, we still bump into the dotted lines. The spaces between the dashes reveal that Christ has definitively broken through our distrust. In the power of the Spirit and in the name of Christ, we trust.

Remember that sin took the form of distrust in God's words, but Christ became sin for us (2 Cor 5:21). He bore the judgment for *our* distrust in the communion behavior of God, which was *himself*, for the eternal Word is the ultimate communion behavior of the Trinity! Just think about the selfless love of God in this—when Paul says that God made him to be sin for us, he is saying that the divine, eternal trust of the Trinity absorbed our distrust at great cost to God. As Oliphint noted some pages ago, God paid the ultimate price for our distrust, "And the price was paid *to God, by God.*"[11] There is no payment we can offer. In the bedlam of sin, we are beggars before the beneficence of the Trinity. And now we are beggars turned to worshipers, for all is paid.

Still, that does not mean that all is fully restored—not yet. Though the devil himself cannot raise his voice to silence the speech of God in redeeming all things, we have our issues to work through. We daily struggle to take God at his word, and to trust others in a world that is still on the mend. But what is critical for us to remember is that, because of the Spirit's work in us, we both *can* and *will* trust in the truth and goodness of God's words—his precepts and promises. In Christ, God has begun a good work in us that he has vied to complete (Phil 1:6).

Our trust in Christ, in the name of God, is brought out prophetically in the Psalms. Consider some of the passages that highlight this.

- "And those who know your name put their trust in you, for you, O LORD, have not forsaken those who seek you" (Ps 9:10).

- "Some trust in chariots and some in horses, but we trust in the name of the LORD our God" (Ps 20:7).

- "For our heart is glad in him, because we trust in his holy name" (Ps 33:21).

- "Then shall I have an answer for him who taunts me, for I trust in your word" (Ps 119:42).

---

11. Oliphint, *The Majesty of Mystery*, 76.

These passages draw our attention not just to trust in God, but to trust in his *name*. The final passage (Ps 119:42) calls us to trust in the word of God, and we have already seen how God's redemptive words are rooted in the eternal Word, so trusting in God's word is related to trusting in God's name, Jesus Christ, who is the incarnate and eternal Son and Word of the Father. In a similar spirit, Isaiah writes, "Who among you fears the LORD and obeys the voice of his servant? Let him who walks in darkness and has no light trust in the name of the LORD and rely on his God" (Isa 50:10). "The name of the LORD"—that is where we put our trust.

In Christ, we are given a name that has taken on a full human nature, which means that every part of who we are as humans has been redeemed *in* him, *in* the name of Christ. Yet, as we noted already, this trust in the name of Christ is simultaneously a trust in the communion behavior of the Father, Son, and Spirit. Trust in the name of Christ is trust in the one person of Christ, who has both a human and divine nature, and his divine nature, as the eternal Word, is tethered to the Father and Spirit. So, trust in Christ is really trust in the eternal Trinity. It is also, by implication, trust in the communion behavior of God, for God *is* the Father speaking the Son in the eternal power and hearing of the Holy Spirit.

This trust in God, in his name, and in his speech (biblical revelation) is what allows us to trust in each other's words, though that is at a lower level of the hierarchy and is by no means as "safe" as trusting in God's written words of Scripture. In fact, we rely on Scripture to tell us when we can or should trust in the words of another creature. And in a fallen world that is still in the process of being redeemed, our trust in the words of another creature (even when our trust is biblically warranted) is still risky. We can trust in God's words unflinchingly, but we must trust in the words of a creature with a measure of caution, knowing that God's creatures are still being redeemed and restored.

This situation is very different when it comes to our relationships with non-Christians, for they are not consciously engaging with the triune God and are not being sanctified by the life-giving Spirit. Their words are not backed by the redeeming Word of the Father, so we must approach non-Christian words with even greater caution. God, of course, can and does give non-Christians trustworthy speech in his common grace, but this is *common* grace, not *special* grace (or saving grace).

We might think of our trust in creaturely words using a metaphor. If our words are a kind of currency (a coinage for communion), then Christians operate in a market that is being redeemed, so there are both authentic and counterfeit coins being traded among persons, and most people are self-consciously (through the work of the Spirit within them) trying to root out the counterfeits because such counterfeits are an affront to the eternal Word, who is worthy of our highest trust. However, non-Christians operate in a market that is not being redeemed. The majority of the coins are counterfeits, and most of the people in the market place are not self-consciously trying to root out these counterfeits, because there is no calling for them to do so. Counterfeits can still serve their selfish ends, so they often pass them along unnoticed. Christians certainly struggle with this, too. Yet, the Christian communicative market is being redeemed and conformed to the holy trust of the Trinity, while the non-Christian market is not. This fact has implications for our use of language each day, depending on the nature of those to whom we speak. That does not mean you should distrust every word that comes from the mouth or pen of a non-Christian, since, as we just said, God's common grace is at work to draw non-Christians to himself. Still, there is a biblically warranted measure of caution that should come along with our reception of the speech of non-Christians, and that caution is exercised with an eye to God's word, the Bible. We use the true and trustworthy words of God in Scripture to sift the words offered to us by non-Christians.

In sum, Christ has restored our trust in God's words, and this then begins restoring our trust in the words of other creatures, but this must always be done in a way that keeps God's words primary. According to the hierarchy of trust, God's speech to us must stand above our speech to each other.

Re-naming the world in himself. Lastly, our naming is restored in Christ because all things are being redeemed *in* him. Salvation and restoration come only through the name of Christ, and we learn in Revelation 21:5 that the exalted Christ is making *all* things new. This means that our naming and labeling take on a Christ-centered and, in fact, trinitarian dimension.

First, our names and labels are now colored by the ultimate name of Christ. In Christ all things are being remade. This has profound implications for the names and labels that we use in pretended isolation from him. All of our descriptions, opinions, and evaluations are under the Lordship of the name of Christ. What does this mean, exactly? We could say many things, but for starters it is clear that no description, opinion, or evaluation (or any other naming feature of language) can be properly understood apart from the name of Christ, the anointed incarnate Son of God.

Consider the example we used in an earlier chapter: the character descriptor *honest.* I might describe my wife as honest, for instance (and she is), but this must be understood in light of Christ's person and work. All of us are by nature children of wrath (Eph 2:3), and if we believe in Christ, then we are united to him and are beneficiaries of his atoning sacrifice. The good that we do after being regenerated by the Holy Spirit, the character traits that we develop, are the direct result of our union with Christ. They are the fruit of the Spirit who dwells in us (Gal 5:22). Honesty, for example, is "good," and if "goodness" is a fruit of the Spirit, then we can say that the Holy Spirit is ultimately responsible for my wife's honesty, as she is bound in loving union with Christ and reconciled to her heavenly Father. So, when I tell my wife that she is honest, I am in a way also telling God that his work in Christ and the Holy Spirit is bearing fruit in her life. In thanking my wife for her honesty, I am simultaneously thanking God for his honesty—the perfect honesty of Christ according to which he professed the truth of God throughout his entire life, in faithful obedience, even to the point of death on a cross. *Honest* is a label I properly give to Christ and then derivatively give to my wife.

Of course, there are examples that are more difficult. When a Christian business is critiqued by its own manager or boss for being *inefficient*, how are we to understand that critique in relation to Christ? Well, the efficiency of a business is an evaluation of its expenditure of resources, its carrying out of tasks, and its offering of services. If those resources, tasks, or services are being wasted in some sense, that business is not being fully effective. Its work, in other words, is not fully effective. We might relate this in a broader sense to the effectiveness of Christ's work. There was no drop of Christ's sweat, no bead of his blood that was not fully effective in procuring our salvation. Christ did not waste his life—he did not waste his time or his resources or his power or his obedience. It was *all* effective. He set his mind to doing his Father's will (John 6:38), and we now have *his* mind. Paul tells us that we have "the mind of Christ" (1 Cor 2:16). This is certainly a wondrously mysterious claim—multifaceted and deep. One of the many potential implications of this claim is that we set our minds to doing God's will for our lives. God has given each of us a purpose and a calling, and that includes the work we do each day. The Christian businessman, in other words, is indwelt by the Spirit who shapes him to Christ's image, and one mark of that image is devotion: fully setting our minds on what God has called us to do. So, in critiquing his own business as being *inefficient*, the business owner is critiquing himself for failing to evoke the mind of Christ. Efficiency and inefficiency, then, are not labels that correspond to secular labor practices. In an ultimate sense, they correspond to and reflect Christ himself, whose atoning life and work are fully efficient, fully effective, in meriting our salvation. When we are efficient with our time and resources, we are conforming our lives to Christ's image in the realm of work, whatever that might be.

The point is, there is no label or name that has value or meaning apart from the name of Christ.

Second, our names and labels are also shaped by and reflective of the Trinity. In fact, every *word* is shaped by and reflective of the Trinity. This is one of the implications of some of the triads we looked at in an earlier chapter: identity, variation, and context (distribution). Poythress calls our attention to this amazing truth towards the end of his book on language.

> We see in God himself the logical origin for the words in language. Words do not come out of nowhere. Out of his bounty, his goodness, God has supplied human beings with all the words in each particular language. He has not given words in isolation, but words that are tied to and related to one another in their meanings, their sounds, and their ability to form constructions that communicate rich truths. And it is not a gift that is unrelated to the Giver. The gift reflects the Giver in mysterious ways. Words, with their ability to describe, reflect God who describes himself, as is hinted at in his self-description, "I am who I am." God describes himself to himself in the communication and communion of the persons of the Trinity, in unity and diversity. And then that unity in diversity is reflected in the unity (contrastive-identificational features), diversity (variation), and interconnectedness (distribution) that exist in any one single word.
>
> When you use a word, you rely on God. Each word shows God's eternal power and divine nature (Rom 1:20). Each word comes to you in a situation that depends on God's creation of you and of your environment. In its coinherence of aspects, each word images the coinherence in God's trinitarian character.[12]

It is hard to overstate the profundity of this—how pervasively God has embedded reflections of himself in the worded world. Even a single name, a single word, is reflective of God's trinitarian character. There is no shortage of examples here, so let us consider just one briefly. The word "road" is common enough for most of us. This word *contrasts* with other words and real-world referents. It is not a bear or a mountain or a person or a plane. It is a pathway that has been cleared for travel, often for vehicles. This negative and positive identity for the word "road" also has *variations*. Each time I pronounce that word, I do so with the slightest of variation. I may draw out the "r" sound or barely pronounce the "d" at the end. People who live in different places in the United States will say this word a bit differently. But my different pronunciations of this word, along with the various

---

12. Poythress, *In the Beginning Was the Word*, 279.

pronunciations of the word in other dialects of American and British English, does not change the fact that we are referring to the same thing. There are also variations in the particular reference for this word in a given context. There are many different roads in the world, and I am likely using this word to refer to only one of them at a given time. Lastly, the word "road" has *context* (distribution) because it always occurs in an utterance or conversation, in verbal or written language, and its reference always has relationships to other referents in the world. A road might be next to a river or stream, for instance, which is next to a town, which is next to a city, and so on. We can do this with every word in every language.

The contrastive identity of a word must be rooted somewhere, and because we live in a world that is reflective of the Trinity at every turn, it makes biblical sense to look to God for the origin or purpose of this contrastive feature of language. In fact, as we saw in an earlier chapter, the Father is contrastively identified by his being the eternal "begetter" of the Son. Only the Father can be described this way. He contrasts with the Son and Spirit in this sense and has a unique identity—though this identity is a *relational* identity, that is, the Father is identified *in relation to* the Son and the Spirit, not in isolation from them. The contrastive identity of the Father is the source for the contrastive identity of creaturely words, which have been gifted to us through his Son, the eternal Word, and his Spirit, the eternal Breath.

The variation of a word is rooted in the Son, who is a unique variant or manifestation of the one divine essence, and relates to his Father as the one who has been eternally begotten by him. As a variant of the divine essence, the Son is not identical to the Father, but they do share the same essence. The Son is as much God as is the Father, and yet he is not the Father. This essential identity with personal difference is the source or origin for the variations we find with any particular word. I may pronounce the word "road" differently from my wife (there is personal variation in our pronunciation), but we are each speaking *essentially* the same word.

Lastly, the context (or distribution) of a word is rooted in the Holy Spirit, who is the context of the loving relationship for the Father and the Son. The Father and the Son love one another *in* the Spirit. In a sense, without the Spirit the Father-Son relationship would be unintelligible, just as a human word without a context is unintelligible.

Thus, while it is certainly true that no label or name has value or meaning apart from the name of Christ, it is equally true that no label or name has value or meaning apart from the Trinity, who stands behind and beneath every name and every word.

REDEEMING COMMUNION BEHAVIOR: BEYOND RE-NAMING

Now, before suggesting some implications for us from this chapter, I want to point out that, while earlier we discussed the effects of the fall on our naming and labeling, language allows God's creatures to do far more than this. In fact, perhaps two of the greatest linguistic abilities for Christians are self-expression and grace-expression (the two often overlap). Let me explain what I mean.

Self-expression. In an obvious way, language (communion behavior) allows all of us to express ourselves—our subjective thoughts, feelings, and emotions. This is as true for Christians as it is for non-Christians. The reason for this was presented in a previous chapter: Language is the heart of the image of God in us.

However, there is certainly a difference between the self-expression of the non-Christian and the self-expression of the Christian, especially when we consider the nature of the word "self" for those redeemed by the Spirit of the living God. The Apostle Paul brings our attention to this in his second epistle to the Corinthians and in his letter to the Ephesians.

> 16 So we do not lose heart. Though our outer self is wasting away, our inner self his being renewed day by day. 17 For this light momentary affliction is preparing for us an eternal weight of glory beyond all comparison, 18 as we look not to the things that are seen but to the things that are unseen. For the things that are seen are transient, but the things that are unseen are eternal. (2 Cor 4:16–18)

> 17 Now this I say and testify in the Lord, that you must no longer walk as the Gentiles do, in the futility of their minds. 18 They are darkened in their understanding, alienated from the life of God because of the ignorance that is in them, due to their hardness of heart. 19 They have become callous and have given themselves up to sensuality, greedy to practice every kind of impurity. 20 But that is not the way you learned Christ!— 21 assuming that you have heard about him and were taught in him, as the truth is in Jesus, 22 to put off your old self, which belongs to your former manner of life and is corrupt through deceitful desires, 23 and to be renewed in the spirit of your minds, 24 and to put on the new self, created after the likeness of God in true righteousness and holiness. (Eph 4:17–24)

The *inner self*, the *new self*—this is what Christians should have in mind when they think of self-expression. The inner self is daily being renewed and prepared by the Spirit for an eternal glory—a glory that far outshines any earthly glory, i.e., any glory from men. The new self has a renewed *mind* and heavenly desires, longing to live a righteous and holy life before the righteous and holy Trinity. For Christians, we might call the inner or new self the *true* self, since that is who we truly are becoming as we move through time and towards eternity, never to relapse again into sin and doubt. The Word, who is truth (John 14:6), indwells us with his Father and Spirit. So, our true self is a self shepherded by the Father (Ps 23:1), conformed to the Son (Rom 8:29), growing in grace by the Spirit (2 Pet 3:18).

This self should be expressed in our language, though certainly the old, outer self does not go quietly to the spiritual grave. We have a war of selves within us, each one fighting for expression through language. The old self must be silenced; the new self must be given a voice in our words and actions. James 1:19–21 applies here.

> Know this, my beloved brothers: let every person be quick to hear, slow to speak, slow to anger; 20 for the anger of man does not produce the righteousness of God. 21 Therefore put away all filthiness and rampant wickedness and receive with meekness the implanted word, which is able to save your souls.

Quick hearing and slow speech applies to the waring selves within us. The old self needs to have his speaking privileges revoked. He needs to receive biblical discipline from the "implanted word." Only when our spirits are guided and directed by the Holy Spirit himself, in accordance with that implanted word, are we to speak. For struggling sinners saved by grace, this means that most of the time we should not offer quick responses in the context of delicate issues or passionate debates. In a similar way, we must check our anger, for ungodly anger (anger that originates in the old sinful self) leads not to the righteousness of God (Eph 4:24) but to wickedness (James 1:21).

Notice here that the Christian and the non-Christian mean something entirely different by the phrase "self-expression." It all comes down to the nature of the self that is being expressed.

Having said that, the inner, new self—the *true* self, for Christians— can be expressed in a myriad of ways. This brings us back to a basic point made earlier: language, as communion behavior, involves both verbal and nonverbal communicative actions. While that definition seems broad, it is biblically appropriate, given that all of the created world and all of our creaturely behaviors *communicate* or "speak" about God. Recall Titus 1:16, where Paul critiques nominal Christians: "They profess to know God, but they deny him by their works." Profession in verbal language is paired here with denial in nonverbal communicative behavior. Both verbal and non-verbal behaviors *communicate*. This is a reminder that all of what we do, in one way or another, communicates or expresses the self—either a self in covenantal submission to the God of grace or a self in covenantal rebellion against him. Certainly, we can focus in on our verbal/or written language, but we must be careful not to let that focus exclude all of the other elements of our behavior that communicate our relationship with the triune God and our enmity with a world that is passing away.

Grace-expression. One of the ways we can honorably communicate our relationship with the triune God in our verbal communion behavior is to *give grace*. This is a striking idea, brought to us in Scripture, again, by the Apostle Paul in his letter to the Ephesians. "Let no corrupting talk come out of your mouths, but only such as is good for building up, as fits the occasion, that it may give grace to those who hear" (Eph 4:29). One of the most profound ways in which the God of language is working to redeem our words is to instill them with power to be instruments of grace. This is in stark contrast to the sinful use of words that was part and parcel of the old, outer self.

OLD, OUTER SELF-EXPRESSION	NEW, INNER SELF-EXPRESSION
Corrupting talk	Holy, righteous speech (in accordance with the Word)
Tearing down	Building up
Inappropriate	Fitting the occasion
Judgment-laden	Grace-giving

Figure 18: Old Self-Expression vs. New Self-Expression

Now, what does it mean for our words to give grace to those who hear them? Grace is found in the triune God, in the Father who gave his Son for us and in the Spirit who infused our lifeless veins with the breath that will carry us into eternal fellowship with the Almighty. Thus, to have our words give grace is to have them point to God. We can do this in several ways because God has done so much for us! Think of all the ways in which words can work to express gracious gifts that reflect the triune God.

Consider words of sympathy, for instance.[13] "I know what that is like" or "That must have been difficult" or "I can sympathize with you." These words impart a shadow of grace, a shadow stretching behind the back of God, who showed unparalleled sympathy for his people in Christ. The writer of Hebrews tells us that "we do not have a high priest who is unable to sympathize with our weaknesses, but one who in every respect has been tempted as we are, yet without sin. Let us then with confidence draw near to the throne of grace, that we may receive mercy and find grace to help in time of need" (Heb 4:15–16). Jesus has been tempted in *every* respect. He was tempted to despair (Matt 26:38), tempted to take from the devil what only his Father could give him (Matt 4:9), tempted to follow the will of men (see John 5:19, where this temptation is implied by the fact that Jesus chooses to do his Father's will). Because Jesus has been tempted in every respect, he can sympathize with us in every way. No matter what we experience, we can utter a simple sentence that brings great comfort: Jesus *knows*. Whatever we experience, whatever we struggle with, he knows. He sympathizes with us as our great high priest.

Our words of sympathy can point to the sympathy of the triune God in the person of Christ—a sympathy that goes beyond what any of us can show to one another. When we utter words of sympathy, we partially identify with the joys or sorrows or frustrations of fellow human beings. But in God's sympathy, he identified completely with the worst of who we are. "For our sake he made him to be sin who knew no sin, so that in him we might become the righteousness of God" (2 Cor 5:21). God went to depths of us—where no light shines. There he uttered his eternal Son in the power of his Spirit and shattered our darkness, as a stone shatters a window pane. All human sympathy is but an echo of this great, self-giving love. When we offer words of sympathy, we thus offer testimony to the God who shows the deepest sympathy with us. When people receive our words and feel a sense of kinship or camaraderie, they are drawn closer to the God who gives

---

13. On our ability to empathize with one another as rooted in the Trinity, see Hibbs, "Solipsism or Empathy? Beating the Devil with His Own Tricks," Place for Truth, August 31, 2015, http://www.placefortruth.org/content/solipsism-or-empathy-beating-devil-his-own-tricks.

himself. In this, our words give grace to those who hear by directing human hearts to the God of grace.

We can say the same about our words and actions that display patience. This is a prime example of how communion behavior includes not just what we say but what we do. I was once standing behind someone in a line at a department store. The cashier was having trouble scanning an item of the woman in front of me. She looked up after a few minutes and said, "I'm sorry. I'm just waiting for my manager." Without thinking much, I said, "That's fine. I'm in no hurry. Don't worry about it." Many of us probably have had numerous experiences such as this one. But do we realize what we are doing? My expression of patience is not a context-less action. I live in the ongoing story of redemptive history, and so do you. When we express patience—either with a sentence or simply by not saying anything and just waiting in line at the grocery store—we are pointing to the grace of God who is patient with us to an unfathomable degree. In 2 Peter 3:9, the apostle writes, "The Lord is not slow to fulfill his promise as some count slowness, but is patient toward you, not wishing that any should perish, but that all should reach repentance." God is patient because of his love for us. Scripture tells us that love is patient (1 Cor 13:4), but it also tells us that God is love (1 John 4:8). Our patience is a finite imitation of God's great patience— a patience that spans millennia. Our patience is also a finite imitation of God's love. So, when we express patience to others, we are pointing to the ever-patient God of love. Thus, our words give grace to those who hear by turning them toward the God of patient love.

We could go on and on with examples, and there would be no harm in doing so. But the point is that our communion behavior can be grace-giving as it points others to the God of grace. We thus use redeemed language (redeemed communion behavior) for new, inner self-expression and for grace-expression, passing along to others in little acts and phrases what God has given us in his Spirit-filled Word.

IMPLICATIONS

There are many implications we could take from this chapter. It is difficult to focus on only a few, but let's try to consider how Christ's bringing communion, restoring trust, and renaming the world in himself affects our everyday use of language.

Bringing communion. Christ's bringing about our communion with God has a profound implication for how Christians understand the word "family." The world looks at family as a matter of blood. They say "Blood runs thicker than water." But Christ's blood runs thickest. If we are in him as adopted sons and daughters, then Christians are an eternal family bound in Spirit-wrought faith. We are a family in a way that transcends earthly concepts. I have brothers and sisters, for instance, with whom I will share an eternal and intimate union, and yet I have never met them. There are legions of souls that are waiting to meet me on the other side of this life. I will have millions of best friends, and together we will lift up our hands and voices to praise and worship the God who made us one with him (John 17:21). What's more, my family is rich. We are wealthy with the greatest currency a creature could ask for: *time*. Our life does not end when the breathing machines turn off, or when the impact of a utility vehicle smashes the driver's side door. We continue. Ours is eternity—with the Father, Son, and Holy Spirit. God will be ours, and we will be his. That will be our never-ending beginning.

Do you think this way when you gather to worship on Sunday morning? Do you look around and see your brothers and sisters? Do you treat them as those with whom you will soon share an eternity of union and worship with the triune God? If we are honest, many of us do not look at others this way. But if God has redeemed communion behavior, if he has redeemed all things by breaking into his worded world with the Word of his Son, then why are our hearts not bent on communing with his sons and daughters?

Consider a common example for some of us. Why are we sometimes silent and awkward when the preacher tells us to turn and greet each other in a Sunday morning service? I am not posing this question to make us feel guilty; I am posing it to help us begin the process of self-inspection. There are spiritual reasons why we keep ourselves from communing with others in the body of Christ. Here are a few that come from my own self-inspection.

- I do not truly see those around me as brothers and sisters (i.e., I do not appreciate the depth and breadth of Christ's work in and through them).

- I think that people are only greeting each other because they are being asked to do so, and therefore the exchanges are not genuine.

- I feel more comfortable *not* engaging with others. I would rather stay seated and silent.

- I am afraid of awkward social interactions (e.g., grabbing the "wrong" hand when going for a handshake).

- I feel bad that I say the same thing to the same people
  each week, when I know I should be trying to learn more
  about those around me.

Noticing these reasons for resisting a simple interaction with people in
the body of Christ is the first step in our ongoing communicative redemption. The next step would be prayerfully searching for the truth of Scripture
in response to each of these reasons, and a final step would be taking action based on the biblical revelation to which the Spirit has led us. This is
one tangible way in which Christ's redemption of language might affect our
regular communications in his body, the church.

Restoring trust. This has an obvious implication for us on the divine-
human and human-human levels. On the divine-human level, we still struggle each day to trust God's word, to fully embrace the validity and surety of
his promises and his direction for our lives. Though we struggle with this,
we can be encouraged that this full realization of trust in the triune God is
not up to us; it has already been accomplished by God himself. The trust
that we have in the words of God is a loving trust—a trust that the God who
has professed to love us and claims us as an inheritance for himself will be
true to his speech. And he always is. That is why Paul can say in in Romans
8:38–39, "I am *sure* that neither death nor life, nor angels nor rulers, nor
things present nor things to come, nor powers, nor height nor depth, nor
anything else in all creation, will be able to separate us from the love of God
in Christ Jesus our Lord" (emphasis added). Paul's certainty does not come
from his own volition. He has not willed himself to be certain. Instead, his
certainty is rooted in God's communion behavior and accompanying action. God has said and done many things, and when he says that we will
not be taken from the hand of God (John 10:28–29), that is enough for
Paul. And it is enough for you and me, too. God will help us, by the power
of our great comforter, the Holy Spirit, to trust in his words again. Though
we are covenantally required to cultivate this trust, God has taken this upon
himself. By giving his Son for us and absorbing our distrust into the eternal
trust of the Father, Son, and Holy Spirit, God himself *is* now our trust. The
triune God of speech dwells within us and carries us to himself. That does
not mean that we are not required to put in any effort, but it does mean that
the power and peace we find in trusting God's words is something for which
God is solely responsible, and that is an encouraging thought.

On the human-human level, however, we encounter many issues. How
can we have trust restored in interpersonal relationships, when each of us is
still being redeemed and is struggling with sin?

The biblical answer here is clear but not exactly comforting: *interpersonal trust in human relationships is a Christ-conforming process.* In other words, every time we trust others, we are putting ourselves on the line. If our trust is well-founded and the person follows through or circumstances do not prevent the promise from being fulfilled, then that is a blessing. But if the person mishandles our trust, or if circumstances prevent a promise from being fulfilled, then we have an opportunity to be conformed to the image of Christ.

We conform to the image of Christ through suffering—a message that is not well received by today's culture. Jesus Christ and the apostle Paul, however, were crystal clear about the role that suffering played in their lives. Repeatedly, Christ tells his disciples that he came to suffer and die for sinners (Matt 16:21; 17:12; Mark 8:31; 9:12; Luke 9:22; 17:25; 22:15; 24:26, 46; Acts 3:18). Christ's suffering was the only suffering that atones for sin. He offered his life as a sacrifice, once for all (Heb 10:10). Paul's suffering, and our suffering, does nothing to atone for sin, but it does conform us to the image of Christ. In fact, tying in with our earlier discussion, we read in Acts 9:16 a striking message from Jesus himself to the apostle Paul, "I will show him how much he must suffer for the sake of my name." The *name* of Christ is what Paul suffered for, and he suffered much. But for Paul, suffering was not something to be avoided; it was something to be embraced and used to draw us closer to the risen Christ, who has suffered on our behalf. In fact, you might say that Christ has suffered for our names, which resulted in his crucifixion. Our suffering for Christ's name, by contrast, results in our betterment and even glorification. Paul tells his readers in the epistle to the Romans that suffering produces endurance (5:3) and that we suffer with Christ so that we might be glorified with him (8:17). What's more, though we are to share in Christ's sufferings, we also share in the comfort that Christ provides through the power of the Holy Spirit (2 Cor 1:5).

All this is to say that having our trust betrayed is an instance of suffering and an opportunity for Christ conformity. That means that even when our trust is abused by others, God is still using that for our good. We should never trust in the words of creatures in the way that we trust in God's words, for people will always disappoint us. But even that disappointment serves a great purpose in God's church, as he builds us up through the suffering we experience in having our trust mishandled by other image bearers. If nothing else, experiencing the brokenness of the world in its mishandling of trust and its self-serving use of deception will bring us to glorify the God who never lies (Titus 1:2)—the God who simply *is* divine interpersonal trust as the Father, Son, and Spirit.

Renaming the world in Christ. One clear implication of the truth that all things have been renamed in Christ is to begin reinterpreting old names in Christ and "re-naming" elements of our lives in light of that sacred name. As we saw earlier in the chapter, all names and labels must be understood in relation to the overarching name of Christ.

Take a common example: Down the street from us is a building with the name "Quakertown Community High School" embossed above the front doors. How am I to understand that name in relation to the name of Christ? It may take some creative thought, but we see the relations if we dig a little deeper.

Quakertown is a small town in suburban Pennsylvania—a tiny patch of the world that was spoken into being by the divine Word and is now held together by the Word of God's power (Heb 1:3). The name of the building signifies its location, a location that is included in God's plan to draw all nations to himself (John 12:32) and to make all things new (Rev 21:5). The location "Quakertown Community" is thus bound to the name of Christ by fitting under his redemptive lordship in time and space. But the high school is not simply the building; it also includes the many students who attend and the teachers who instruct them and the staff that maintain the grounds. All these people are offered the name of Christ for their redemption and have either chosen to accept it or reject it. They are a community of persons who have a covenantal relationship with the tripersonal God of the Bible.

What's more, the name "High School" denotes education: the imparting of knowledge and wisdom. But Christ is the knowledge and wisdom of God (1 Cor 1:24), so any knowledge and wisdom the high school students receive from their teachers or friends is ultimately a gift of God that is delivered through his Son, the eternal Word, who took on flesh in the person of Christ. The entire name "Quakertown Community High School" stands upon the eternal truth of the Trinity in the second person of the Godhead. To some, the name of this high school is little more than a locative label. But to us who have been redeemed in the name of Christ, it is a marker of what the Father and Spirit have done and are continuing to do through the Son, through Christ. Knowing this changes my perception of the name of the school.

In addition to reinterpreting old names in light of the name of Christ, we must keep the name of Christ in mind when we devise new names. Our firstborn son we named Isaac Matthew. We were self-conscious about the biblical root of his names, but it was not until after we had named him that I realized how deeply his name is connected to the name of Christ. Isaac, of course, was the son of God's promise (Gen 15:4; 17:19) to Abraham, and God upheld his promise. Isaac was born into the line of God's people.

Matthew, the tax collector of Jesus's day (Matt 9:9), was not the result of a fulfilled Abrahamic promise. Because of his occupation, he would have been viewed with suspicion, even scorn, by the Jewish people around him. Both Isaac and Matthew, however, share their acceptance of God's providential grace. Isaac did nothing to merit the covenantal fulfilling of his own birth, neither did Matthew do anything that warranted an invitation to discipleship. Grace came to these men in two different ways, each uniting them to Christ. In Isaac's case, the promise made to his father was a foreshadowing of salvation. Christ was there in the promise, for he would be the greater son of Abraham, the one who would come and redeem the entire covenantal line. In Matthew's case, the promise came in flesh and bones; it spoke to him directly. Isaac came first, drawn into the promise of Christ; Matthew came second, drawn by the voice of Christ. Isaac was born into the promise; Matthew wandered into it. The insider and the outsider both came to the name of Christ. It is fitting, then, that we named our son Isaac Matthew. His name is a constant reminder to us of the wondrous work of God in the lives of men who do not deserve his loving kindness.

There are countless examples that we could explore, but I believe the point is clear enough: every name and label must be brought under the lordship of Christ, the name above all names.

In ending this chapter, I would remind us of how profound it is to have redemption come by the Word into God's worded world. By the Son and Spirit who speak love and glory to one another, our heavenly Father has infiltrated the world that speaks ill of him. The Word of God—the eternal Son come in the flesh—broke through our linguistic rebellion and then indwelt us as spiritual infants learning to mumble in the tongue of grace. We still have much to learn. Every day there is a list of language lessons for all of us, drawn from the pages of Scripture. But no matter how much we learn about our own communion behavior, our use of language, we will not see the fulfillment of it until we reign together with the God who speaks. That brings us to the final chapter.

✱ DISTINCT COMMUNION WITH EACH PERSON OF THE GODHEAD:
↳ FATHER: BY MEDITATING ON & REVELING IN HIS DEEP LOVE FOR US.
↳ SON : BY MEDITATING ON HIM AS OUR GRACIOUS MEDIATOR.
↳ SPIRIT : BY CONSTANTLY RESTING UPON HIS CONSOLATION.

9

The Consummation of Language

WE HAVE SEEN CREATION in language, the fall in language, and redemption in language. The consummation of language, the consummation of communion behavior, is pure, unbridled fellowship with God himself and with our brothers and sisters in Christ. This is end that God has in mind for those he loves. The Father, Son, and Spirit have in store for us a communion beyond comprehension, a loving intimacy that outweighs any earthly love.

Even now, the triune God loves us with a love that refuses to let us go. George Matheson (1842–1906) put this truth in poetic form. And notice how he draws our attention to our finding ultimate fulfillment in the Trinity.

> *O Love That Wilt Not Let Me Go*
> O Love that will not let me go,
> I rest my weary soul in thee;
> I give thee back the life I owe,
> That in thine ocean depths its flow
> May richer, fuller be.
> O light that followest all my way,
> I yield my flickering torch to thee;
> My heart restores its borrowed ray,
> That in thy sunshine's blaze its day
> May brighter, fairer be.

O Joy that seekest me through pain,

I cannot close my heart to thee;

I trace the rainbow through the rain,

And feel the promise is not vain,

That morn shall tearless be.

O Cross that liftest up my head,

I dare not ask to fly from thee;

I lay in dust life's glory dead,

And from the ground there blossoms red

Life that shall endless be.

The redeeming love that the Trinity has for us right now promises to carry us into deeper, endless, uninterrupted communion life with the God who speaks. That is the consummation of language, of communion behavior.

This can often seem like a dream to us. It can be hard to put concrete hope in a promise so lofty. John Owen wrote, "for sinners to have fellowship with God, the infinitely holy God, is an astonishing dispensation."[1] We tend to gloss over that adjective without a second thought. *Astonishing*—that is what this is and always will be. There is nothing we can study or read that will make this divine truth any less astonishing.

Still, that does not mean that we cannot come to understand a bit more about why this is the end or *telos* of communion behavior. As we have seen throughout this book, the Trinity is a speaking God, and language (i.e., communion behavior) is essential to him. Our complete communion with the triune God has deep and profound implications for some of the themes we have been developing in the previous pages.

UNINTERRUPTED COMMUNION

It is sometimes easy to think that our union with the Trinity must be little more than a silent union, as if eternity would be comprised of our sitting quietly in the presence of a blinding light. But given what we have seen in Scripture about the nature of God as communicative, and language as the heart of the image of God in us, this would not appear to be the case. The Father, Son, and Holy Spirit did not dwell in silent isolation for eternity past. There was, to be sure, continuous and unfathomably rich interpersonal

1. Owen, *Communion with the Triune God*, 91.

discourse—constant, divine communion behavior. We mentioned earlier that this communion behavior was the personal exchange of love and glory. We cannot say much more about this divine "language" of the Godhead, but we certainly should not say anything less.

This divine, interpersonal linguistic communion of the three persons in one essence—this is the communion into which we are gathered, either at Christ's return or at the moment of our own death. We are thus ushered into ongoing divine discourse. This is not to say that we become divine; we are and always will be creatures. But we will be closer to God than we have ever been before. And here is the important part: *we will be speaking with God for eternity.* The restoration of communion behavior by the person of Christ rekindles trust in divine language; the consummation of communion behavior solidifies the communion bond between us and God, a bond that will continue to be upheld by language. In eternity, we will not be sitting silent in heavenly rooms. We will be speaking with the Father, Son, and Holy Spirit about things we cannot yet dream of. We can only speculate about the content of those holy conversations, but make no mistake: there *will be* conversations between ourselves and the Trinity. And the discourse will have no end.

This beautiful, breathtaking reality is hard to fathom precisely because our time on earth is spent in the context of *interrupted communion.* John Owen penned a striking work of theology on our communion with the triune God. In that work, he tells us in what way we have distinct communion with each person of the Godhead.

For Owen, we have communion with the Father by meditating on and reveling in his deep *love* for us.[2] As two scholars recently put it, "Owen sees the gospel itself wrapped up in the love of the Father for his elect."[3] This love is all the more mysterious when we consider the absence of want in God. This love of the Father is from him "who is in himself all sufficient, infinitely satiated with himself and his own glorious excellencies and perfections; who has no need to go forth with his love unto others, nor to seek an object of it without himself."[4] We will be speaking with our heavenly Father for all eternity—conversing in loving fellowship about his heart for us, how his love makes us lovely, how we find joy and peace in that love, and how we stand upon it to give love to others. We will forever *speak* with our Father. And he will speak to us.

2. Owen, *Communion with the Triune God*, chap. 4.

3. Barrett and Haykin, *Owen on the Christian Life*, 59.

4. Owen, *Communion with the Triune God*, 124.

We have communion with the Son by meditating on him as our *gracious mediator.* Our communion with the Son is marked, for Owen, by sweetness, delight, safety, and comfort.[5] These marks of our communion with the Son, however, all point to our communion in his bestowal of *grace*—the grace of Christ's personal presence, the grace of his acceptance of us, and the grace of his Spirit bearing fruit in our lives.[6] In the grace of Christ, we speak to him in prayer right now, by the power of the Holy Spirit. In eternity, our speech with Christ will be filled with passionate ruminations on his enveloping and uplifting grace—his full-orbed acceptance of us in himself. We will forever *speak* with the Son, our great high priest and elder brother. And he will speak to us.

Lastly, we have communion with the Spirit by constantly resting upon his *consolation.*[7] This consolation, of course, is rooted in the Spirit's testimony to the Son. "Only by this testimony to the Son can the Spirit's role as Comforter be accomplished, for there is no true rest and consolation outside of Christ."[8] In other words, as the Spirit testifies in our hearts to the truth of Christ's person and work, he moves us and prepares us for uninterrupted communion with the Trinity. The work of the Spirit in us brings us not to fear but to hopeful anticipation of present and future joy in God. As one scholar put it, "Enjoyment of God is found in recognizing the Spirit's movement in one's life, preparing one for the eternal and unhindered communion with God."[9] In eternity, our speech with the Holy Spirit will be wrapped up in delight and joy at being brought into the presence of a holy God. We will be unable to cease expressing our gratitude for the Spirit's comfort and guidance, which is alone responsible for leading us into endless fellowship with himself, with the Son, and with the Father. So, in eternity, we will *speak* with the Spirit. And he will speak with us.

My point in all of this is that John Owen was adamant about our eventual *uninterrupted communion* with the Trinity, a communion that has begun at the moment of our salvation but will not be consummated until Christ returns or until we walk through the door of death and recline at the table with the triune God himself. This communion at every point presupposes *language*; it presupposes interpersonal discourse. Kelly Kapic notes, "[Owen] believes true communion involves the 'mutual communication' of good between two persons, allowing each to delight in the other. Owen's

---

5. Owen, *Communion with the Triune God*, 139–142.

6. Barrett and Haykin, *Owen on the Christian Life*, 68.

7. Barrett and Haykin, 75–85.

8. Kapic, *Communion with God*, 198.

9. Kapic, 201.

conception of communion rules out unending monologue or isolated autonomy."[10] In ruling out "unending monologue," Owen simultaneously affirms unending dialogue. We will be forever conversing with the Father, Son, and Holy Spirit.

What is all too obvious, however, is that we struggle right now to maintain personal communion with the triune God through language, through prayer and through meditation on God's words in Scripture. And so instead of embracing the Father's love, we fear him or view him as far off. Instead of embracing the grace of the Son, we rely on our own efforts to be holy and good. Instead of resting in the Holy Spirit's consolation, we seek comfort from earthly things that pass away. On earth, our communion with the Trinity is *interrupted* by the sin that our God is faithfully and steadfastly rooting out of our hearts. Our incessant interruptions in communion with the triune God make uninterrupted communion seem like a dream rather than a goal towards which we are moving.

But let us constantly remind ourselves: the goal of redemption towards which we are moving is a goal of *communicative* or *linguistic unity*. We are moving towards oneness with the triune God, but that oneness is not a silent or static oneness, void of loving, interpersonal exchange. Quite the opposite: it is a discourse-based and dynamic oneness.

Richard Baukham has recently written about how the oneness that is referenced by Jesus in John's Gospel (John 17:11, 21a, 22b–23b) is, first, a "oneness of personal community" in God himself (Father, Son, and Spirit) and, second, a oneness of believers with God and with each other.[11] The oneness that we will have with the Trinity and with our brothers and sisters in Christ is thus rooted in the concept of *community*. Now, we are not saying that the Trinity is a community in any human sense, for each of the persons of the Godhead shares the same divine essence. We must always guard against taking something creaturely (the concept of community for separate human beings) and applying it unwittingly to the Creator. As the church has historically confirmed, God is *one essence in three persons*. The sense in which the Trinity is a community cannot be rationally understood by us or reduced to human categories. But the New Testament everywhere affirms that the unity of essence does not preclude distinct communication amongst the Father, Son, and Spirit; nor does it preclude the distinct communication that we have with each divine person. The concept of community presupposes communication. It presupposes language. So, when we are united with the Trinity for eternity, our union will be what we might call a

10. Kapic, 152.
11. Baukham, *Gospel of Glory*, 33, 34–36.

linguistic or *communicative* union. It will be a union in which the Father, Son, and Spirit communicate with us, and we with them. That will be the nature of our uninterrupted communion with the Trinity.

GLORIOUS GOVERNING IN LIGHT OF GOD'S SPEECH

Following from this discussion is a need for us to rethink what eternity will be like. This is more than a suggestion that we think positively as Christians; it is a clarion call from Scripture to be heavenly minded (Col 3:2).

Carl Trueman used to joke with us in church history classes about Dante's *Divine Comedy*, comprised of three books: *Inferno*, *Purgatorio*, and *Paradiso*. When mentioning the *Inferno*, which describes Dante's descent into the nine circles of hell, Trueman would usually say something about how people are attracted to a story of devastation and horror. Yet, what people usually do not know is that this book is only the first of three and was never meant to stand alone. It was followed by *Purgatorio* (an exploration of purgatory) and *Paradiso* (an exploration of paradise). Of the three poems, however, the *Inferno* is by far the most widely read. Why? Well, the joke was that *Purgatorio* was lest horrific and thus less engaging, and *Paradiso* was purged of the drama we expect from great stories. The underlying assumption—though this was, of course, delivered in humor—was that there would be little going on in paradise. Our eternal communion with the Trinity would thus amount to us twiddling our thumbs in God's presence and exchanging superficial niceties with him and with each other.

This is not what Scripture suggests paradise will be like. On the one hand, we will be engulfed by worship and will thus engage constantly with God and with each other via communion behavior. Again, we cannot fathom what these acts of worship and conversations will entail, but we can at least be certain of their depth and passion and their effect on us as creatures fully restored to their speaking God. On the other hand, we will also take up *glorious governance* through language, in alignment with God's words, fulfilling but far transcending Adam's original purpose of governing God's creation.

Adam, remember, was tasked with governing creation by trusting in the words of the triune God. His work was what we might call *linguistically directed* by God's divine speech. Based on the revelation that God had given of himself in the created world and in Adam's own being (natural revelation) as understood through the direct verbal revelation of God to him (special revelation), Adam and Eve were told to steward all that God had made. They were to multiply and have dominion over God's created world.

Their dominion was meant to reflect the Trinity linguistically, in ways we have already noted. Their naming and labeling, for instance, would reflect particle, wave, and field observer perspectives and the elements of contrast, variation, and distribution—all of which are rooted in the Trinity.

In the new creation, God's people will again partake in glorious, linguistically mediated governance. As noted above, we will be in ceaseless, uninterrupted fellowship with God. In his divine discourse with us—whatever that might entail—we will be working to steward the created order in ways that transcend our imagination.

I would love to say more about this; I would love to ruminate on the glorious, God-honoring work that will be set before us in communion with the Trinity, but I simply cannot. Paul quoted the prophet Isaiah in remarking on the untold riches of the gospel: "What no eye has seen, nor ear heard, nor the heart of man imagined, what God has prepared for those who love him" (1 Cor 2:9). God's glorious work for us is beyond the shoreline of human imagination. But make no mistake: there will be glorious, God-honoring work for us to do, and we will do this work fully attentive to the divine speech of God in the Father, Son, and Holy Spirit.

LIVING IN THE NAME

Finally, I would encourage us to reflect on what it means to live *in a name* for all of eternity. Eternity has, in a sense, already begun. Christ has come and ushered in the end of the age. As many Reformed theologians have taught, there is an "already-but-not-yet" dimension to redemption.

We are already *in* the name of Christ, though we are not yet with him in glory. There is deep mystery about how we understand the former element. Paul's frequent use of the expression "in Christ" has drawn much scholarly attention throughout history.[12] I have always found a somewhat older text by James Stewart to be quite helpful. As he saw it, being in Christ means being in union with him through the Spirit of Christ (Rom 8:9–11; 1 Cor 6:11; Phil 1:19), i.e., the Holy Spirit. Yet, what does this Spirit-wrought union with Christ mean? Stewart's answer is,

> Just as it might be said that the human body is in the atmosphere which surrounds it on every side, and yet that atmosphere is also within it, filling it and vitalizing it, so it may be said of the Christian soul that it both exists in the Spirit and has the Spirit within it. Here, then, is the key to the phrase "in Christ." Christ

12. For recent examples, see Peterson, *Salvation Applied by the Spirit* and Campbell, *Paul and Union with Christ.*

is the redeemed man's new environment. He has been lifted out of the cramping restrictions of his earthly lot into a totally different sphere, the sphere of Christ. He has been transplanted into a new soil and a new climate, and both soil and climate are Christ. His spirit is breathing a nobler element. He is moving on a loftier plane.[13]

A nobler element—that is what we breath as Christians. Our life is found in a person who is pure and perfect. All of our existence is bound in a lifeline to Christ. So, when we say that we are *in Christ*, we mean that he is our holistic environment. That is what Stewart and the Apostle Paul seem to be getting at here.

Yet, as we saw earlier, we are in his *name*. This is a slightly different focus. In other words, there is a nuanced difference in meaning between being in *the person* of Christ and being in *the name* of Christ—though these meanings are bound up with one another. What might it mean, specifically, to be in the *name* of Christ?

In light of the fact that names are markers of identity (identities which comprise the whole person to whom the name is attached), it seems clear that to be in the *name* of Christ is to find our identity—with its attendant motivations, passions, and purpose—in his name. That is, our identity is first and foremost in the name of Christ, not in our own names considered independently from him. Our identity is found *within* his identity.

There is an "already" and "not yet" dimension to our identity being embedded, as it were, in Christ's name. In the "not yet" sense of redemption, our own creaturely names have yet to blossom in the name of Christ; they have yet to open themselves fully to *his* identity. In simple terms, we constantly consider ourselves independently from Christ. This is rooted in the linguistic nature of sin, for not trusting in God's words, and in the eternal Word, means we attempt to introduce separation from the God who defines us. On this side of paradise, our lives are fissured with doubt and distrust as we strive, by the power of the Spirit, to put our faith in God's words—indeed, to trust in *the Word*, who has accomplished all things on our behalf. But the "already" element of our redemption is certain. In paradise, there will be no fissures, no doubt, no distrust. We will simply *be* in the name of Christ. Our identity will flower in the warming light of his name. The petals of our personality will extend in glorious worship of who he is. In short, we will find our identity *in* his identity.

Think of it this way: we are not who we are apart from Christ. We are who we are only in him; in *his* name, we find *our* name. Thus ends the

13. Stewart, *A Man in Christ: The Vital Elements of St. Paul's Religion*, 157.

ancient war with our sinful human ego. Strivings for security and praise in the world melt away; attempts to find identity apart from God evaporate. In their stead blossom strength and worship for the name above all names, the name in which we find our own names truly spoken by the speaking Trinity, the God of language. Put differently, in paradise we will be who we are only in relation to Christ, to whom we are bound by the Holy Spirit and the love of our heavenly Father. Our identity will be irrevocably rooted in the Trinity. Every person, in a sense, will carry Immanuel inside of them, for God will be with us in the most pervasive way possible. This will not eclipse the Creator-creature distinction or mean that we become divine. Rather, our identity will be established as it always should have been: in relation to the Trinity. We will do all things only *with* God, only *in the name* of Christ. There will be no other name vying for power or authority. There will be one name, and we will be one *in that name*.

This beautiful reality will culminate in our seeing God face to face, which has ever been the hope of God's people since the fall. *Seeing* is the culmination of linguistic hope and identity in the name of Christ. Ben Jonson (1573–1673), in a poem addressing the Trinity, once wrote the following lines in earnest prayer, which all of us can echo:

> Eternal Spirit, God from both proceeding,
>
> Father and Son—the Comforter, in breeding
>
> Pure thoughts in man, with fiery zeal them feeding
>
> For acts of grace!
>
> Increase those acts, O glorious Trinity
>
> Of persons, still one God in Unity,
>
> Till I attain the longed-for mystery
>
> Of seeing your face,
>
> Beholding one in three, and three in one,
>
> A Trinity, to shine in Union—
>
> The gladdest light, dark man can think upon—
>
> O grant it me,
>
> Father, and Son, and Holy Ghost, you three,
>
> All co-eternal in your majesty,
>
> Distinct in persons, yet in unity
>
> One God to see.

This sight of God is not meant to be understood as of greater importance than God's linguistic relationship with us; instead, it is the *complement* to linguistic trust. A life of faith in God's word culminates in the eternal vision (and continued discourse) with God.

IMPLICATIONS

The practical implications of this chapter are vast, but they can also be expressed quite simply: *every day we are called to be a people of hope, knowing that God's word will bring us into union with the Trinity, and there we will find our identity eternally established.*

Still, that is a lofty truth to carry with us into the mundane of daily life. Is there anything, more specifically, that we can say about practical implications? I believe so.

Communion. The goal of our communion with the Trinity calls our attention to the communion we can already have with the triune God right now through prayer. Starting and ending our days with prayer is, in a sense, starting and ending our days with communion. And this prayer should be drawn from the well of God's word. Simply setting up a routine of daily prayer based on Scripture is far more than an exercise in piety; it is your personal attempt to engage with the God who speaks—the God with whom you will speak for all of eternity. Neglecting prayer—even amidst the chaos of life—is effectively neglecting our *need* (not want, but *need*) for communion with the Father, Son, and Holy Spirit. Keep speaking to God. Speak every day. That is what prayer is: earnest speech with the triune God.

Governing. Knowing that we will one day govern all things in accordance with God's speech helps us also to look for practical ways in which we can govern the world around us with Scripture. We have touched on this in previous chapters. Consider our relationship with animals, which many of us can relate to. We own a dog and cat, both of which were rescued. Every day, we say something to each of them, calling their names, giving them directions or commands (often ignored). These are creatures that were meant to be stewarded by us in light of God's speech. As I look forward to eternal communion with God, I think about how my speech to these animals each day is related to the way in which I will use speech in eternity: guiding and shepherding these animals to help them enjoy the best of the life God has given them. This may seem petty to some people (especially to those who do not like dogs and cats), but to think of it this way would be, I argue, unbiblical. Using language to govern and guide the animals that God has created is an image-bearing behavior that reflects, in a distant sense, the way in which God governs and guides us through divine speech. Certainly, the relationship between ourselves and dogs is not analogous to the relationship between God and his image-bearers. But there is a relationship there. How might our speech change if we became more conscious of what we were doing when we spoke to animals?

Living in the Name. Lastly, we can apply what it means to find our name in the name of Christ by retraining ourselves to understand our identity. Each day, the secular, sinful world assumes that every human identity is independent of God. In the forms we sign, for example, there is no indication that our primary identity is found in the name of Christ. It would be humorous, though theologically accurate, if I were to sign my name on tax forms as follows:

CHR Pierce Taylor Hibbs IST

My name, after all, only has meaning and significance because it is embedded in the name above all names—the name that will have no end. There is a profound sense in which, apart from the name of Christ, no person has a lasting name. Those who do not bind their name to the name of Christ have no eternal anchor for their identity. They have a temporal identity, of course, but this is nothing if they have no eternal identity in Christ.

Because we are constantly encouraged by culture to identify ourselves by our behaviors or by our preferences, we must constantly work to retrain ourselves in knowing who we are. I am nothing by myself, and neither are you. We are what we are only in the name of Christ. It is time we start working that truth into our daily routines, constantly reminding ourselves that who we are cannot be understood apart from who God is, and apart from what Christ has done and is still doing in us through the Spirit.

10

Conclusion: Principles for Living in a Worded World

IN THIS BOOK, I have tried to explore how language is central to reality. This is primarily because the Trinity is a speaking God. Language, divine interpersonal discourse, is an essential attribute of God. In light of this, God's use of language to create and redeem all things has a profound effect both on the nature of reality and our interpretation of experience. As we saw in an earlier chapter, reality is *linguistic* or *communicative* because it has been created through the communion behavior of the triune God. All of reality "speaks" about this God. This is how Scripture encourages us to interpret the world around us—not as a gathering of impersonal elements and random events but as a comprehensively integrated web of revelation. Everything in this world reveals God. Moreover, for Christians, the linguistic nature of God, of ourselves, and of reality calls us to trust in God's words above all else and to look with longing at the consummation of our communion with the Trinity.

I noted in the introduction that there has been little, if anything, novel in what I have done in these pages. Truth be told, I am doing only what my teacher and friend has already done, perhaps with a different focus. He once wrote,

> Speaking is a perspective on everything God does. The activities of God can be expounded in more than one way, that is, from multiple perspectives that are still faithful to who he is. One of those perspectives is the perspective of speaking, as we see from Hebrews 1:3: "he [the Son] upholds the universe by the word

177

of his power." The entire course of God's sustaining activity in providence is here declared to be an operation of his "word," his speech. Thus, we have obtained a verbal perspective on absolutely everything that happens.[1]

I hope I have continued to encourage us to take a verbal perspective on everything that happens, everything that is, and everything that will be. In this context, let me now end the book with some principles we might follow as we continue living in God's worded world.

1. The world is not what it seems. The secular world constantly encourages us to see the world as an impersonal atmosphere that is essentially non-revelational or non-communicative. The sunlight, to a secular mind, is simply a concentration of light particles that have travelled millions of miles through the darkness. A non-Christian sees nothing about sunlight that is transcendent or revelatory of the God who speaks. But I look at the morning light and I see speech. I see something that God has created through communion behavior that "speaks" to me about who God is in his grace, kindness, and glory. We must continue to combat the secular, sinful assumption that the world is not communicative of God. It *is*—every part of it. So, when I say, "The world is not what it seems," I am really saying, "The world is more than it seems."

2. Rejecting the testimony of God's worded world and of his holy word is an act of self-deception. This is related to the previous point, but there is an apologetic dimension here. Cornelius Van Til and his followers have reminded us constantly that all people know God (Rom 1). We are covenantally bound to the Father, Son, and Spirit because God has revealed his divine nature in everything that has been made (Rom 1:19–20). As Greg Bahnsen, one of Van Til's students, once put it, unbelief—i.e., rejecting the testimony of God's worded world and his written Word—is an act of self-deception. It is "deception of the self, by the self, and for the sake of preserving one's self-conception."[2] We can understand this self-deception in terms that we have discussed in this book. To disbelieve in God is to feign what we might call *revelational illiteracy.* To disbelieve in God is to pretend that the world around us is not communicating about the one who has spoken it into being. But because God himself has told us in Scripture that he has spoken all things into being and upholds all things with the word of his power, we know that being illiterate in God's linguistic world, a world that is everywhere revealing him, is impossible. Because we are created in God's image and likeness, we have been created *as literate* of God's speech. We

1. Poythress, *In the Beginning Was the Word*, 282.
2. Bahnsen, *Van Til's Apologetic*, 449.

have been created to receive the revelation of God in his worded world, and to understand that world through the lens of Scripture, God's special word of salvation. The point in this is that engaging with non-believers is not about telling them what they do not know; it is about calling them to recognize the voice that they have been suppressing. It is calling them to hear and respond to the speaking Trinity, who is revealed all around them. We must approach and engage with non-believers knowing that God is *already* speaking to them in the world around them. But they will not hear this speech until they receive God's saving special revelation by the work of the Holy Spirit. The salvation of an unbeliever, we might say, is a language lesson given by God himself, in which the Spirit brings someone to profess the truth of Christ and find reconciliation with the Father.

3. The Bible is all you need. Following from the second principle is the truth that Scripture—God's special, saving word—is what people need in order to interpret the worded world in a way that is faithful to God. Even though we live in a worded world, a world which everywhere speaks of God, we have trouble "hearing" that revelation. In fact, we *cannot* truly hear what the worded world has to say about God until, by the power of the Spirit, we accept the Word himself in the saving work of Christ. As sinful and confused creatures, we need a divine language lesson in order to see God, ourselves, and the world for what they truly are. We need to be reborn in the Spirit (John 3) and adopted in the Word of our Father.

What's more, Scripture is not only necessary for our salvation; it is also necessary for our entire view of reality. Philosophers typically discuss metaphysics or ontology—the nature of what exists. But the Bible has its own metaphysic, its own claim as to the nature of all that exists. This is what we have been exploring throughout this book. *God's speech is the ground for all that is created and has been sustained.*[3] The very first page of the Bible tells us that all we see and experience came about because God spoke, and God upholds his spoken world with the Word of his power (Heb 1:3). Scripture is not limited to discussing matters of religious behavior or moral ideals; it is a holistic message of what reality is like. I have tried to express this message in these pages by pointing out the *linguistic* element of reality. This comes directly from the pages of Scripture. We do not need to look to ancient or modern philosophers or scientists to discern the nature of the world. It's all in the good book.

4. Mind the hierarchy of trust. Every day we are assaulted with requests for trust. There was, is, and always will be one word that demands our

---

3. For details, see Hibbs, "World through Word: Towards a Linguistic Ontology," 345–64.

allegiance, the word of God. In every decision we make, the hierarchy of trust is at work. We are constantly either taking the word of God above the words of others or vice versa. There is no such thing as a decision that does not engage with this hierarchy.

It is also a great encouragement to know that the exhaustive trust of the divine persons (Father, Son, and Spirit) is the ground of our trust in God's words and our trust in creaturely words. God *is* trust in himself, of the highest order. He is completely trustworthy, so we can take the Father at his Word, the Son, and do so by the power of the Holy Spirit—never for an instant doubting that God is who he says he is or that he will do what he has promised. When we begin to doubt God's words, we can pray that the Spirit will return us to childlike faith, a faith that rests in utter trust. This is critical for many of us. We do not consider ourselves children in God's eyes frequently enough. In our youth, we can sprint along a cliff line, careless as a cloud. As we live longer in a fallen world, we develop an awareness of the dangers around us. This is fitting in one sense, but unfitting in another. Awareness of dangers (of all sorts) should help us to be circumspect; such an awareness should *not*, however, imprison us with fear, for we are children of an all-powerful and loving God. It would do us all good to return to childhood before the God upon whose word we stand. That word will always be trustworthy because God is always trustworthy. In fact, his trustworthiness is the anchor of our *hope*. But to cling to that hope, we must be like children.

5. *Reality can be viewed linguistically as having features of grammar, phonology, and reference.* This last principle is one that I hope to develop in the future more fully. For now, I would simply point out that because we can view all things through the lens of language, there are components of language that might help us perceive parts of the world we had not noticed before.

Take grammar, for instance. Grammar is often considered a system of structural rules and morphological patterns. Grammar is an ordered system that we use to communicate in any given language. In a sense, the world around us is part of God's "grammar," that is, part of his systematic and purposeful plan. A street, we might say, has a syntax—an order of houses with yards and roadside parking spaces. Each parking space has a sort of morphology to it. In other words, the length of parking spaces follows a determined pattern, which is implemented by the local township, all of which is under God's control. The patterns and structures all around us—the buildings and vegetation, the fields and flowers, the cars and bridges—are a sort of grammar for reality. Everything is integrated into God's systematic plan. It all functions according to the systematic wisdom of God's Son, by the all-powerful Spirit.

We can also see the world around us in terms of phonology, in terms of sound. We might consider, for instance, what sounds are *phonetic* vs. what sounds are *phonemic* to us. Phonemic sounds have a particular meaning within a society. The sound of baseball bat striking a ball is a phoneme to contemporary Americans. It has a meaning that extends and reveals a larger pattern of discourse in terms of human action. The sound of the bat hitting the ball draws us into the baseball game, which is comprised of players with different roles and is supported by fans and spectators. Sometimes, of course, we hear sounds that we cannot place or understand as meaningful. The sound of silverware falling on the floor appears to be mere noise, though all sounds that are unintelligible to us are still intelligible to God and thus have phonemic meaning to him. In that sense, every sound is a phoneme to God.

The world might also be viewed in terms of reference. We typically think of words referring to objects in reality, but objects in reality also have a reference. As we saw in an earlier chapter, all of reality speaks about the triune God who made it, so there is a sense in which the objects of reality—all real world referents—have God as their ultimate reference. The world around us is analogous to a tapestry of words that speak of God. Reference is thus not something that belongs basically to language; it belongs to God himself.

As I mentioned, I hope to develop further ways in which we can use language to better understand the world around us. What I have said about the grammar, phonology, and reference of the world is just a start and needs much more development. God willing, I will do so in the future.

In this book, it is my prayer that you have learned something more about the greatness of the speaking Trinity, our one God in three persons, and how language is related to everything. If nothing else, perhaps this book will lead you to think more deeply about the nature of God and the world in which we live.

Recommended Reading

THE FOLLOWING BOOKS AND articles constitute a "first step" towards essential reading for a biblical, trinitarian understanding of language. This brief selection of works, most of which comes from the four authors I mentioned in the Introduction, has been a great blessing to me in expanding my understanding of the divine roots of language and its importance in everyday life. I hope they will continue to serve generations to come.

Bahnsen, Greg L. *Van Til's Apologetic: Readings and Analysis*. Phillipsburg, NJ: P&R Publishing, 1998.

Bavinck, Herman. *Our Reasonable Faith*. Translated by Henry Zylstra. Grand Rapids, MI: Wm. B. Eerdmans, 1956.

———. *Reformed Dogmatics, Vol. 2, God and Creation*. Edited by John Bolt. Translated by John Vriend. Grand Rapids, MI: Baker Academic, 2004.

———. *Reformed Dogmatics, Vol. 2, God and Creation*. Edited by John Bolt. Translated by John Vriend. Grand Rapids, MI: Baker Academic, 2004.

Beale, G. K. *A New Testament Biblical Theology: The Unfolding of the Old Testament in the New*. Grand Rapids, MI: Baker Academic, 2011.

Berkhof, Louis. *Systematic Theology*. New ed. Grand Rapids, Mich.: William B. Eerdmans, 1996.

Bosserman, B. A. *The Trinity and the Vindication of Christian Paradox: An Interpretation and Refinement of the Theological Apologetic of Cornelius Van Til*. Eugene, OR: Pickwick, 2014.

Bray, Gerald. *God Has Spoken: A History of Christian Theology*. Wheaton, IL: Crossway, 2014.

Calvin, John. *Institutes of the Christian Religion: A New Translation of the 1541 Edition*. Translated by Robert White. Carlisle, PA: Banner of Truth, 2014.

Frame, John M. *A History of Western Philosophy and Theology*. Phillipsburg, NJ: P&R, 2015.

———. *Systematic Theology: An Introduction to Christian Belief*. Phillipsburg, NJ: P&R, 2013.

———. *The Doctrine of the Knowledge of God. A Theology of Lordship.* Phillipsburg, NJ: P&R, 1987.

———. *The Doctrine of the Word of God.* Phillipsburg, NJ: P&R Publishing, 2010.

Gaffin Jr., Richard. "Systematic Theology and Hermeneutics." In *Seeing Christ in All of Scripture: Hermeneutics at Westminster Theological Seminary,* edited by Peter A. Lillback. Philadelphia: Westminster Seminary Press, 2016.

Grudem, Wayne. *Systematic Theology: An Introduction to Biblical Doctrine.* Grand Rapids, MI: Zondervan, 2000.

Gunton, Colin E. *The Promise of Trinitarian Theology.* 2nd ed. London: T&T Clark, 1997.

Hibbs, Pierce Taylor. "Closing the Gaps: Perichoresis and the Nature of Language." *Westminster Theological Journal* 78 (2016): 299–322.

———. "Imaging Communion: An Argument for God's Existence Based on Speech." *Westminster Theological Journal* 77, no. 1 (Spring 2015): 35–51.

———. "Panic and the Personal God." *Journal of Biblical Counseling* 29, no. 3 (2015): 36–41.

———. "We Who Work with Words: Towards a Theology of Writing." *Themelios* 41, no. 3 (December 2016): 460–76.

———. "Where Person Meets Word Part 1: Personalism in the Language Theory of Kenneth L. Pike." *Westminster Theological Journal* 77, no. 2 (Fall 2015): 355–77.

———. "Where Person Meets Word Part 2: The Convergence of Personalism and Scripture in the Language Theory of Kenneth L. Pike." *Westminster Theological Journal* 78, no. 1 (Spring 2016): 117–34.

———. "Words for Communion." *Modern Reformation* 25, no. 4 (August 2016): 5–8.

———. "Words for Communion." *Modern Reformation* 25, no. 4 (August 2016): 5–8.

Hill, Wesley. *Paul and the Trinity: Persons, Relations, and the Pauline Letters.* Grand Rapids, MI: Eerdmans, 2015.

Kelly, Douglas. *Systematic Theology: Grounded in Holy Scripture and Understood in Light of the Church.* Vol. 1, The God Who Is: The Holy Trinity. Ross-shire, Scotland: Mentor, 2008.

Letham, Robert. *The Holy Trinity: In Scripture, History, Theology, and Worship.* Phillipsburg, NJ: P&R Publishing, 2004.

Levering, Matthew. "The Holy Spirit in the Trinitarian Communion: 'Love' and 'Gift'?" *International Journal of Systematic Theology* 16, no. 2 (2014): 126–42.

Oliphint, K. Scott. *Covenantal Apologetics: Principles and Practice in Defense of Our Faith.* Wheaton, IL: Crossway, 2013.

———. *Reasons for Faith: Philosophy in the Service of Theology.* Phillipsburg, NJ: P&R Publishing, 2006.

———. "Simplicity, Triunity, and the Incomprehensibility of God." In *One God in Three Persons: Unity of Essence, Distinction of Persons, Implications for Life,* edited by Bruce A. Ware and John Starke, 215–35. Wheaton, IL: Crossway, 2015.

———. *The Majesty of Mystery: Celebrating the Glory of an Incomprehensible God.* Bellingham, WA: Lexham Press, 2016.

Pike, Kenneth L. "Language and Life 4: Tristructural Units of Human Behavior." *Bibliotheca Sacra* 114, no. 456 (January 1958): 36–43.

———. *Language in Relation to a Unified Theory of the Structure of Human Behavior.* 2nd ed. The Hague: Mouton, 1967.

————. *Linguistic Concepts: An Introduction to Tagmemics.* Lincoln, NE: University of Nebraska Press, 1982.

————. *Linguistic Concepts: An Introduction to Tagmemics.* Lincoln, NE: University of Nebraska Press, 1982.

————. *Talk, Thought, and Thing: The Emic Road toward Conscious Knowledge.* Dallas, TX: Summer Institute of Linguistics, 1993.

Poythress, Vern S. "God and Language." In *Did God Really Say? Affirming the Truthfulness and Trustworthiness of Scripture,* edited by David B. Garner. Phillipsburg, NJ: P&R Publishing, 2012.

————. *God-Centered Biblical Interpretation.* Phillipsburg, NJ: P&R Publishing, 1999.

————. *In the Beginning Was the Word: Language—A God-Centered Approach.* Wheaton, IL: Crossway, 2009.

————. *In the Beginning Was the Word: Language—A God-Centered Approach.* Wheaton, IL: Crossway, 2009.

————. *Logic: A God-Centered Approach to the Foundation of Western Thought.* Wheaton, IL: Crossway, 2013.

————. *Philosophy, Science, and the Sovereignty of God.* Phillipsburg, NJ: P&R Publishing, 1976.

————. *Reading the Word of God in the Presence of God: A Handbook for Biblical Interpretation.* Wheaton, IL: Crossway, 2016.

————. *Redeeming Philosophy: A God-Centered Approach to the Big Questions.* Wheaton, IL: Crossway, 2014.

————. *Redeeming Philosophy: A God-Centered Approach to the Big Questions.* Wheaton, IL: Crossway, 2014.

————. *Redeeming Science: A God-Centered Approach.* Wheaton, IL: Crossway, 2006.

————. "Reforming Ontology and Logic in the Light of the Trinity: An Application of Van Til's Idea of Analogy." *WTJ* 57, no. 1 (March 1, 1995): 187–219.

Smith, Ralph A. *Trinity and Reality: An Introduction to the Christian Faith.* Moscow, ID: Canon Press, 2004.

Stăniloae, Dumitru. *The Holy Trinity: In the Beginning There Was Love.* Translated by Roland Clark. Brookline, MA: Holy Cross Orthodox Press, 2012.

Trueman, Carl R. "The Trinity and Prayer." In *The Essential Trinity: New Testament Foundations and Practical Relevance,* edited by Brandon D. Crowe and Carl R. Trueman, 199–214. London: Apollos, 2016.

Van Til, Cornelius. *Christian Theistic Evidences.* Edited by K. Scott Oliphint. 2nd ed. Phillipsburg, NJ: P&R Publishing, 2016.

————. *In Defense of the Faith, Vol. 2, A Survey of Christian Epistemology.* Phillipsburg, NJ: Presbyterian and Reformed, 1969.

————. *Introduction to Systematic Theology: Prolegomena and the Doctrines of Revelation, Scripture, and God.* Edited by William Edgar. 2nd ed. Phillipsburg, NJ: P&R Publishing, 2007.

————. *The Defense of the Faith.* Edited by K. Scott Oliphint. 4th ed. Phillipsburg, NJ: P&R Publishing, 2008.

————. *The Defense of the Faith.* Edited by K. Scott Oliphint. 4th ed. Phillipsburg, NJ: P&R Publishing, 2008.

Vanhoozer, Kevin J. *Is There a Meaning in This Text? The Bible, the Reader, and the Morality of Literary Knowledge.* Grand Rapids, MI: Zondervan, 1998.

————. *Remythologizing Theology: Divine Action, Passion, and Authorship.* New York: Cambridge University Press, 2010.

Vos, Geerhardus. *Anthropology.* Edited and translated by Richard B. Gaffin Jr. Reformed Dogmatics 2. Bellingham, WA: Lexham Press, 2014.

————. *Biblical Theology: Old and New Testaments.* Carlisle, PA: Banner of Truth, 2014.

Warfield, B. B. *Biblical and Theological Studies.* Edited by Samuel G. Craig. Philadelphia: Presbyterian and Reformed, 1968.

Waterhouse, Viola G. *The History and Development of Tagmemics.* The Hague: Mouton, 1974.

Bibliography

Bahnsen, Greg L. *Van Til's Apologetic: Readings and Analysis.* Phillipsburg, NJ: P&R, 1998.

Bavinck, Herman. *Our Reasonable Faith.* Translated by Henry Zylstra. Grand Rapids, MI: Wm. B. Eerdmans, 1956.

———. *Reformed Dogmatics.* Vol. 2, *God and Creation.* Edited by John Bolt. Translated by John Vriend. Grand Rapids, MI: Baker Academic, 2004.

Beale, G. K. *A New Testament Biblical Theology: The Unfolding of the Old Testament in the New.* Grand Rapids, MI: Baker Academic, 2011.

Berkhof, Louis. *Systematic Theology.* New ed. Grand Rapids, Mich.: William B. Eerdmans, 1996.

Bosserman, B. A. *The Trinity and the Vindication of Christian Paradox: An Interpretation and Refinement of the Theological Apologetic of Cornelius Van Til.* Eugene, OR: Pickwick, 2014.

Bray, Gerald. *God Has Spoken: A History of Christian Theology.* Wheaton, IL: Crossway, 2014.

Calvin, John. *Institutes of the Christian Religion: A New Translation of the 1541 Edition.* Translated by Robert White. Carlisle, PA: Banner of Truth, 2014.

Conn, Harvie M., ed. *Inerrancy and Hermeneutic: A Tradition, a Challenge, a Debate.* Grand Rapids, MI: Baker, 1988.

DeYoung, Kevin. *Taking God at His Word: Why the Bible Is Knowable, Necessary, and Enough, and What That Means for You and Me.* Wheaton, IL: Crossway, 2014.

Frame, John M. *The Doctrine of the Knowledge of God.* A Theology of Lordship. Phillipsburg, NJ: P&R, 1987.

———. *The Doctrine of the Word of God.* A Theology of Lordship. Phillipsburg, NJ: P&R, 2010.

———. *A History of Western Philosophy and Theology.* Phillipsburg, NJ: P&R, 2015.

———. *Systematic Theology: An Introduction to Christian Belief.* Phillipsburg, NJ: P&R, 2013.

Gaffin Jr., Richard. "Systematic Theology and Hermeneutics." In *Seeing Christ in All of Scripture: Hermeneutics at Westminster Theological Seminary*, edited by Peter A. Lillback, 39–51. Philadelphia: Westminster Seminary Press, 2016.

Grudem, Wayne. *Systematic Theology: An Introduction to Biblical Doctrine.* Grand Rapids, MI: Zondervan, 2000.

Gunton, Colin E. *The Promise of Trinitarian Theology.* 2nd ed. London: T&T Clark, 1997.

Hibbs, Pierce Taylor. "Closing the Gaps: Perichoresis and the Nature of Language." *Westminster Theological Journal* 78 (2016) 299–322.

———. "Imaging Communion: An Argument for God's Existence Based on Speech." *Westminster Theological Journal* 77, no. 1 (Spring 2015) 35–51.

———. "Panic and the Personal God." *Journal of Biblical Counseling* 29, no. 3 (2015) 36–41.

———. "We Who Work with Words: Towards a Theology of Writing." *Themelios* 41, no. 3 (December 2016) 460–76.

———. "Where Person Meets Word Part 1: Personalism in the Language Theory of Kenneth L. Pike." *Westminster Theological Journal* 77, no. 2 (Fall 2015) 355–77.

———. "Where Person Meets Word Part 2: The Convergence of Personalism and Scripture in the Language Theory of Kenneth L. Pike." *Westminster Theological Journal* 78, no. 1 (Spring 2016) 117–34.

———. "Words for Communion." *Modern Reformation* 25, no. 4 (August 2016) 5–8.

Hill, Wesley. *Paul and the Trinity: Persons, Relations, and the Pauline Letters*. Grand Rapids, MI: Eerdmans, 2015.

Kelly, Douglas. *Systematic Theology: Grounded in Holy Scripture and Understood in Light of the Church*. Vol. 1, *The God Who Is: The Holy Trinity*. Ross-shire, Scotland: Mentor, 2008.

Letham, Robert. *The Holy Trinity: In Scripture, History, Theology, and Worship*. Phillipsburg, NJ: P&R, 2004.

Levering, Matthew. "The Holy Spirit in the Trinitarian Communion: 'Love' and 'Gift'?" *International Journal of Systematic Theology* 16, no. 2 (2014) 126–42.

Lillback, Peter A., and Richard B. Gaffin, Jr., eds. *Thy Word Is Still Truth: Essential Writings on the Doctrine of Scripture from the Reformation to Today*. Philadelphia: Westminster Seminary Press, 2013.

Nagel, Thomas. *Mind & Cosmos: Why the Materialist Neo-Darwinian Conception of Nature is Almost Certainly False*. New York: Oxford University Press, 2012.

Oliphint, K. Scott. *Covenantal Apologetics: Principles and Practice in Defense of Our Faith*. Wheaton, IL: Crossway, 2013.

———. *The Majesty of Mystery: Celebrating the Glory of an Incomprehensible God*. Bellingham, WA: Lexham Press, 2016.

———. *Reasons for Faith: Philosophy in the Service of Theology*. Phillipsburg, NJ: P&R, 2006.

———. "Simplicity, Triunity, and the Incomprehensibility of God." In *One God in Three Persons: Unity of Essence, Distinction of Persons, Implications for Life*, edited by Bruce A. Ware and John Starke, 215–35. Wheaton, IL: Crossway, 2015.

Pike, Kenneth L. "Language and Life 4: Tristructural Units of Human Behavior." *Bibliotheca Sacra* 114, no. 456 (January 1958): 36–43.

———. *Language in Relation to a Unified Theory of the Structure of Human Behavior*. 2nd ed. The Hague: Mouton, 1967.

———. *Linguistic Concepts: An Introduction to Tagmemics*. Lincoln, NE: University of Nebraska Press, 1982.

———. *Talk, Thought, and Thing: The Emic Road toward Conscious Knowledge*. Dallas, TX: Summer Institute of Linguistics, 1993.

Poythress, Vern S. *God-Centered Biblical Interpretation*. Phillipsburg, NJ: P&R, 1999.

———. "God and Language." In *Did God Really Say? Affirming the Truthfulness and Trustworthiness of Scripture*, edited by David B. Garner, 93–106. Phillipsburg, NJ: P&R, 2012.

———. *In the Beginning Was the Word: Language—A God-Centered Approach.* Wheaton, IL: Crossway, 2009.

———. *Logic: A God-Centered Approach to the Foundation of Western Thought.* Wheaton, IL: Crossway, 2013.

———. *Philosophy, Science, and the Sovereignty of God.* Phillipsburg, NJ: P&R, 1976.

———. *Reading the Word of God in the Presence of God: A Handbook for Biblical Interpretation.* Wheaton, IL: Crossway, 2016.

———. *Redeeming Philosophy: A God-Centered Approach to the Big Questions.* Wheaton, IL: Crossway, 2014.

———. *Redeeming Science: A God-Centered Approach.* Wheaton, IL: Crossway, 2006.

———. "Reforming Ontology and Logic in the Light of the Trinity: An Application of Van Til's Idea of Analogy." *Westminster Theological Journal* 57, no. 1 (March 1, 1995) 187–219.

Smith, Ralph A. *Trinity and Reality: An Introduction to the Christian Faith.* Moscow, ID: Canon, 2004.

Stăniloae, Dumitru. *The Holy Trinity: In the Beginning There Was Love.* Translated by Roland Clark. Brookline, MA: Holy Cross Orthodox, 2012.

Thomas, Francis-Noël, and Mark Turner. *Clear and Simple as the Truth: Writing Classic Prose.* 2nd ed. Princeton, NJ: Princeton University Press, 2011.

Trueman, Carl R. "The Trinity and Prayer." In *The Essential Trinity: New Testament Foundations and Practical Relevance*, edited by Brandon D. Crowe and Carl R. Trueman, 199–214. London: Apollos, 2016.

Van Til, Cornelius. *Christian Theistic Evidences.* Edited by K. Scott Oliphint. 2nd ed. Phillipsburg, NJ: P&R, 2016.

———. *In Defense of the Faith.* Vol. 2, *A Survey of Christian Epistemology.* Phillipsburg, NJ: Presbyterian and Reformed, 1969.

———. *The Defense of the Faith.* Edited by K. Scott Oliphint. 4th ed. Phillipsburg, NJ: P&R, 2008.

———. *Introduction to Systematic Theology: Prolegomena and the Doctrines of Revelation, Scripture, and God.* Edited by William Edgar. 2nd ed. Phillipsburg, NJ: P&R, 2007.

Vanhoozer, Kevin J. *Is There a Meaning in This Text? The Bible, the Reader, and the Morality of Literary Knowledge.* Grand Rapids, MI: Zondervan, 1998.

———. *Remythologizing Theology: Divine Action, Passion, and Authorship.* New York: Cambridge University Press, 2010.

Vos, Geerhardus. *Anthropology.* Vol. 2, *Reformed Dogmatics.* Edited and translated by Richard B. Gaffin Jr. Bellingham, WA: Lexham, 2014.

———. *Biblical Theology: Old and New Testaments.* Carlisle, PA: Banner of Truth, 2014.

———. *Theology Proper.* Vol. 1, *Reformed Dogmatics.* Edited and translated by Richard B. Gaffin Jr. Bellingham, WA: Lexham, 2014.

Warfield, B. B. *Biblical and Theological Studies.* Edited by Samuel G. Craig. Philadelphia: Presbyterian and Reformed, 1968.

———. *Inspiration and Authority of the Bible.* 2nd ed. Phillipsburg, NJ: P&R, 1980.

Waterhouse, Viola G. *The History and Development of Tagmemics.* The Hague: Mouton, 1974.